D0837673

LEON EDEL has been active as a critic, writer, and teacher for more than a quarter of a century. His reputation as the foremost authority on Henry James was firmly established in 1962, when he won both the Pulitzer Prize for Biography and the National Book Award for Nonfiction for Volumes II and III of his life of James. Leon Edel is also known for his forays into literary history, his pioneering of literary psychology, and his editions of the works of Henry James, including THE COMPLETE TALES and THE COMPLETE PLAYS. Widely honored, he has been elected to the American Academy of Arts and Sciences, the British Royal Society of Literature, and the National Institute of Arts and Letters, which gave him an award for "creative writing in biography." New York University created its Henry James Chair of English and American Letters for him, and he is also Citizens Professor of English at the University of Hawaii. Mr. Edel is the author of HENRY DAVID THOREAU, JAMES JOYCE: THE LAST JOURNEY, LITERARY BIOGRAPHY, and THE MODERN PSYCHOLOGICAL NOVEL. With Edward K. Brown he is co-author of a biography of Willa Cather.

BY LEON EDEL

The Life of Henry James:

HENRY JAMES

THE TREACHEROUS YEARS: 1895—1901

LEON EDEL

 A DISCUS BOOK/PUBLISHED BY AVON BOOKS

Designed by Marshall Lee.

AVON BOOKS
A division of
The Hearst Corporation
959 Eighth Avenue
New York, New York 10019

Copyright © 1969 by Leon Edel
Published by arrangement with J. B. Lippincott Company.
Library of Congress Catalog Card Number: 53-5421
ISBN: 0-380-39677-7

First Discus Printing, August, 1978
Second Printing

DISCUS TRADEMARK REG. U.S. PAT. OFF. AND IN
OTHER COUNTRIES, MARCA REGISTRADA, HECHO EN
U.S.A.

Printed in the U.S.A.

Never say you know the last word about
any human heart!

Henry James

HENRY JAMES

THE TREACHEROUS YEARS:
1895—1901

Contents

BOOK TWO *The Black Abyss*

1 8 9 5

BOOK THREE *The Turn of the Screw*

1 8 9 6 - 1 8 9 8

BOOK FOUR *The Great Good Place*
1898-1899

BOOK FIVE *The Sacred Fount*
1899-1901

Illustrations

Woolson, Aunt Kate, Mrs. Kemble, Alphonse Daudet, Alice
James. From a photograph in the possession of Mr. John James

LAMB HOUSE: INTERIOR   218

Part of the hall and "telephone room," from an unpublished
photograph by Alvin Langdon Coburn supplied by him for this
volume. ". . . In his hall at Rye . . . caps and hats, each with
its appropriate gloves and sticks . . ."—*H. G. Wells*

BROTHER JONATHAN   271

Jonathan Sturges (1864–1911), from a drawing by Albert Sterner
in the Princeton University Library. On the back is a note by
Mary Sturges Wilson: "Posthumous drawing made from notebook sketches Mr. Sterner had kept from his days in Paris in
1891 when he and my brother were closely associated in the
Latin Quarter."

THE YOUNG SCULPTOR   357

Hendrik C. Andersen, from the portrait painted by his brother,
Andreas Andersen

HENRY JAMES IN ITALY 1899   358

On the steps of the Palazzo Borghese, Rome. Photograph by
Count Giuseppe Primoli, from a print in the Houghton Library.

THE BROTHERS   359

Henry and William James near Rye in the summer of 1900,
shortly after the novelist had removed his beard. From a snapshot in the Houghton Library

A RAGE OF WONDERMENT   360

From the caricature by Max Beerbohm in the Ashmolean
Museum, reproduced by permission of Mrs. Eva Reichmann.
". . . Standing often, in double pairs, at the doors of rooms."

INTRODUCTION

"THE TREACHEROUS YEARS" IS THE PENULTIMATE SECTION OF MY *LIFE* of Henry James which has been appearing in "serial" form since 1953. It focuses on the 1890's and principally on the novelist's spiritual illness between 1895 and the beginning of the new century, and describes how he rid himself of his private demons by writing about them. The novels and tales of these years have always had a distinctive place in the Jamesian canon; they can be best understood when examined as a part of the inner experience that brought them forth. In substance, they deal with children and ghosts—with the phantasmagoric—and the ways in which the imagination endows reality with realities of its own. In form and structure, they constitute a remarkable series of technical experiments devoted to modes of indirect narration and the refining of the novelist's omniscience. In these works James parts company with the nineteenth century and points the way to the innovations of Joyce and Virginia Woolf and the "interior journey" of Proust.

What we can discern is that on the level of art James was probing the same human experience—and in an analogously systematic if unconscious way—as Sigmund Freud, who was making his discoveries at this very moment in Vienna. And also at this same moment, in Paris, James's fellow-artist, Marcel Proust, was engaged in examining that part of reflective experience which relates to association and memory. Proust, in the footsteps of Bergson, discovered for himself and demonstrated how a calling up of the past (which Freud was asking of his patients) establishes man in time, can give him an identity and reveal to him the realities of his being. Thus in three different cities of the Old World three different men were embarked at this singular moment of the history of mind and psyche on journeys into a personal "dark backward and abysm." Freud had the advantage of studying his patients as well as himself; Proust worked alone; and of the three James wrote with a profound intuition but with the least self-awareness. His series of unrelated stories about children took them chronologically from the cradle to maturity; in a certain sense it is as if we were studying the case history of the growth of a single child. By offering us the inner history of his little Maisie or of his young governess, James was in reality re-dreaming and using for art the essential materials of his own childhood; and in turn, using art as a form of catharsis for the lingering wounds within his psyche. He performed self-therapy rather than self-analysis; but he offered us the materials by which we can glimpse his extraordinary private history.

During the years dealt with in these pages Henry James may be said to have suffered a kind of "nervous breakdown." It was in part a failure of confidence, although his belief in his art never seems to have faltered. Yet while living through his depression and mourning for "the death of childhood," James kept before him an ideal of the invincibility of his craft. He was able to "function" so long as he kept to this belief. And in returning to earlier, to earliest experience, he rediscovered the means by which he had long before armed himself for life. He healed his wounds, and recovered his strength, finding new sources of power within himself. The steps by which this occurred, and the heroic effort required, constitute not only a fascinating chapter of literary history, but a striking "case" of literary psychology. To have rendered in fictional form— and in complete independence—those very subtleties of the human personality and of the unconscious which Freud systematically studied, is achievement enough. But because James sought the truths of the self, and was not concerned with psychological speculation, he was able to touch matters that would be explored beyond Freud in modern ego psychology. Above all, he performed on himself what Freud was busily demonstrating—he showed man's capacity to heal himself by a retreat to earlier experience.

It seems to me that the evidence here offered supports the hypotheses of those who have sought to show that creation—when it does not degenerate into the pathology so common in our midst today—is a work of health and not of illness, a force for life and life-enhancement, not a mere anodyne or "escape" or a symptom of neurosis. Recent experiments have shown that man's dreams are necessary to his well-being, that "dream deprivation" can lead to serious illness. Might we not speculate that the health-giving dreams and disciplines of transcendent imaginations contribute to the maintenance of universal well-being when communicated to the culture and the race? Seen in this way, the inner troubles and conflicts, the morbidities and sufferings of Proust or James, Virginia Woolf or Kafka, or that very sick artist whose wit and humor have given us the poetry of *Finnegans Wake*, represent victories of life over death, triumphs of art over despair.

Perhaps I should add a word about my biographical method, since it seems to have puzzled some of my critics, chiefly those in the academic world. I have accepted the axiom of modern psychology that there is sequence and consistency in the stuff of man's imagination; that an artist's work is less accidental than it has seemed; and that even as form and discipline represent conscious effort on the part of an artist, there exists an equally consistent unconscious effort—an inescapable use of the buried materials of life and experience—to which the artist constantly returns. Biography has for too long occupied itself with the irrelevancies of daily life and overlooked the essential keys to character and personality: I refer to the ways in which an artist fashions the myth by which he lives. The physical habits of the creative personality, his "sex life" or his bowel movements, belong to the "functioning" being and do not reliably distinguish him from his fellow-humans. What is characteristic is emotional life and the way in which the emotions dictate—other elements and mysterious forces aiding— the exercises of the demonstrative and symbol-making imagination. A writer of novels and tales, in particular, in the act of creating universal works is at the same time telling us personal parables about himself. "Poetry," said Thoreau in a moment of great insight, "is a piece of very private history, which unostentatiously lets us into the secret of a man's life." It is the quest for this secret that I regard as the justifiable aim of literary biography. All the rest is gossip and anecdotage.

Readers of *The Middle Years*, the volume preceding this one, will notice that I have gone back in time in the present volume to the beginning of the 1890's. The previous section covered the years 1882 to 1895; the present section takes up certain parts of my story between 1890 and 1895 hitherto omitted in the interest of a sustained "story line." My retrospective method has incidentally enabled me to make use of certain materials not available to me when I was writing the earlier sections of the life of Henry James.

Leon Edel

New York
1968

An Excess of Simplicity

1890-1895

THE SCENIC IDEA

ON THE CLOCK-STROKE OF FIFTY—IN 1893—HENRY JAMES HAD had his first attack of gout. But he had hobbled bravely in a split boot to stand at the grave of his beloved Fanny Kemble, for whom he lit one of the brightest tapers on his personal altar of the dead. Then, in quick succession, he had had three further attacks, one while he was staying in the Hotel Westminster in Paris. He had dragged about his room, cushioning the offending toe and reading proofs of three books to be published that spring. The years were catching up with him—but not with his fertility. In a burst of alliteration he had told Edmund Gosse he was "moody, misanthropic, melancholy, morbid, morose." The malaise was however more than gout. He set it down in his notebooks. "The most beautiful word in the language?—Youth!" Henry James had begun to have a sense of ebbing time, of shrinking opportunities.

Everything spoke of the flight of youth. The old motherly

Queen was now—had long been—grandmotherly. Her once-young son, the Prince of Wales, had grown bald and heavy with the good things of life while awaiting his turn in the royal succession. People grew old; institutions grew old; the very century had grown old. Everyone talked of *fin de siècle*. It was a malady of unrest in which the pulse quickened and the calendar grew large on the wall. The Victorian age was coming to an end and Henry James had called his new volume of tales *Terminations*. Three of the tales were about writers, dying or moribund, ignored by the worka-day world. If we read personal overtones in the title, we can do the same for the volume that followed. This was called *Embarrassments*.

I

Moody, misanthropic, melancholy, morbid, morose—embarrass-ment seemed a mild word indeed for such states of feeling. But James had been trying to be a playwright since 1890 and his life in the theatre in 1893 had not gone well; there had been endless delays; and his financial resources continued to dwindle. Moreover his days were filled with personal relations not of his choosing. He was paying a heavy price for quitting his beautiful ivory tower of fiction. He had told himself there would always be a line of retreat —to his many-windowed flat in Kensington, to the peace of his writing desk. Nothing could prevent him (he assured himself) from dipping his pen "into the *other* ink—the sacred fluid" of the novel. At various intervals during the five years of his theatre-life he spoke of "this quiet, this blessed and uninvaded workroom," where he was sole master. "Among the delays, the disappoint-ments, the *déboires* of the horrid theatric trade nothing is so soothing as to remember that literature sits patient at my door." He had only to lift the latch, he said, "to let in the exquisite little form that is, after all, nearest to my heart and with which I am so far from having done."

Literature sat patiently at his door—but he kept it waiting.

Something in the theatre held him. He could not tear himself away. He might complain of "the vulgarities and pains" of stage production, yet he continued to suffer both. Perhaps he felt there could be no turning back; a kind of pride of endeavor possessed him. The "vulgarities" fascinated him too much. He had seen that dull, egocentric, vain stage-folk could be brilliant before the footlights. Their charm could be turned on and off like the gaslight. There was a great deal of reality—and dream—behind the proscenium. Women were ethereal creatures to put into fiction; but in the stage wings they were flesh and blood, with greasepaint covering the flesh, and beads of sweat on top of the paint. And then there were the crudeness of the managers and the pettiness of the actors, their monstrous vanity. He had worshipped Coquelin's art at the Théâtre Français during memorable evenings in the late 1880's; meeting him now in London James saw only a monster of conceit. If he spoke of his contempt for the stage and for the players, he was less willing to recognize that there was a kind of contempt of himself too for having truck with the perpetual self-exhibitionism around him. He was not being true to himself as the artist of the study. And he rationalized his persistence in a little autobiographical story called "Nona Vincent" in which a young playwright sees a play through production while he is counselled by a wise married lady and struggles to fit an actress into her part.

The scenic idea was magnificent when once you had embraced it—the dramatic form had a purity which made some others look ingloriously rough. It had the high dignity of the exact sciences, it was mathematical and architectural. . . . It was bare, but it was erect, it was poor, but it was noble. . . . There was a fearful amount of concession in it, but what you kept had a rare intensity. You were perpetually throwing over the cargo to save the ship, but what a motion you gave her when you made her ride the waves—a motion as rhythmic as the dance of a goddess!

As always, his tales of this time, little fables out of his own experience, tell us much more than his busy, anxious letters. There is one tale in particular, of 1892, which contains a clear translation of the facts of his case into fictional fantasy. It is called "Greville Fane," and is numbered among the stories James called "anecdotes." A busy lady writer of popular novels decides that writers are made, not born. To prove this she announces she will rear her son to be a novelist. The consecrated child takes to cigarettes at ten "on the highest literary grounds." By the time he is a young man his "rings and his breastpins, his cross-barred jackets, his early *embonpoint*, his eyes that look like imitation jewels" indicate to the narrator that he is working hard at "life"—and at living up to his mother's expectations. She had conveyed to him the idea that "the great thing was to live, because that gave you material." He is so busy living—at his mother's expense—that his books remain unwritten; he is always gathering material. His mother has had a secret dream that her son might have a *liaison* with a countess; he persuades her without difficulty that he has had one. He dips into cheap French novels and talks glibly about the craft of fiction, making a better show at this than his mother "who never had time to read anything, and could only be vivid with her pen." In the end she writes herself to death to support the obese product of her "system."

James was in effect saying that he could never educate himself into being a playwright. And in another tale, one of his finest and briefest, called "The Real Thing," he seems also to say that the "real thing" in art is not simply a learning of particular laws, that one is either an amateur or a professional. An upper-middle-class couple, husband and wife, having lost their money, decide that since they are socially "the real thing" they can serve as models to a fashionable painter. In his studio, in spite of their smart appearance, they are inanimate objects; nothing can turn them into human beings usable for illustration. But the artist's Italian house-boy and cockney maidservant, with a mere hint of the right clothes, can posture to perfection. They seem more real than "the real thing." The real thing, James says in this story, remains simply the real thing; only the imagination transfigures.

II

In spite of these insights, he got a rude shock when he offered a scenario for a play called *Guy Domville*, written in 1893 amid twinges of the gout, to Edward Compton and his wife. The Comptons had asked for a romantic play for their provincial repertory. James offered them a three-act drama of a young man destined for the priesthood who has to abandon his vocation and return to the world because he is the last of his line. He owes it to his family name to marry and produce children. The scenario provided a touching love affair; and at the end James planned to have the novice reject the world—and the woman—for the monastery. The Comptons promptly expressed alarm that there would be no happy ending. James replied that renunciation of love was "the only ending I have ever dreamed of giving the play," indeed, he said, "it *is* the play." Would it not be "ugly and displeasing" to the audience to marry off someone who has one foot in a monastery? The Comptons argued it would please English audiences very much. James answered stiffly, "my subject is my subject to take or to leave." The Comptons did not take it.

James had a second thought. "Do I mean something that your audience can't understand? It is a complete surprise to me to suppose so, for I have been going on with a great sense of security." He had been in the same predicament long ago with Howells when *The American* was serialized in the *Atlantic Monthly*. Howells had urged that the marriage of the hero and the aristocratic lady should take place, and James had replied, with a touch of hauteur, "They would have been an impossible couple . . . I should have felt as if I were throwing a rather vulgar sop to readers who don't really know the world."

He repeated to the Comptons that "to make a Catholic priest, or a youth who is next door to one, *marry*, really, when it comes to the point, *at all*, is to do, to spectators a disagreeable and uncomfortable thing." What the Comptons could not convey to James was that the artistic discomfort was his own; it would not be the audience's. They nevertheless gave James serious pause. He wrote: "I have a general strong impression of my constitutional inability to (even in spite of intensity and really abject effort) realise the sort of simplicity that the promiscuous British public finds its interest in. . . . Even when I think I am dropping most diplomatically to the very rudiments and stooping, with a vengeance, to conquer, I am as much 'out of it' as ever, and far above their unimaginable heads." He could not conceive of the coarse. Nor did he recognize that an audience was entitled to a happy ending in a romantic work—that this was the tradition of romance. He had neglected "the romantic property of my subject" in the novel of *The American*, as he came to see many years later. In the 1890's, however, his confusion between the romantic play he was writing and his sense of reality was strong. Moreover it was hard for him, as a bachelor, to bestow a bride on his hero. Thus when he went, in June 1893, to see *The Second Mrs. Tanqueray* and heard the pistol shot in the third act, he told himself the Comptons did not know what they were talking about. If George Alexander was willing to have an unhappy ending—and the English audience applauded it—why should not his unhappy ending in *Guy Domville* be equally acceptable? He took his play to Alexander and laid his cards on the table. He told George Alexander that his ending did not "belong to the class of endings conventionally termed 'happy.' " He drove his point home—"no *banal* union comes off between Guy and Mrs. Peverel." Alexander did not seem troubled. Like James he accepted the evidence of *Mrs. Tanqueray*.

James was thus enabled to feel that he had adhered to the code of the artist as he had defined it in one of his letters to Mrs. Bell. One had to give the audience "what one wants oneself—it's the only way; *follow* them and they lead one by a straight grand highway to abysses of vulgarity." To his brother William he had written, "One must go one's way and know what one's about and have a general plan and a private religion." To drag after the public, he said, "simply leads one in the gutter." An artist would have public enough if he could arouse an "audible vibration." He would not make his fortune in the theatre but, he added, "I know what I shall do, and it won't be bad."

III

By 1894 he admitted to himself that four of his comedies, which he had passed around the London theatres for two years, stood little chance of production. He accordingly published them as *Theatricals*, in two volumes, with two rueful Addisonian prefaces, acknowledging that it was "an humiliating confession of defeat" to have to print unproduced plays. It was the first time during his "dramatic years" that he spoke of "defeat." He printed the comedies handsomely, with wide margins and much white space, and the names of the characters above rather than beside the speeches, in the French manner. The prefaces are filled with subdued and eloquent rage: the rage of "the perverted man of letters freshly trying his hand at an art of which in opposition to his familiar art, every rule is an infraction, every luxury is a privation, and every privilege a forfeiture." Like his hero in "Nona Vincent" he likened himself to a ship's captain caught in a storm, obliged to throw most of his cargo overboard. This was his way of saying that the cuts imposed upon him by the managers were so drastic that in the end there was "no room in a play for the play itself." James's prefaces boiled down to a denunciation of the theatre and the "theatre's laws." The implication was that plays by literary men should be produced as they are written: the literary man knew what he was about. In all this Henry James seems to have taken his cue from his knowledge of Balzac's misadventures in the theatre. Balzac too, with his strong novelistic sense, had treated the theatre with complete disdain. Accustomed to dictate to publishers, he had refused, until too late, to compromise with managers. "The sole thought of the manager, the producer, the actor, is to turn the play into something other than the one you wrote," Balzac had said. The words were now being echoed by Henry James.

William James read his brother's plays when they came out and found them "unsympathetic." He urged Henry to work for "emotionality and breadth," and he offered a pointed criticism. He had noticed that the comedies depended wholly on verbal play and on the characters' not understanding what was said to them, so that they were constantly having to explain themselves. To such criticisms James's answer was—he put it into one of the prefaces—that the stage demanded of him "an anxious excess of simplicity." It is the word "anxious" which catches our eye.

IV

George Alexander had accepted *Guy Domville* for reasons that had nothing to do with its ending. It was a costume play which allowed him to be romantic in the first act, disillusioned in the second act, and visionary in the third: he saw himself in a series of costumes which would display his fine legs. He liked the quantity of tailoring that would be necessary, the breeches and jackets with long sleeves fringed with lace. He would be able to strike those poses which his audience found agreeable and which filled his matinees with sighing ladies so that any play he produced was assured of a month's run. Most audiences at the St. James's wouldn't know who Henry James was; but they knew their George Alexander of the handsome profile and the well-turned-out costume.

The play, however, had to wait its turn. First *Mrs. Tanqueray* had to complete its run; then late in 1894, Alexander had to keep a pledge to Henry Arthur Jones and do *The Masqueraders*. This play did not succeed; and Alexander finally sat down to a critical reading of *Guy Domville*. It was a "hideous, supreme ordeal." Whole scenes were cut and speeches were mangled. Alexander had "a theory of the play so beggarly in its meagreness and crudity, that it is absolutely nauseating." James swallowed his pride. He told Elizabeth Robins however that his play had been "abbreviated and simplified out of all *close* resemblance to my intention."

And then quite irrelevantly Alexander came down with German measles and the novelist fretted through another fortnight, during which he read with admiration Ibsen's *Little Eyolf*. He saw in *Little Eyolf* fine opportunities for the Ibsen actress, Miss Robins. "Really uttered, *done*, in the gathered northern twilight, with the flag down and the lights coming out across the fjord, the scene might have a real solemnity of beauty." Then Alexander was well again and at the beginning of December 1894 the novelist had been summoned to the St. James's for rehearsals.

THE NORTHERN HENRY

I

HENRY JAMES HAD FIRST HEARD OF HENRIK IBSEN—"THE NORTHERN Henry," as he later referred to him—from Edmund Gosse. "You must tell me more," he had written in 1889. The essayist and critic, who had begun as a specialist in the literature of northern Europe, obliged his friend; and in 1890 we find James writing to him: "How provincial all these poor dear Norsefolk, including the Colossus himself. They all affect me like intensely domestic fowl plucking behind a hedge—the big bristling hedge

of Germany." By 1891 he had read excerpts from *Brand* and
Peer Gynt in translation and in January of that year he attended
his first performance of Ibsen's *A Doll's House,* in which Elizabeth
Robins played Mrs. Linde. But in April 1891 James still protested.
He found *Rosmersholm* dreary; *Ghosts* shocked him. "Must I
think these things works of skill?" he queried Gosse. They seemed
to him of a "grey mediocrity." They were simply "moral tales
in dialogue—without the objectivity, the visibility of the drama."
He added: "I can't think that a man who is at odds with his
form is ever a first-rate man. But I may be grossly blind."

A few days after this he went to see Elizabeth Robins in her
own production of *Hedda Gabler.* The play had "muddled and
mystified" him when he read it; now he was fascinated. Ibsen was
actable, and Hedda—in the hands of the young American actress
—was indeed "uncanny." He had sat through three performances
and had promptly written an article, "On the Occasion of *Hedda
Gabler,*" which placed him on the side of the Ibsenites in the
brewing battle between the defenders of the Norwegian playwright and the Victorians of the old school. He recognized that
Ibsen had "sounded in our literary life a singularly interesting
hour." He could not, however, overcome his sense of Ibsen's "bare
provinciality." Indeed he always had for him uncomplimentary
adjectives along with his compliments. He spoke of the dramatist's
"charmless fascination," his "aesthetic density"; he was not
happy with his evocation of "a spare strenuous democratic
community." He was "ugly, common, hard, prosaic, bottomlessly
bourgeois"—and yet "of his art he's a master." James would have
been happier, one judges, if Henrik Ibsen had emulated Shakespeare and written about kings and queens. But with these reservations, he recognized two things. The first was that Ibsen would be
the "adored" dramatist of the acting profession; he made it possible for actors "to do the deep and delicate thing." The second—
and this touched him personally—was Ibsen's extraordinary skill
in projecting a situation, in choosing a crucial hour in the lives of a

group, and yet within that hour making the audience aware of the entire psychological history and "the whole tissue of relations" between his people. In this sense Ibsen's influence on the later novels of Henry James was profound: it was Ibsen's "admirable talent for producing an intensity of interest by means incorruptibly quiet, by that almost demure preservation of the appearance of the usual, in which we see him juggle with difficulty and danger and which constitutes, as it were, his only coquetry." The sentence that follows, in the article on *Hedda*, shows exactly where Ibsen the artist had touched the artist in Henry James: "There are people who are indifferent to these mild prodigies; there are others for whom they will always remain the most charming privilege of art."

What James did not discern at first—and it had to be pointed out to him—was that Ibsen achieved his effect through his symbolic power. James had complained of "the absence of style, both in the usual and larger sense of the word." This might have made Ibsen "vulgar," for he was "massively common and 'middle-class,' but neither his spirit," wrote James, "nor his manner is small." These remarks prompted William Archer, the most dedicated of drama critics in the 1890's and one of Ibsen's translators, to a rejoinder. In a long letter he praised James for having written "one of the very few really sane and luminous things that have been said on the subject in English," but he assured him that in the original Ibsen was a master of style—if style, on the stage, meant giving to every word a vital function. The real secret of Ibsen, Archer told James, was that he was "the greatest *poet* who has as yet enslaved himself to the conditions of realistic, or perhaps I should rather say everyday, drama." In this sense Ibsen had a "gigantic imagination," for he could seize a few fragments of experience and endow them with the depth and complexity of life. "Remember," Archer told James, "it is not as a realist, but rather as a symbolist, that I chiefly admire Ibsen." James was to remember this, for in a complementary piece, "On the Occasion of *The*

Master Builder," two years later he spoke of "the mingled reality
and symbolism of it all" that "gives us an Ibsen within an Ibsen."

There was indeed an imaginative link between the dramatist
who had used a wild duck as symbol of man's imprisonment
within his instincts and civilization and the novelist who would
invoke the wings of a dove for a sinister drama—a future "death in
Venice."

II

The record of James's flirtation with Ibsen makes amusing reading
in his correspondence with Miss Robins and Mrs. Bell. *The Master Builder* arrived in London act by act. James, reading the
translation piecemeal, as it was sent to him, was driven "from
bewilderment to madness." He looked for a leading role for Miss
Robins, but saw only the Master Builder. "The fact remains that
the quinquagenarian architect *must* be the heroine," he teased.
"Miss Elizabeth must do *him*." And then there were the usual
reservations: "It is all most strange, most curious, most vague,
most horrid, most 'middle-classy' in the peculiar ugly Ibsen sense."
But when he saw Miss Robins's great triumph in the play—he had
attended the rehearsals—he recognized the triumph of Ibsen as
well. In his article he wrote of "the hard compulsion of his
strangely inscrutable art." And writing about *Little Eyolf*, he
spoke of "the small Ibsen *spell*, the surrender of the imagination
to his microcosm, his confined but completely constituted world."
Finally, seeing *John Gabriel Borkman*, some time later, he praised
"the sturdy old symbolist" and his "admirable economy," but as
before contended the plays had "no tone but their moral tone."
He complained of "so dry a view of life, so indifferent a vision of
the comedy of things."

Unable to read Ibsen in the original, James never consecrated to
him the full-length article he might have written. However, as late
as 1908, in the preface to his novel *The Awkward Age*, we find
him still holding to his fundamental view, although he pretends to
put the words into the mouth of a devil's advocate against the

theatre. This advocate's argument is that playwrights like Ibsen and Dumas are forced in the theatre to renounce the fine for the coarse; in this James was arguing in reality his own difficulties with the stage. Ibsen was clear, he said, only on a thesis as "simple and superficial" as that of *A Doll's House,* but was confused and obscure from the moment he tried to say something finer, as in *The Wild Duck.* Even *Hedda Gabler,* for all its appeal, was enfeebled by remarkable vagueness. These criticisms voiced, the novelist nevertheless recognized—as imaginative artists will—all that had meaning for his own work in the plays of the northern Henry.

The subterranean influence of Ibsen on James's fiction belonged to the future; a direct influence could be discerned on two plays projected in 1893, the year when he was involved in the piecemeal study of *The Master Builder* and its final production. Coming on Ibsen at the very moment when he himself was turning playwright, James seems to have asked himself whether he should enroll under the Norwegian's experimental—and avant-garde—banner or go his own way. Ibsen, still a playwright for the small coterie in London, was hardly a model for a novelist who wished to find a large audience. Miss Robins obtained her hearings for Ibsen through subscription evenings, special performances, subsidized management: he was hardly a model for an artist whose eye was on the box office. Nevertheless, James had had Ibsen in mind in the spring of 1893 when he planned *Guy Domville.* He shaped the play for a handful of characters and chose a critical moment in the hero's history, when Guy is confronted with a moral decision; and late that year, dreaming before his Christmas fire, he first sketched the scenario for what ultimately became *The Other House.* Here he planned a "bourgeois" drama and "provincial" characters in the manner of Ibsen—creating a tense and violent "Bad Heroine" who seemed ideally suited to the special talents of the actress who had played Hedda in England. But *The Other House* did not become a play in the 1890's. And *Guy Domville* was not to be produced until 1895.

SAINT ELIZABETH

THE BATTLE FOR IBSEN, WHICH OCCURRED DURING THE YEARS HENRY James was writing plays, brought him close to Elizabeth Robins and their friend in common, Florence Bell. We can glimpse these interesting ladies in James's theatrical tale of "Nona Vincent," written immediately after his experiences with *The American* in 1891. Miss Elizabeth is embodied in the ambiguous, faltering actress with the two-toned name of Violet Grey—for she had her gray side as well as her violet. And Mrs. Bell, who was a wise and worldly English cosmopolite, is the quiet Mrs. Alsager—very sage and purposeful—who helps the young dramatist find a producer. Miss Robins had played Claire de Cintré in James's play—and had played her very badly. James had wished that Mrs. Bell, or the American beauty—the friend of the Prince of Wales—Mrs. Mahlon Sands, might show the tense and earnest Miss Robins what was wrong with her acting. Miss Robins had but recently come to England; she had had considerable professional experience, and had toured across the United States with Barrett and Booth, but she could not play a Jamesian renunciatory lady. "I am unhappy about Miss Robins's hair—but I wish she could see you!" James had written to Mrs. Sands. The ending of "Nona Vincent" hinges on Violet Grey's finally having a talk with Mrs. Alsager and turning her role from failure into great success. A young and energetic actress in her twenties, Miss Robins was a presence of charm and vitality, but she was strenuous: she lacked the repose of the older ladies, and their calm. A young woman like Miss Robins invited chivalry and gallantry; but usually James could relate to her only in a courtly manner.

I

In a later time, long after James was dead, Miss Robins published the letters Henry James wrote her during the years of his dramatic

obsession and their common espousal of Ibsen. She called the
book *Theatre and Friendship*. In spite of her own gloss, and the
atmosphere she created in the book of a deep and cherished
intimacy, the correspondence is lively and impersonal. The letters
are humorous, good-natured, filled with persiflage and elaborate
courtesies; many are simply the equivalent of modern telephonic
communication—appointments, comments, shared public enthusi-
asms. What one discovers in the book is the skill with which Miss
Robins used James's letters to her friend Florence Bell to support
and enhance those written to herself. One-fourth of the volume
belongs to Mrs. Bell, and by far the warmest letters in it are
addressed to her. The book is indeed a record of a triangular
theatre-friendship. Miss Robins and Mrs. Bell were devoted
friends. They wrote to each other daily, since Mrs. Bell was much
out of London in her north-country home. James on his side wrote
to both about the other—and about himself.

The friendship between Miss Robins and James was one of
backstage camaraderie and common dedication. The novelist, in
his play-writing phase, nourished a dream of writing a great part
for her; and he seems to have had her in mind when he was
creating the child murderess in *The Other House*. A handsome
hard-working woman, Miss Robins could be all fire and passion—
and perversity—as Hedda or Hilda; but she could do little with
other parts and other plays. She knew this and became an Ibsen
specialist, although James repeatedly warned her that she was
narrowing her career. She listened but went her own way. Leonard
Woolf, who knew her at a later time, characterized her as "gentle,
soft, frail—and *iron*." In the 1890's she was far from frail; but
there was plenty of iron. She gave an effect however of softness.
"In talking with her one continues to *batter* one's self against that
quiet individuality of determination—not to say perversity of it—
which takes for me, at least, all sense of effect and fruit from my
words." Thus James to Florence Bell. "She sees her life in a
certain way—and that's the end of it. But she *will*, all the same, I

think, arrive." Miss Robins did "arrive"; but not in the usual theatre-sense.

The actress had a way of disarming those who talked with her—and she talked mainly to the great. She was all attention; she turned on them her lustrous blue eyes; she created an effect of hearing and understanding everything. By means of her quiet intensity she had managed with extraordinary skill, within a week after landing in London, to involve a dozen leading stage figures, among them Beerbohm Tree and Oscar Wilde, in her personal affairs and ambitions. Only Bernard Shaw cut through her pose, and for a long time Elizabeth Robins feared and detested him. He rode rough-shod over her Joan of Arc manner—he dubbed her "Saint Elizabeth." He understood her way of using her environment and of making herself the center of it. "The beautiful puritan charm, the St. Elizabeth sanctity, the pure-toned voice, the unstagey beauty of movement"—these were the qualities Shaw found in her playing in *Pillars of Society*. He had interviewed her when he was still a round-the-town journalist, and before they had ended their talk Miss Elizabeth "swore she would shoot me if I said anything she didn't approve of." The situation he describes in a letter to Miss Robins at the time of *The Master Builder* was typical of the actress's way of arousing response in men and then retreating from them:

You send me for a cab, and contemptuously reward me with a lift, during which, being so near you, I cannot help being in love with you in a poetic and not in the least ignoble way; but though I do not venture on the faintest expression of my impulse, you discover it by a sort of devilish divination, and instantly I am seized and flung out of the vehicle into the mud, with wheels flying over me this way and that and horses dancing and stumbling on my countenance.

Shaw was indulging in characteristic verbal caricature; but the episode (of which there is a record in his shorthand diaries) is illustrative. Elizabeth Robins, with her large liquid eyes and her inner toughness, regarded men as creatures to be manipulated. She could love women; men were to be conquered and "used," and her secret love affair with the critic William Archer—a story yet to be told—was a kind of collaboration in the theatre as much as a passion, a case of mutual professional respect transmuted into affection. There is even a mention of a child somewhere in her legend; and a bundle of love letters from the later poet laureate John Masefield. But while she kept a voluminous archive, she covered her tracks carefully. "This mania for secrecy will undo you," Shaw wrote to her. She remained secretive all her life. "What the world wants from her is not noble conduct but acting," he told a friend. Miss Robins preferred the noble conduct. And Shaw discerned one thing more—that Elizabeth Robins was a great actress only when she was acting her own life. He recognized that the emotion, so powerfully infused into Ibsen, was "really yourself and not your acting." In this the dramatist touched the deepest truth of her career. He put his finger on her greatest secret, and the heart of her success. In later years, Henry James also came to understand this. He told a friend she had been wise ultimately to leave the stage—to abandon the false position of being engaged "without a scrap or shred of artistic feeling, in an occupation which was all art."

II

In America Miss Robins had been married to an actor named George R. Parkes; her widow's weeds proclaimed the fact when she arrived in England. That part of her life however was one of the best kept secrets of all. Parkes had wooed Miss Elizabeth in the 1880's at the stage door when they were both players at the Boston Museum. He offered her much attention and gallantry; he was ready to be her flunky—and in her lonely youth, seeking to win a place on the stage, she was appreciative and even affectionate in her cold ambitious way. Photographs of Parkes suggest an elegant

if flaccid "masher" of the time; and Miss Robins, who had resisted
a number of wooers, finally—after much conflict and secrecy—
married Parkes almost as if it were a business arrangement. They
rushed from the ceremony to their respective theatres. Nothing
could interrupt their careers. Matrimony was to be a kind of
companionship and indeed Miss Robins treated her husband as if
he were a younger brother. Between them they earned a comfortable income; they lived at good hotels; but Miss Robins always got
better parts and more press notice than young Parkes, a fatal thing
in most stage marriages. Moreover Mrs. Parkes spent much of her
day sewing her costumes, dressing her hair, studying her roles.
Being a tremendous bluestocking, she also studied German and
French at night and read serious philosophical books. Her husband was baffled and frustrated. But it is clear that he was also a
man of little resource, more capable of tantrum than of self-assertion. He tried consistently to domesticate Elizabeth. He urged her
to give up the stage and become a home-keeping wife. He planted
her for a long hot summer in a dreary house at Medford with his
dull mother and dull sisters. Elizabeth Robins paced the veranda
like a caged lioness—like Hedda Gabler. Thus within months of
her marriage she had lived out A Doll's House and Hedda several
years before she heard the name of Henrik Ibsen. The ending of
this domestic strife was indeed to be like one of Ibsen's stark
tragedies.

Parkes had always kept a suit of stage armor in his hotel room,
although he never explained why. One day the armor was missing
—and so was Parkes. Only Miss Robins knew what he had done,
for in the letter he wrote and mailed to his wife he did not spare
her any details. He was ending everything. He could not continue
a loveless marriage: and as a sadistic refinement he told Elizabeth
the time at which he would be drowning himself, weighed down
by the armor, in the Charles River. When she received the letter it
was past the fatal hour. For ten days the actress did not know
whether she was a widow or the subject of a grim joke. She lived in

the glare of newspaper headlines and a police search. The body was finally recovered in Boston harbor. Parkes had tied the armor to his feet to pull him down. Ultimately it had dropped away and the corpse had floated to the surface.

The widow's weeds which Elizabeth wore when she arrived in London in 1888 were a symbol of her shock and feeling of guilt. In later years she forgot her troubled life with Parkes. She wrote of him in private memoranda as if their love had endured and as if his ghost were at her side. Fortunately she was young and her sense of self was strong. During a later suffragette phase she even nourished a curious fantasy that George would have approved of her militancy. She destroyed some of his letters but carefully packaged and sealed others in her archive. Fifty years after the tragedy she could not bring herself to part with these sad relics which included a batch of clippings from the Boston newspapers. She died in her ninetieth year in 1952 with the seals unbroken.

Miss Robins's *Hedda* had been "uncanny" to James, because the stifled exasperated lady of Ibsen's play embodied the desperate desolation of the veranda in Medford; and when Hilda Wangel knocked on the door and sounded the fate of the Master Builder, Miss Robins was playing the "Saint Elizabeth" who expected men to serve her as her husband had done during his wooing, by total abdication of the self. Her success in *The Master Builder* was also related to a more remote part of her experience. At sixteen she had been taken by her metallurgist father to spend a summer in a mining camp at Summit in Colorado. The "Little Annie" gold mine was a profound adventure of her adolescence (she was at a later phase to go to the Klondike during the gold rush to be with her favorite brother Raymond Robins). It was as if Ibsen had known Miss Robins and her Colorado life when he provided his northern Hilda Wangel with an alpenstock and made her talk of great heights and castles in the air.

Miss Robins was intelligent and intuitive. She knew exactly on what plane to pitch her friendship with Henry James. She did not give him too great a feeling of mystery; she aroused no anxieties. In her cultivated simplicity she made him feel at home when he called, served him a cup of cocoa, listened to him until late in the night while he talked of his play troubles—and offered him the quiet encouragement of her blue eyes.

They were often at the theatre together. They went to see Coquelin and Duse. James's letters to her are pitched on a plane of bemused euphoria: "Saturday evening will suit me down to the ground—or as I ought in your case to say, up to the skies: and I shall be eager—and not later than *nine*." During the period when Ibsen's plays were arriving piecemeal from Norway, and James was writing mystified letters, unable to figure out what role Miss Robins would play, we have Miss Robins reporting to Mrs. Bell: "Third instalment of the Ibsen play. I am more in a maze than ever. . . . I had a cosy chat over the fire with H.J. yesterday. I told him bits and read him bits (intensely private of course) under seal of secrecy except so far as you're concerned. He comes Tuesday of next week to hear if the Ibsen heroine has appeared yet and what she's like. He'll faint when he hears!" James found *The Master Builder*, on reading it, "most *un*promising for Miss Elizabeth or for any *woman*." He felt the play to be a man's play, the Master Builder's. But Miss Robins had quietly studied Norwegian—she had travelled in Norway before coming to England, in the company of the widow of the violinist Ole Bull—and did not have to rely on the hurried translations of Archer and Gosse. James little dreamed, as he later recognized, with what magic and witchery the actress would render Hilda Wangel: nor would he ever know that all of herself was in the part. She was perhaps unconsciously acknowledging this when, in a lecture on Ibsen three decades later, she remarked, "Make no mistake, you must let Ibsen play you, rather than insist on your playing Ibsen." Everyone agreed there was something demonic in the way in which Miss Robins played some of her Ibsen roles.

The Isabel Archer side of Miss Robins understandably appealed to Henry James even though she came closer to possessing the histrionic self-absorption and self-centeredness of his actress Miriam Rooth in *The Tragic Muse*. (James with a flourish inscribed that novel to her as "From her friend and colleague" during the run of *The American*.) He befriended her as a compatriot and as a woman of temperament. What he never discovered was that Miss Robins had, behind her mask of the stage, the mind of a journalist. She thus had a Henrietta Stackpole side to her as well. From her earliest days she had regarded all of her experience as potential "copy." In the end, when there were no more Ibsen parts for her to play, she abandoned the stage and under the name of C. E. Raimond wrote a series of sensational best-selling novels based on questions of the day—euthanasia, votes for women, white slavery. Dressed in a Salvation Army costume she gathered material for the latter work at first hand from the prostitutes in Piccadilly. She doubtless would have kept this secret side of her endeavors undisclosed had not Mrs. Patrick Campbell come upon some of her bundles of proof or perhaps a manuscript in her flat. Mrs. Pat could never keep a secret and Miss Robins was forced to admit that she was C. E. Raimond. The *nom de plume* embodied much more than met the eye. The initials C. E. R. were those of her father; and Raymond was the youngest and best-loved of the three brothers she helped raise. She absorbed thus into her career and existence the males who had meant most to her. She clung to her mass of papers, her minute diaries recording dates and meetings. Had James known that Miss Robins dreamed of turning all that happened to her into copy, he probably would have kept a much greater distance. What saved Miss Robins was her innate discretion—and her indirectness. She began too late to write her memoirs: the first volume barely covers her pre-Ibsen experiences in England. Virginia Woolf gave her the happy title for the book—*Both Sides of the Curtain*; but the picture of both sides had been too abundantly preserved. Drowning in the clutter of her days, Miss Robins produced a confused memoir of her earliest English

years and never wrote the volume which would have counted most:
that of her Ibsen triumphs and her wide friendships.

III

Mrs. Alsager in the tale of "Nona Vincent" has a large comfortable house in London, "simply a sort of distillation of herself" and her "shy sincerity." She is married to an indulgent wealthy husband and she throws "her liberty and leisure into the things of the soul—the most beautiful things she knew." This lady listens to the dramatist's play, introduces him to a producer, helps him to success; and as we have seen ultimately shows the leading lady how to do her part. The attributes of Mrs. Alsager would fit a number of James's literary lady-friends; but they fit best of all Florence Bell, wife of the colliery owner and ironmaster Hugh Bell. She had grown up in France and from childhood had often sat in a box at the Comédie Française; she cherished the French stage and the French language. James and Mrs. Bell thus had common Gallic ground. A lady of delicate perceptions, she was warm, attentive, generous; busy always with her three children and two stepchildren (one of whom was the indomitable Gertrude Bell, explorer of Arabian deserts), she divided her time between her Yorkshire home at Redcar and her big house at 95 Sloane Street. When she was in London, James found her house a welcome place to spend a late afternoon, and Mrs. Bell was an eager listener to his plays. He had given her a copy of the privately printed dramatization of *Daisy Miller*, which normally he would not have shown to anyone; he allowed her to read the manuscript of *The American*; and she was an interested participant in all his stage adventures. "Lady of the full program and rich performance," James was to say of her, and indeed this was the role in which he appreciated her. They had met in the mid-1880's and already had the habit of going to theatres and discussing plays when Elizabeth Robins came into their lives. James accepted Mrs. Bell's opinions of his plays because she had shown some ability as a playwright herself; she had a flair for comic dialogue and could write witty closet comedies. One of them, written in French, had been performed at the Théâtre Français by Coquelin. Others on occasion were performed in London and were the delight of amateur companies in the provinces. On attending an evening bill of these chamber comedies James urged Mrs. Bell to "follow the inclination of your mind, which is full of drollery and humorous resource." And he also offered advice: "Avoid simplicity as you would poison and the 'obvious' as you would the devil."

Their interest in Miss Robins was almost that of watchful parents trying to cope with a wilful daughter. They agreed about Miss Robin's "unworldly careering." Reporting from Brighton to Mrs. Bell after seeing Elizabeth in *A Doll's House*, James said she had not been at her best, but it had been good to see her on the stage after an idle spell. "She ought to take more what she can get —to do, whenever she can, *any*thing she can—be it Norwegian or not." He added, "Too little, alas, however, comes in her way—and she is, after all, indifferent (so it seems to me)."

A great opportunity did come her way in the spring of 1893. Mrs. Patrick Campbell, slightly younger than Miss Robins and then less known, was offered the part of Paula Tanqueray in Pinero's play which Alexander had in production. But Mrs. Pat was under contract elsewhere and had to turn it down. Alexander, impressed by Elizabeth's playing of *The Master Builder*, invited her to take the part and she agreed. It was "the kind of thing that comes along once in an actress's lifetime, seldom oftener." In the interval Mrs. Pat was released from her contract. With a show of renunciation worthy of a Jamesian heroine, Elizabeth decided that Mrs. Pat had more claim to the part than she did and surrendered it to her. From the point of view of self-sacrifice and nobility it was a handsome and gallant—indeed a Saint Elizabeth—action; it would have been understandable in a great actress who had already had great parts. It was also something the majority of dedicated actresses would not do. Given the long waits for roles in

the theatre, and the shuffles and changes, what had occurred had
not demanded so much sacrifice on Miss Robins's part. Moreover
Mrs. Pat was young enough and promising enough to have other
chances, as she did some years later, when she created Eliza in
Shaw's *Pygmalion*. Miss Robins seemed to have thought neither of
the future nor of her own great needs. She wrote to Mrs. Pat that
she was consoled at losing the part by the fact that it had come to
her fellow-actress. In terms of a stage career this was not a loss but
a surrender. Miss Robins had made of the incident one of her
Ibsenite moments—the "noble conduct" which she put above her
art. And she signed her strange letter of renunciation with these
words: "There is to my mind no woman in London so enviable at
this moment, dear savage, as *you*." Miss Robins's friend and
literary executor, Dr. Octavia Wilberforce, was to grant many years
later that this decision showed that Elizabeth was not "one
hundred per cent actress"—but after a further thought she added,
"Elizabeth wasn't a hundred per cent anything."

Henry James was in Paris at that moment and seems to have
gained the impression that the loss of the part was simply a bit of
bad luck. He felt Miss Robins had behaved "admirably well." But
here again others understood more clearly: Mrs. Pat herself, who
was to be forever grateful, though not always loyal, recognized
that the bluestocking in Miss Robins was in conflict with the
actress. "The peculiar quality of Elizabeth Robins's dramatic gift,"
she said, "was the swiftness with which she succeeded in sending
thought across the footlights; emotion took a second place, personality a third."

OSCAR

I

THE BULKY FIGURE OF OSCAR WILDE HAD CROSSED HENRY JAMES'S
path at infrequent intervals during the previous decade. They had
met long before—in 1882—in a drawing room in Washington,
during Oscar's circus-like tour of America. James had confided to
friends at the time that he thought Wilde "an unclean beast," and
found him "repulsive and fatuous." Thereafter he referred to him
usually in terms of the animal kingdom. There was however no ill
will or animosity between them. Oscar simply irritated James; and
the novelist regarded with curiosity and a certain amused condescension the public antics and public wit of the younger man.
Wilde on his side spoke with respect but with understandable
reservations concerning the fastidious American. His own relaxed
amateurism, his emphasis on talk and performance rather than on
creation, caused him to feel that James treated art as "a painful
duty" rather than as one of the amusements of life. They had no
common bonds of temperament; and they represented two diamet-
rically opposed attitudes toward life and the imagination. If Wilde
insisted on putting his talent into his art and his genius into his
life (as he later told André Gide), Henry James did exactly the
opposite. James's drawing-room wit was merely the surplus of his
genius—and he lived for his art. He was eleven years older than
Wilde; he worked hard and was highly productive. Wilde had a
lazy facility that James found "cheap"—the cheapness of the actor
who knows how to provoke applause: he had written very little and
the American deplored the public display which had made the
young Wilde the subject of Gilbert and Sullivan and of George du
Maurier in *Punch*. There has been speculation that Gabriel Nash,
the talkative aesthete in *The Tragic Muse*, incorporated some of

Wilde's qualities: if this was so, James had drawn a singularly generous portrait. Nash's cultivated ineffectuality might be that of Wilde; his wit is that of Henry James, and so is his sentience. Whether James read *The Picture of Dorian Gray* when it came out in 1891 we do not know. What we do know is that Wilde turned to the theatre at the very time that James did; and from this moment on, they were—from James's point of view—rivals, or fellow-contenders in the same arena.

In 1892 Henry James went to the opening of *Lady Windermere's Fan*, Oscar's first play, filled with a great curiosity. The play, he wrote to Mrs. Bell, "strikes me as a mixture that will run, though infantine to my sense, both in subject and in form. As a drama it is of a candid and primitive simplicity, with a perfectly reminiscential air about it." It contained things one had always seen in plays, and from this point of view there was nothing to analyze or discuss. "But there is so much drollery—that is 'cheeky' paradoxical wit of dialogue, and the pit and gallery are so pleased at finding themselves clever enough to 'catch on' to four or five of the ingenious—too ingenious—*mots* in the dozen, that it makes them feel quite '*décadent*' and *raffiné* and they enjoy the sensation as a change from the stodgy." They thought they were hearing the talk of the *grand monde*—"poor old *grand monde*"—and they felt altogether "privileged and modern." There was a perpetual attempt at epigram, and many of these fell flat, "but those that hit are very good indeed. This will make, I think, a success—possibly a really long run." There was no characterization; all the personages talked "equally strained Oscar" and the central situation "one has seen from the cradle." As for Oscar's curtain speech, it may have been impudent but it was "simple inevitable mechanical Oscar", that is, said James, the usual trick "of saying the unusual—complimenting himself and his play." James thought it wrong of the newspapers, which had criticized Oscar's levity, to be taking his remarks and his attitude seriously. To be deadly serious about his lack of seriousness seemed to James simply stupid. "Everything

Oscar does is a deliberate trap for the literalist, and to see the literalist walk straight up to it, look straight at it and step straight into it, makes one freshly avert a discouraged gaze from this unspeakable animal."

Two days later he wrote a further account of the occasion for Henrietta Reubell in Paris; she was a friend of Oscar's and he frequented her salon in the Avenue Gabriel. "I was at the *première* on Saturday last and saw the unspeakable one make his speech to the audience, with a metallic blue carnation in his buttonhole and a cigarette in his fingers. The speech, which, alas, was stupid, was only to say that he judged the audience felt the play to be nearly as charming as he did. I expected something much more *imprévu*." James quoted some of the Oscarisms he had liked. "There's nothing like the devotion of a married woman—it's a thing no married man knows anything about." "Yes. London is all sad people and fogs. I don't know whether fogs produce the sad people, or the sad people produce the fogs!" "There is nothing so unbecoming to a woman as a nonconformist conscience." And "To love a good woman is a middle-class education." The epigrams however sounded familiar to James, "and the idea of the play, of which the treatment is beneath discussion, is one that has been knocking about for fifty years."

"*Ce monsieur,*" James wrote, "gives at last on one's nerves." One suspects however it was not only Wilde who made James nervous. It was his own recognition that Wilde had an infallible sense of his audience, which he lacked.

11

During James's gouty winter in Paris word reached him that Wilde's second play, *A Woman of No Importance*, was about to be put on. When he heard of its subject he became worried; the play sounded singularly like his own unproduced comedy, *Tenants*, which dealt with a woman "unimportant" in the same sense as Wilde's, and with her illegitimate son. A letter was posted promptly from the Hotel Westminster to Miss Robins: "One thing I do wish you would do—tell me three words about Oscar W's piece—when it is produced; and if in particular the *subject* seems to discount my poor three-year-older that Hare will neither produce nor part with." Miss Robins however was busy arranging an Ibsen season for the early summer. She did not reply. James wrote again, sending a subscription to her season and cautioning her once more on figuring in public "as an Ibsen-actress only." Also he renewed his appeal—he would welcome, he said, "a spark of ecstasy over Oscar W's tragedy. I am consumed with curiosity . . . but I eat my heart out in silence." Miss Robins continued silent, and James turned to Mrs. Bell for "any stray crust or two about Oscar's play . . . *don't* neglect Oscar." A few days later another letter to Mrs. Bell: "If you have a hearing of the entrancing Oscar may I have an echo of it? I read with wonderment Archer's strange rhapsody over him in the *World*. However, I sit in darkness."

He was satisfied only after his return to London and then rested easy, for he found Wilde's play "an *enfantillage*," he told Miss Reubell, "a piece of helpless puerility." Yet his own *Tenants*, which he had thought Wilde's play might resemble, could be similarly criticized. He too had assembled all the Victorian stage clichés: a retired army officer, his illegitimate son, his ward, the love of the army man's legitimate son for the girl, the confrontation of the legitimate and illegitimate sons—a goodly collection of stereotypes, which James had adapted from a tale in the *Revue des Deux Mondes*. He had actually written the play before seeing any of Wilde's comedies, and he was attempting a similar though more serious kind of comedy. The truth James did not face was that Wilde's successes in the theatre—and his own failures—stemmed directly from the attitudes the two men brought to the stage and to their audiences. James's comedies were full of unexpected situations and drolleries, and his wit was often superior to Wilde's; but it lacked Wilde's common touch, his sense of what would amuse. James was not only too subtle, but also too earnest, in his endeavor; and when he tried to be less subtle, he became banal. Wilde's humor was inherent in his comic situations and in his air of improvised fantasy out of which his social caricature sprang. James's humor was all on the surface, it was built into the speeches, not the action.

We thus have the spectacle of two gifted writers each attempting in his own way to put a kind of intellectual comedy on the stage. Wilde accomplished this by being offhand and casual, as if he were shrugging his shoulders. James anxiously cared; indeed he cared too much, as his series of *Theatricals* and their apologetic prefaces show. His subtlety was a fine theatrical instrument; and it had to be used finely. He was blunting it under the misguided belief that he must discover common ground with audiences whose needs he could not experience. He had never had to face such problems in writing his tales.

III

Back in London James went to see Eleanora Duse with her "exquisite delicacy and truth and naturalness." He also had some evenings at the visiting Comédie Française with Rhoda Broughton, the sharp-tongued Victorian novelist, seeing Sarah Bernhardt. Duse had neither the temperament—nor the vulgarity—of Sarah, "but a pathos, a finish, an absence of the tricks of the trade that are strangely touching and fascinating. No beauty—no wigs, no clothes, scarcely any paint—but a delicate refinement and originality. The total is rare." In a sense one might have said that Sarah resembled Wilde. The qualities of Duse were in himself.

He went also to see Miss Robins in an Ibsen series and praised her work; but he felt he was being exposed to a heavy dose of northern gloom. Then on the stage of the St. James's he watched Mrs. Pat play Paula Tanqueray, with the consequences we have seen. It gave him renewed courage. He determined to stake everything on *Guy Domville*.

THE YOUNG BARD

HE HAD GONE, LATE IN 1891, TO DRESDEN, HURRIEDLY CROSSING THE
Channel to stand in a dreary little suburban cemetery at the grave
of his young compatriot, Wolcott Balestier. Balestier had been an
unabashed success-seeker, a literary publisher who had helped
James with the financial details of the dramatized *American*. He
had come abroad bringing his own exuberance and the praises of
William Dean Howells; and in a few months had made friends
with most of the established English writers, and with the new
"infant prodigy"—for so James called him—Rudyard Kipling. Balestier worked in picturesque but insalubrious quarters beside
Westminster Abbey. Somewhere he had taken a drink of contami-
nated water; and now he was dead of a virulent typhoid in a
strange city, his dream of rivalling (in partnership with William
Heinemann) the great publishing Baron Tauchnitz abruptly
ended. James had developed a deep affection for him, and had
willingly accompanied Heinemann to Germany to bring solace to
the youth's mother and sisters.

Wolcott Balestier was the first of several young men who came
to figure in Henry James's middle life as beloved acolytes, and
"The Middle Years," the tale he wrote at this time of a dying
novelist and a young admiring doctor who attends him, seems to
reflect something of their relationship, broken so early by Balestier's death. In later years, James wrote annually to Wolcott's
mother on the anniversary of Dresden, mourning the young man
with the emotions of the years, almost as if he had lost a son.
"Strange and sad it seems to me when you bring home to me that
it's eight years since we laid Wolcott to rest in those unforgettable
Dresden days!" he wrote to Mrs. Balestier in the last year of the
century. "His photograph hangs here beside me as I write—and he
looks down at me meeting my eyes, as if he knew I am speaking of

him. My memory, my affection, thank heaven, holds him fast—for all the swift, awful sweep of the deep stream of time, swifter, more noiselessly lapsing with each year." As late as 1911 James could still remind himself that Wolcott would have been fifty had he lived. Only with 1914 did he accept the thought that his young friend, so long dead, was well out of the terrible world into which he himself had survived.

Both Henry James and Edmund Gosse wrote memorials to the young Balestier. Gosse's portrait suggests the characteristic English view of the young American as an attractive if pushing publisher from overseas bringing to the British Isles the promise of high American royalties. James rebuked Gosse for this. He thought one portion of the sketch "ungracious." "To the young," he told Gosse, "the early dead, the baffled, the defeated, I don't think we can be tender enough." In his own brief memoir, which served as preface to Balestier's posthumous novel *The Average Woman*, James paid him perhaps the highest tribute of all: "He had the real cosmopolitan spirit, the easy imagination of differences and hindrances surmounted." Thus he placed him on a footing with himself. On this impersonal ground—but also on the deeper ground of the love he had felt for the young man—James lit still another taper on his private altar of his remembered dead.

I

The cemetery in Dresden was an ugly alien place for a young American to lie. The rite seemed "monstrous" to James for the poor "yesterday-so-much-living boy." He listened to the service read by a chaplain "with soft, yet not offensive sonority," and handed to one of Balestier's sisters a pot of English flowers which Mrs. Edmund Gosse had given him; she let fall this bit of English fragrance and earth into the foreign grave that would henceforth house her brother. The ceremony was soon ended, and James came away with Balestier's other sister, Caroline. She had asked him to ride with her in one of the big black-and-silver funeral coaches

with German footmen also in black and silver. She had whispered
that she wanted to talk with him.

Caroline Balestier was a trim young woman with tiny features
and tiny hands and feet. She was admirable in her grief, in "the
intense—almost manly—nature of her emotion." James described
her as concentrated and passionate, filled with force and courage.
She was a worthy sister to "poor dear big-spirited, only-by-death-
quenchable Wolcott." What Caroline had especially to say to the
novelist in the baroque coach we can only surmise. What we know
is that a month later (on January 18, 1892), Henry James, playing
his paternal role with becoming gravity, gave Caroline Balestier in
marriage to the young poet and story-teller, the great success of
London, Rudyard Kipling. It was a quiet, almost a secret wedding
—the family in mourning, the mother and other sister confined to
their beds with influenza. Only four persons were present besides
the bride and groom. "Oh the 'ironies of fate,' the ugly tricks, the
hideous practical jokes of life," Henry had written from Dresden.
Here was another irony, this marriage of the poet of Empire, from
India, with this daughter of the New World. It mainly illustrated
for James "the ubiquity of the American girl." "I today, at All
Souls, Langham Place, 'gave away' Caroline Balestier to Rudyard
Kipling—a queer office for *me* to perform—but it's done—and an
odd little marriage," James wrote to his friend Morton Fullerton.

II

It was to seem always to James an odd little marriage, but he was
to count the Kiplings as his friends from first to last and to follow
the interval of their life in America, in Vermont, with fascination.
The novelist and the young genius had met in 1890. "I liked
Rudyard," he told Rhoda Broughton. He called him "the young
Bard." Later he called him "the star of the hour," "the infant
monster," "the little black demon." "That little black demon of a
Kipling," he wrote to Robert Louis Stevenson, "will have perhaps
leaped upon your silver strand by the time this reaches you—he

publicly left England to embrace you, many weeks ago—carrying literary genius out of the country with him in his pocket."

In the first flush of his admiration for Kipling and before he had been a principal at his marriage, Henry James had praised his precocity by writing an introduction to the American edition of *Mine Own People*. He had done this as a favor to Balestier, who arranged for the preface, probably because he felt that so new a writer needed introducing in the United States. James's introduction was hedged with precautions: he intuitively felt he must not commit himself too far. He spoke of this "strangely clever youth who has stolen the formidable mask of maturity," he characterized him as having "an identity as marked as a window-frame." Kipling was "shockingly precocious"; he had delight in battle; he was cheeky about women, "and indeed about men and about everything." James noted his love of the private soldier and the primitive man; he felt it a bit of good news that "in the smoking-room too there may be artists." He prophetically remarked however that if invention should ever fail Kipling "he would still have the lyric string and the patriotic chord, on which he plays admirably." He observed that "Mr. Kipling's actual performance is like a tremendous walk before breakfast, making one welcome the idea of the meal, but consider with some alarm the hours still to be traversed."

Disillusionment set in quickly. James had praised Kipling's "extraordinarily observed" stories of barrack-room life; but he began to have doubts when he read *The Light That Failed*—"there," he wrote, "the talent has sometimes failed," even if that talent was enormous. Kipling's violence was deep-seated. He had outdone the brutal stories of Rider Haggard and triumphed; but James could not stomach the new violence. By 1893 Kipling was living in America near Brattleboro and writing James of the winter cold, the rude conditions, the delights of being driven "over stone walls in an oxcart" and how he had met Henry Adams in New York, finding him "painfully civilized" and wearing a tall silk hat, a thing Kipling hadn't seen since he left England. James confided to a friend that he believed the writer well satisfied—"he needs nothing of the civilized order." And he went on, "He charged himself with all he could take of India when he was very young, and gave it out with great effect; but I doubt if he has anything more of anything to give. All sorts of things—i.e. symptoms and indications—seem to me to point to that. But what he *did*—in two or three years, remains wonderful."

This was James's verdict in July 1893, and a year later, when he read *The Jungle Book*, Henry James exclaimed: "How it closes his door and sets his limit! The rise to 'higher types' that one hoped for—I mean the care for life in a finer way—is the rise to the mongoose and the care for the wolf. The *violence* of it all, the almost exclusive preoccupation with fighting and killing is also singularly characteristic." In 1894 he repeated that he expected nothing more from Kipling "save some beast stories."

For a while James had hoped Kipling might have in him the seeds of an English Balzac. Presently he came to recognize that there was in him "almost nothing of the complicated soul or of the female form or of any question of *shades*." The novelist and poet of civilization had looked carefully upon the poet of the jungle and the barrack-room and by the turn of the century he delivered his final judgment to his old Cambridge *confidante*, Grace Norton: "My view of his prose future has much shrunken in the light of one's increasingly observing how little of life he can make use of. Almost nothing civilised save steam and patriotism —and the latter only in verse, where I *hate* it so, especially mixed up with God and goodness, that that half spoils my enjoyment of his great talent." James had been alienated from Kipling "in proportion as he has come steadily from the less simple in subject to the more simple—from the Anglo-Indians to the natives, from the natives to the Tommies, from the Tommies to the quadrupeds, from the quadrupeds to the fish and from the fish to the engines and screws. But he is a prodigious little success and an unqualified little happiness and a dear little chap." He also remarked, "And, *such* an uninteresting mind."

Kipling destroyed many of his letters. But a typed copy of one from James, acknowledging *Kim*, of 1901, suggests the verbal legerdemain the latter practiced in his relationship with his *confrère*. James rejoiced, he wrote, "in such a saturation, such a splendid dose of you." He had read *Kim* "with comment and challenge . . . in other words I have some small reserves and anxieties—as to your frequent *how* of performance." Yet he did not allow these things to matter: he had "surrendered luxuriously to your genius. . . . I take you as you are. It might be that I wished you were quite different—though I don't." Continuing this counterpoint of ironic qualification and praise James added, "You are too sublime—you are too big and there is too much of you. I don't think you've cut out your subject, in *Kim*, with a sharp enough scissors, but with that one little nut cracked—so!—the beauty, the quantity, the prodigality, the Ganges-flood, leave me simply gaping as your procession passes. What a luxury to *possess* a big subject as you possess India!" He ended with the suggestion that Kipling "chuck public affairs, which are an ignoble scene [by which he meant his patriotic verses at the time of the Boer War] and stick to your canvas and your paint box. There are as good colours in the tubes as ever were laid on, and *there* is the only truth. The rest is base humbug."

A ROMANTIC FABLE

I

THE RECIPIENT OF HENRY JAMES'S CONFIDENCES—HIS AMBITIONS
and misgivings in the theatre—had been his old friend Robert
Louis Stevenson. To faraway Samoa, Henry James dispatched
from time to time a record of his hopes and his doubts. While he
had boasted in London of the "honourable" run of *The American*
he had candidly told Stevenson in 1891 that it had been a "public
humiliation," moreover "the papers slated it without mercy." The
word "dishonour" crept into another letter. "I am working with
patient subterraneity at a trade which it is dishonour enough to
practise, without talking about it: a trade supremely dangerous
and heroically difficult—*that* credit at least belongs to it."

But even Stevenson, whom James loved with a tenderness of
memory unique among his friends, had by this time become a
wraith. James remembered how he had visited the Stevensons in
1885 at Skerryvore, their house near Bournemouth, and how ill
Louis had been at the time. He rejoiced in his friend's newfound vigor in the South Seas yet he could no longer invest him with reality.
Some of James's most touching letters were written during these
years to the absent Stevenson and they are among his finest literary
letters—the virtuoso performances of a stylist aware that he is writing to a stylist. The refrain is constant. James felt as if he were writing to a company of ghosts—"You are too far away, you are too
absent—too invisible, inaudible, inconceivable." He teased his
friend, told him he had become "a beautiful myth" and also a kind
of "unnatural uncomfortable *mort*." It is true that the visual-
minded James wanted always to see—and Stevenson's adventures
in Polynesia seemed to belong to fairy tales. Again and again Henry
James pleaded for more description of "people, things, objects,

faces, bodies, costumes, features, gestures, manners"—what he called "the personal painter-touch." He had seen some snapshots; these only whetted his appetite. When John Hay had sent him some of Henry Adams's letters from the Pacific, including an account of his visit to Stevenson, James complained that Adams too had not given him "the *look* of things." (He found however a very good self-portrait in what Adams wrote—"what a power of *baring* one's self—hitherto unsuspected in H.A.")

James regularly sent Stevenson books and papers. When he came upon the Napoleonic volumes of Marbot, they were dispatched in haste for Stevenson's enjoyment. James sent him Bourget and Anatole France, and talked of Thomas Hardy, whose *Tess* he considered "vile," and of the genius of Kipling. There is, in all his letters, a great embracing tenderness. He told Stevenson his friends brandished laurel over his absent head and he called him a "buccaneering Pompadour of the Deep" and "a wandering wanton of the Pacific," and when Stevenson misdated a letter by two years James twitted him as "my dear time-deluded islander." He saluted Stevenson's family as "your playfellows—your fellow-phantoms. The wife-phantom knows my sentiment. The dim ghost of a mother has my heartiest regard." He grieved over Louis's "permanent secession." He was too far away—he had become a legend—but a legend of "opaline iridescence."

II

From beyond the seas there had appeared in London at the moment of Balestier's death the ghostly figure of Henry Adams and that distant ghost from James's Newport youth, John La Farge. They brought news of Tusitala—Stevenson's native name—and his installation in his rough-hewn quarters on the Samoan hilltop.

James had not seen Adams since before the suicide of Clover, his wife, in 1885; the three had had happy times together abroad in 1879 and in Washington in 1882. Now the melancholy historian

was in the British capital again, remembering how he had come
there with his father, Charles Francis Adams, during the Civil
War. In his *Education*, Adams uses the word "extinct" repeatedly
as he describes the emotions of this time. Thinking of Polynesia,
he found himself wishing, during a week he spent in a nursing
home in Wigmore Street, that he might "sleep forever in the
trade-winds under the southern stars, wandering over the dark
purple ocean, with its purple sense of solitude and void." Life, he
wrote, "had been cut in halves" for him. He brought his countenance of despair to Henry James in De Vere Gardens.

James tried to cheer him up out of his own melancholy. Adams
found him on one occasion excited by Kipling's marriage which he
had witnessed six days before; the two friends gossiped about the
poet and his American bride. Adams found Kipling a bohemian, a
wanderer "of the second or third social order"; he felt he had
"behaved well about his young woman," had married in the face
of family opposition. James gave him the impression that Caroline
Kipling was "without beauty or money or special intelligence."
James also told Adams how his friend John Singer Sargent had lost
his temper when he had been scolded by a Cotswolds farmer for
riding his horse over the farmer's spring wheat. Sargent had been
enraged when the farmer suggested he was no gentleman. The
painter had returned to the farmhouse, called out the farmer, and
given him a thrashing. Now he faced a jail term for assault.

All this, Adams reported to a friend in Washington, "much
distresses Henry who has a sympathetic heart. As Sargent seems
not to distress himself, I see no reason why James should do so.
But poor James may well be a little off his nerves, for besides
Balestier's death, the long nervous illness of his sister is drawing
slowly to its inevitable close, and James has the load of it to carry."
Adams had called at Alice James's house on Campden Hill and
had sat for two hours with her companion and friend, Katharine
Loring of Beverly. We gather from Alice's journal that among the
subjects of their talk was the helplessness of English doctors when
faced with American patients.

To Elizabeth Cameron, his Washington *confidante*, Adams wrote, "I feel even deader than I did in the South Seas, but here I feel that all the others are as dead as I. Even Harry James, with whom I lunch Sundays, is only a figure in the same old wall-paper, and really pretends to belong to a world which is as extinct as Queen Elizabeth. I enjoy it." Henry James on his side wrote to his and Adams's Scottish friend, Sir John Clark, the laird of Tillypronie: "I like [Adams] but suffer from his monotonous, disappointed pessimism." Adams was "a man of wealth and leisure, able to satisfy all his curiosities, while I am a penniless toiler—so what can I do for him? However, when the poor dear is in London, I don't fail to do what I can."

Each thus seems to have believed he was comforting the other. In reality they made each other uncomfortable.

III

When Stevenson told James that he had been visited by Adams and La Farge, the novelist had replied: "Henry Adams is as conversible as an Adams is permitted by the scheme of nature to be; but what is wonderful to me is that they have both taken to the buccaneering life when already 'on the return'—La Farge many times a *père de famille*."

Stevenson came on horseback to visit the western wanderers, swimming his horse through a river to get to them. He had accordingly to borrow dry clothes from the American consul so he could dine with them. He described the way in which he was clearing the land and creating his Vailima home in the hills above the sea; and how he and his wife had not yet managed to arrange their food supplies. (It was very much what had happened earlier to the Stevensons at the Silverado mine in California.) Adams and La Farge, returning the visit, sent food ahead, and after a long weary tramp arrived and spent several hours. At the end, the frail and sickly Stevenson seemed greatly refreshed, while Adams was completely exhausted. Stevenson's fragility, Adams observed, "passes description, but his endurance passes his fragility." The eye of

Quincy and Lafayette Square never understood the carefree ways of the bohemian; and Mrs. Stevenson in her dirty workaday *mumu* had seemed to him to be a lady in a nightdress. The Stevensons' mode of existence was "far less human than that of the natives"; compared with their shanty Adams considered the native houses palaces. He decided that Stevenson's ability to live in this "squalor" was due to his education. "His early associates were all second-rate; he never seems by any chance to have come in contact with first-rate people, either men, women or artists." This was spoken like an Adams; it was like his judgment of the second- or third-rateness of Kipling. How he reconciled Stevenson's knowing the first-rate Henry James we do not know. Adams moreover felt uncomfortable in a belief that Stevenson, with his gregarious nature, had contempt "for my Bostonianism." Stevenson however had written to James, "we have had enlightened society; a great privilege—would it might endure."

To Sir John Clark again, Henry James voiced his wonder "how Adams and La Farge could either of them have failed to murder the other." He had finally decided that "each lives to prove the other's self-control." La Farge, passing through London briefly on his way back to America, felt that James did not understand Adams: and probably there had been peace in Polynesia between the restless La Farge and the melancholy Adams only because La Farge was busy absorbing the painter's visual world and the South Sea colors and Adams, in his effort to get outside himself, was trying very hard to keep pace with him. James wondered afresh at "La Farge's combination of social and artistic endowments." He characterized him to Stevenson as "a strange and complicated product." He was delighted however to find that neither his charm nor his talk had changed; for a moment the years fell away —they were in Newport again, on the shining sands, walking to the Paradise Rock. "I was all young again," La Farge wrote to Adams.

It was probably with a sense of relief that Henry James had seen Adams off to America in February of 1892. Adams had hardly emerged from his cabin to take the sea air, he later wrote, "when I fell into the arms of Rudyard Kipling and his new wife, and wife's sister, and wife's mother." "Henry James," he wrote to a friend, "is responsible for this last variation on my too commonplace existence." Adams quickly changed his mind about Kipling; he wasn't second- or third-rate; indeed he judged him one of the rare Englishmen he had met whom he did not experience as condescending to an American. "Fate was kind on that voyage," he was to remember in the *Education*, "Rudyard Kipling, on his wedding trip to America, thanks to the mediation of Henry James, dashed over the passenger his exuberant fountain of gaiety and wit—as though playing a garden hose on a thirsty and faded begonia."

I V

That had been almost two years before, and in the midst of the rehearsals of *Guy Domville*, on December 17, 1894, Henry read in the newspapers that Stevenson was dead. The news had travelled slowly from the distant place where he had been buried on his hilltop—Tusitala, the teller of tales—buried for his permanent sleep under the bright and starry sky. "This ghastly extinction of the beloved R.L.S.," James wrote to Gosse that evening, "it makes me cold and sick—and with the absolute, almost alarmed sense, of the visible material quenching of an indispensable light." It was a cruel and exhausting emotion. James experienced it as if in the place Stevenson had occupied "there had descended an avalanche of ice." It was perhaps a relief for Louis—he had suffered enough, "but for us the loss of charm, of suspense, of 'fun' is unutterable."

The next few days were filled with strange rumors and alarums: a report came that the original dispatch was wrong and that Louis still lived; and amid these uncertainties, Henry wrote to Mrs. Sitwell, "We must wait—and yet I hate to—for I'm too afraid." He was right. Soon enough word came to him directly from Fanny Stevenson. Louis's "secession" had been indeed permanent.

Into James's deep mourning for the newest of his dead there was now introduced a curiously unexpected note. Henry James found himself named one of Stevenson's executors. He had not been consulted, but the will did provide alternatives; and James, who had been his father's executor, had no relish for the task and regarded himself as unsuitable. "It would be a dreadful disaster to his heirs," James wrote, asking to be excused. He explained that when his sister had died there had not even been a question of his being her executor, and he begged off as being "utterly and absolutely the creature in the world most abjectly and humiliatedly unfit for the discharge of any such duties."

The long letter which he wrote to Mrs. Stevenson is one of his finest epistolary elegies. Louis had died "in time not to be old— early enough to be so generously young and late enough to have drunk deep of the cup." The note from the first is that of a requiem: "What can I say to you that will not seem cruelly irrelevant and vain? We have been sitting in darkness for nearly a fortnight, but what is *our* darkness to the extinction of your magnificent light." And the image of the light is taken up again a few sentences further—"he lighted up a whole side of the globe, and was himself a whole province of one's imagination." James added:

To have lived in the light of that splendid life, that beautiful, bountiful being—only to see it, from one moment to the other, converted into a fable as strange and romantic as one of his own, a thing that *has* been and has ended, is an anguish into which no one can enter with you fully and of which no one can drain the cup *for* you. You are nearest to the pain, because you were nearest to the joy and the pride."

James had been haunted, he said, by a sense that he would never see Louis again, but it had been one of the best things of life to know him there, beyond the seas, and "one heard him and felt him and awaited him and counted him into everything one most

loved and lived for." James saw his death as having its glorious side
—"struck down that way, as by the gods, in a clear, glorious hour,"
for he had had the best of life, "the thick of the fray, the loudest
of the music, the freshest and finest of himself. It isn't as if there
had been no full achievement and no supreme thing. It was all
intense, all gallant, all exquisite from the first."

From the eloquence of this tribute James returned to the rehearsals of his play; but they seemed at the moment "tawdry and
heartless." Stevenson's ghost "waves its great dusky wings between
me and all occupations," he told Edmund Gosse.

PREPARATIONS

HE HAD LOOKED FORWARD TO THE FIRST READING OF "GUY DOMVILLE"
when he would expound the play to the English actors in the
French tradition. The ritual appealed to him: it touched the
histrionic side of his own nature, and that side of his authorship
which would lead him later to expound his novels in his famous
prefaces. He had a year or two earlier, during one of his Parisian
visits, obtained entrée to the Théâtre Française (with the aid of
Alphonse Daudet) during a series of rehearsals of a play by Jules
Le Maître. But he accepted too readily that what was the rule in
the Maison de Molière should be the rule in the free-and-easy
English theatre. On the morning of the first reading (at the
beginning of December 1894), he arrived at the St. James's with
an acute laryngitis; his voice had sunk to a whisper, and he had the

chagrin of sitting in the dark empty theatre while George Alexander read the play for him. Then, day after day, for four weeks he came in the wet and cold to the West End with great punctuality to participate in "the poverty and patchiness of rehearsal." It involved him in a great deal of anguish; and also some amusement. In his tale of "Nona Vincent" the young dramatist somehow had expected every actor "to become instantly and gratefully conscious of a rare opportunity." Things were different in Alexander's theatre; everything was done with a quiet efficiency. The manager was a masterly technician. He had assembled a highly professional cast, a group of polite, dedicated, co-operative actors. Ellen Terry's gifted sister, Marion, had the lead opposite Alexander; the second male part was entrusted to Herbert Waring, who had recently played Solness with Miss Robins in *The Master Builder*. The other parts were in equally competent hands; one small part was played by the talented man of the stage H. V. Esmond, whom James judged to be the one true actor in the piece. The villain, however, who bore the quasi-satanic name of Lord Devenish, was played by W. G. Elliott, who had come to the stage from amateur theatricals, and on whom the stamp of the amateur remained. He grimaced too much, he was too "stagey." His memoirs suggest that James tried to tell him he should play his part in a more human way, for he quotes James as saying he should make the dissolute peer "as much of a gentleman as is feasible—possible—to you."

James judged the actors to be "comfortable and decorous." He told Miss Robins the rehearsals were "very human and tranquil." He alternated between approval and doubt about Alexander: the manager did have a distinct flair, and much skill; yet he was all profile and posture, with an almost metallic suavity. As regards the material things, Alexander spared no expense. The sets were devoid of flimsiness. Doors could be banged without shaking the set. The hedges of the garden in the first act seemed real. The white parlor of the third act impressed by its sense of having been lived in (and was to do service in a number of Alexander's later productions). The costumes were faithful to the late eighteenth century in too much detail. James was euphoric one day and in the depths of despair the next. He spoke of his "beastly hours at the beastly theatre." He complained that rehearsals cut a gaping hole in his days; yet he never missed a rehearsal. Fatigue did overtake him, so that he could speak of his "demoralizing and exhausting and incongruous ordeal"; and he was overtaken finally by nervousness and panic.

"I am too preoccupied, too terrified, too fundamentally distracted, to be fit for human intercourse," he told a hostess who invited him to dinner during the yuletide of 1894. "I would be a death's head at the feast." On the last day of the year, with the first night but five days away, he wrote a long letter to Miss Reubell in Paris telling her he was about to sit through the dress rehearsals. They were going through the play twice a day to give the actors ease of costumes. This he found amusing, he said, and promptly qualified it with "as amusing as anything can be, for a man of taste and sensibility, in the odious process of practical dramatic production. I may have been meant for the Drama—God knows!—but I certainly wasn't meant for the Theatre." This had been the refrain of his tales of the coarse and the fine.

James felt he had staked everything on this production. He was not a mere dramatist with a play which might or might not succeed. He was a celebrated novelist laying all his reputation—all his earnings—in front of a roulette wheel. "One can have a big danger, in the blessed theatre, even with a small thing," he explained to his architect friend, Edward Warren. He told Miss Robins the production would be "a very creditable performance, and a very finished production"; however he seemed to discern "a bad theatrical wind" rising. A play at the Garrick had just failed, and "I have a superstitious sense that such influences are contagious." He began to discuss with Edmund Gosse what he would do on the first night. During the production of The American, in the provinces, James had had the run of the backstage. Alexander wanted no nervous authors anywhere near the dressing rooms or in the wings. James first said he would go to a pub near-by and Gosse promised to come between the acts to tell him how things were going. Thinking upon this, the novelist realized he needed more distraction during the waiting periods. Finally he decided he would go to see some other play.

With the actors James was tenderly affectionate at the end. "I don't want to worry you," he wrote to the leading lady a few hours before the opening, "on the contrary; so this is only a mere word on the chance I didn't say it a couple of nights ago *distinctly* enough that your business of the end of Act I—your going and leaning your face against the pillar of the porch—couldn't possibly be improved. Please believe from me that it is perfectly beautiful and *right*—like, indeed, your whole performance, which will do you great honour." He closed his note: "Rest quiet, this weary day, at least about *that*."

THE THREE CRITICS

ON THE DAY OF THE OPENING—JANUARY 5, 1895, A SATURDAY— Henry James's nervousness was unbearable. He went for a long walk through London parks and streets. The weather was cold and dreary. In the late afternoon he returned to 34 De Vere Gardens in a state of panic. He now tried epistolary exercises to calm himself. Minnie Bourget had written to wish him luck. He answered: "It is five o'clock in the afternoon and at 8.30 this evening *le sort en est jeté*—my poor little play will be thrown into the arena—like a little white Christian virgin to the lions and the tigers." Madame Bourget had mentioned that a friend of hers, an American lady named Edith Wharton, sent good wishes and James replied, "I cling to *you* . . . with the agitated clutch of this instant, and please say to Mrs. Wharton that I cling a little, if she will permit it, even to *her*." He added, "I offer Mrs. Wharton all thanks for her sympathy." In concluding he invoked prayer, "*Domine in manus tuas. . . .*" He spoke thus again a few minutes later in scribbling a hasty almost illegible note to his brother. Alluding to William's interest in spiritualism, he counted on "psychical intervention from you—this is really the time to show your stuff." He added, "This is the time when a man wants a religion." George Alexander had told him that there had been a large advance sale of seats, "but my hand shakes and I can only write that I am your plucky, but all the same lonely and terrified HENRY." He added after the signature the date and the hour. It was 5:45 P.M. A new play by Oscar Wilde had opened at the Haymarket that week. James decided it would help speed the dragging clock to go to see it.

I

Mr. Bernard Shaw, the drama critic of the *Saturday Review*, who earlier that week had attended the first night of Oscar's play, was preparing on this evening to go to *Guy Domville*. He was new in his job: he had assumed his duties on the first of January. Shaw was thirty-eight and comparatively unknown. He had been a music critic for some years but to the musical public he signed himself "Corno di Bassetto." He had also recently produced a play, *Widowers' Houses*; it had attracted little attention. A second play, about prostitution, *Mrs. Warren's Profession*, had been banned by the Lord Chamberlain. Shaw was known however in socialist circles as an indefatigable pamphleteer and a speech-maker to workingmen's clubs; and he was a familiar figure among the journalists. A lanky Irishman, he was thin, with red scraggly whiskers and bushy brows and the pallor one sees in red-haired persons. He had for some years sought every possible public platform deliberately to overcome shyness and teach himself to be fluent and authoritative. He spoke now on a variety of subjects and with increasing ease: Marx and Wagner, wages, common sense, food—the joys of being a vegetarian, the barbarism of meat-eating—the importance of Henrik Ibsen. He had learned to face audiences and to amuse them by paradox and persiflage; he offered a mixture of wisdom and vulgarity. By trial and error he discovered himself most comfortable when he built a wall of words between himself and the world. Paradoxes came to his lips as naturally as epigrams to his compatriot, Oscar.

Shaw had arrived in London from Ireland in 1876—that is in the same year that Henry James had come from Paris to settle in Bolton Street. Shaw was then just twenty; James was thirty-three. Two years later Henry James had won renown at the moment Shaw was writing a novel appropriately titled *Immaturity*. James was a finished cosmopolite by the time he reached London; Shaw was a young man from the provinces, from John Bull's other island, a clumsy Dubliner with a shrewd sense of practical affairs and a love of music. During the 1880's, when James had written a novel on a social theme, *The Princess Casamassima*, Shaw was busy helping to found the Fabian Society and in the parks and on the Embankment had begun his socio-economic discourses. He had read Karl Marx in the British Museum and also studied closely the operatic scores of Richard Wagner. He was a bohemian and a philanderer; ladies pursued him; he wooed them with words. And yet, as with James, who was also interested in women but kept a proper distance, there was something eternally virginal and fresh in Shaw. His eyes sparkled; his wit flashed. His sexual investment was in his intellect and in the power of language. He lived for ideas, for common sense, for histrionic display. No man of his time seemed more involved with the world or had more opinions on anything and everything, and no man—as Leonard Woolf in particular has shown in his memoirs—was more distant and dissociated in his personal relations. Shaw liked the clash of minds and knew the vitality of ideas. He also liked to make logic out of life's inconsistencies. People however were more difficult. His way of meeting them was to charm them by being charmed with himself.

Henry James on the other hand lived for the subtle contradictory ironies of life; his pursuit was neither that of logic nor of consistency; he knew the meaning of ambivalence and he lived for art. Shaw railed at ugliness and poverty and wanted to change the world. James was troubled by the crudities of existence but hoped to exorcise them by devotion to beauty. He held with Balzac that the artist must take the world as it is; he held with Voltaire that he must cultivate his own little garden; his task was to make—not to remake. Shaw was an articulate revolutionary who performed his revolutions on paper; and he tried to make the world his classroom. Yet he knew only too well the nature of art. "You cannot be an artist until you have contracted yourself within the limits of your art," he wrote to a friend shortly after the production of *Guy Domville*. At the same time James was writing, "Art should be as hard as nails." Both the American and the Irishman were ambitious, both were concentrated egotists—Shaw with an open and good-humored though often garrulous public aggressiveness, James with his aggressiveness concealed behind a façade of discretion, civilization, privacy. Shaw in a word was then journalist and preacher; James was the dedicated artist.

What was happening now, however, in the waning years of the century, was that James was attempting to woo the world in a manner closer to Shaw's nature than to his own. Both wanted to conquer the theatre. When someone in 1892 had booed *Widowers' Houses*, which Shaw had called "an original and didactic realistic play," the dramatist subdued the audience with a three-minute speech and changed the boos into applause. In the theatre

the two men were at this moment equal failures. The difference
was that James had a reputation at stake, and Shaw had still a
reputation to make. And for the moment the would-be playwright,
Bernard Shaw, was a critic of other men's plays. Thus it was that
on this first Saturday in January of 1895 the Irish critic donned his
corduroy jacket and made his way from Fitzroy Street to St.
James's through the cold and wet, to see the American novelist's
much-anticipated play.

II

The critic of the *Pall Mall Gazette* was also new at his job. He was
a thin, undernourished, wispy man, with short legs, long mustaches and a squeaky voice, named H. G. Wells. He had been
offered the post on the newspaper a few days before, and had just
reviewed Wilde's play at the Haymarket. Child of a backstairs
marriage, he knew that the upper classes always dressed for important occasions and one of his first questions, when his editor gave
him the tickets for *An Ideal Husband* and for *Guy Domville*, was,
"One wears evening dress?" The editor answered, "Oh yes, tomorrow night especially," for the Oscar Wilde *première* would draw
all of London society. Wells describes in his reminiscences how he
rushed to a tailor and had a suit made in twenty-four hours, in
time for the Haymarket opening. He had actually only been to a
theatre twice, and when he told his editor this, the reply had been,
"Exactly what I want. You won't be in the gang. You'll make a
break." Apparently his first review, written late into the night, had
satisfied the editor. Wells now went to Henry James's play, in his
new dress suit, with greater assurance. He was to explain later that
he never really cared much for the theatre. He had been trained as
a scientist. Make-believe was not for him.

Wells's childhood might have been written by Charles Dickens.
His mother was a housemaid, his father a gardener who later
became a shopkeeper. He had served an apprenticeship in a drap-
er's shop; later he was a chemist's assistant. He was bright, bril-

liant, articulate. He had become an usher in a grammar school and in spite of bad health and poverty had obtained a scholarship. At the University of London he sat at the feet of T. H. Huxley, and had taken a degree in 1888. Having embarked on a career in science, he discovered now he had a flair for journalism. Magazines accepted his pieces and paid him decently; and he had just written a novel called *The Time Machine* which was shortly to be published and would make him famous. His job on the *Pall Mall Gazette* was to be short-lived, and the only regular job (save for the early apprenticeship) he ever held. No one would have predicted on the night of *Guy Domville* that this immaculately dressed little man was to be the founder of modern "science fiction" and perhaps the most brilliant literary and political journalist of his time. He was also to have a long and as he called it "a sincere and troubled friendship" with the author of *Guy Domville*, whom he considered "a sensitive man lost in an immensely abundant brain."

Like Shaw, Wells was interested in working-class movements. Both were atheists and socialists. Wells was to say later that Shaw had not had as sustained and constructive a mental training as he had had, and this was true; however the Irishman had been saturated with good conversation, good music and "the appreciative treatment of life." Thus in the theatre that night "the new men" of his time were sitting in judgment on Henry James's play. Wells felt, however, that he was the newest of the new men: that science put him in the forefront and that, in their devotion to art, Shaw and James belonged together and lagged behind. Wells put the difference between himself and Shaw as follows: "To him, I guess, I have always appeared heavily and sometimes formidably facty and close-set; to me his judgements, arrived at by feeling and expression, have always had flimsiness." Wells always accused Shaw of philandering with Fact.

In that formally dressed audience on this first night, however, it was Shaw who burst through fact: he broke the ranks of the boiled

shirts and the black and white ties in the stalls with his modest
brown corduroy jacket. It was Wells who, more rebellious than
Shaw, had conformed to job and society by dressing the part
assigned to him. The two men who were to be "prophets" of their
generation met on this evening for the first time.

III

Still another "new man" sat in the audience at the St. James's that
evening as critic of *Guy Domville*. He was wholly unknown—an
assistant editor of a magazine called *Woman*, given to signing his
articles "Barbara" (if he reviewed books) or "Marjorie" (when he
wrote town talk) and "Cécile" (when he reviewed plays). His
name was Enoch Arnold Bennett. Like Shaw and Wells he had
come to London from the provinces, from the Midlands, where he
had been a potter's son, but had grown up to middle-class comfort
and philistinism. If Shaw had sublime self-assurance and Wells
was an uncertain aspirant in literature, and in considerable conflict
about his place in society, Bennett was a simple shy aspirant,
insecure and uncertain, with a marked stammer. He wore a boiled
shirt, and probably would not have dreamed of wearing anything
else. He knew the solid materialistic world in which he had moved
from decent poverty to the professional class, for his father had
succeeded in leaving the pottery and making himself into a solici-
tor. Enoch Arnold Bennett had worked first as a shorthand clerk
in his father's office. A year after Wells came down from university, Bennett arrived in London determined to make himself into a
man of the world. He wanted to write.

Of that brilliant series of cartoons in which Max Beerbohm
caricatured London celebrities, none was more successful than his
drawing of Bennett's Old Self saying to the Young Self: "All gone
according to plan, you see"; to which the Young Self replies, "My
plan, you know." Bennett had published a tale in the *Yellow Book*
after his arrival in London and borrowed £300 to buy himself a
share in the magazine *Woman*, thereby becoming assistant editor.

Later he was its editor. In this school of practical journalism he learned to be a commentator on London life. He was to become a famous novelist, and like Wells a giver of opinions to the average man through the medium of the press. But where Wells was brilliant and erratic, prophetic and often Olympian, Bennett spoke with a kind of plodding honesty, a supreme matter-of-factness. He was six months younger than Wells and the two were not to meet for some time. Wells would remember that "we were both hard workers, both pushing up by way of writing from lower-middle-class surroundings, where we had little prospect of anything but a restricted salaried life, and we found we were pushing with quite surprising ease." They were both liberal and skeptical, but Bennett, even more than Shaw or Wells, felt himself in James's camp. He had an ideal of art, a desire to be a story-teller; he saw the world brighter than it was. He wanted success and all the glitter of success; unlike Shaw and Wells he believed in the fairy tale of achievement, and he was to live the tale to the full.

James, the product of an American aristocracy of the mind, would have held it an irony that in this theatre, where his future as a playwright was to be decided, the plebeians were already sitting in judgment on him: men whom he would get to know reasonably well—one of them intimately—and whom he in turn would criticize when they came to practice his own art of fiction. On this occasion (as we can see now in the long retrospect) the Edwardian world-to-come was already present to review a play of the Victorian world. The names of Shaw, Wells and Bennett were to be linked constantly in the coming decades and were to be—with certain others—among the supreme names of the new time.

At the Haymarket, Henry James fidgeted uneasily as Oscar Wilde's newest epigrams burst from the stage like well-timed firecrackers. "Men can be analysed, women merely adored"; "Only dull people are brilliant at breakfast"; "Morality is simply the attitude we adopt towards people whom we personally dislike."

The play did not have the soothing effect James had expected
Perhaps no play existed which could alleviate the panic Henr
James felt. The newest success of Oscar Wilde seemed alarmingl
to spell his own doom.

THE LAST DOMVILL

I

THERE WERE IN REALITY TWO AUDIENCES AT THE FIRST NIGHT O
Guy Domville. Literary and artistic London came to see a
Alexander production of a James play: it seemed a happy combi
nation; and then many of the members of that audience wer
friends of the novelist. The world of art was represented by suc
figures as Leighton, Burne-Jones, Watts, du Maurier (doubly fa
mous now as the author of *Trilby*), Sargent and members of th
Broadway group such as Millet and Parsons; letters were repre
sented by Edmund Gosse, Mrs. Humphry Ward, Mrs. W. K
Clifford, W. E. Norris, members of the critical "establishment,"
and other late-Victorian luminaries; there were several well-know
actresses in the audience, not least Miss Robins; there were repre
sentatives of the English aristocracy who had always admire
James. These constituted the first audience, which came prepare
to applaud and to praise. The second audience had queued up i
the winter damp and sat in the gallery seats. It had never heard o
James; it had come to be entertained by Alexander. "Alex" coul
be relied upon to put on a good show.

The theatre itself, where gaslight had just given way to electricity (as the programs announced), was warm and cheerful; and by the time the little curtain-raiser had been acted, and the orchestra had fussed through an overture, the distinguished and well-dressed were in their places. The curtain rose on a set visually pleasing, the garden of a wealthy young widow, Mrs. Peverel, near Richmond in 1780. The aim had been to suggest peaceful rural charm, and there was a close-cut privet hedge, with clustering rose bushes and honeysuckle trailing around quaint lattice windows. In this pleasant setting James developed with great simplicity and charm of dialogue the dilemma of young Guy, devout and dedicated on the eve of his departure for France, strong in his determination to become a Benedictine monk. He has been tutor to Mrs. Peverel's son; he loves Mrs. Peverel; his love for the Church however has not permitted him to recognize his deeper feelings. Mrs. Peverel is devoted to him, and thinks of him as an earthly saint. She has accordingly resigned herself to the thought that she must lose him to the Mother Church. Guy is also attached to a neighboring squire, Frank Humber, who pays court to Mrs. Peverel. Since he will not have the widow for himself, Guy is prepared—like Miles Standish or Cyrano de Bergerac—to plead his friend's cause.

All this James set forth with directness and charm; it won both audiences: the gallery, knowing Alexander as a romantic hero, lived in hope that he would throw over the Church and marry Mrs. Peverel—the Comptons had warned James of this two years earlier. The more sophisticated members of the audience experienced, after seasons of tawdry and violent drama, the delicacy of James's dialogue. Guy Domville's conflict quickly became, however, much more than that of spiritual love versus the spiritual life. Upon the quiet of this garden there enters Lord Devenish, the Mephistopheles of the drama. He brings the news that Guy's kinsman has just fallen from a horse and been killed—"he was mostly too drunk to ride." Guy is the last of his line. He must renounce religion, take over the encumbered estates, make an advantageous marriage. The line must not be allowed to die out.

Mrs. Peverel's hopes revive and she urges Guy to take the worldly course. Lord Devenish also urges this as envoy of the newly-widowed Mrs. Domville, now reduced to the dower-house but possessed of a marriageable daughter. Guy speaks in touching lines of his devotion,

Break with the past, and break with it this minute?—turn back from the threshold, take my hand from the plough?—The hour is too troubled, your news too strange, your summons too sudden!

The act was filled with such lines, and Bernard Shaw's ear was sensitive to them. He was delighted with the play's literary qualities. Like the other critics however he was troubled by the rude shifts in feeling. For the Guy who speaks of his vocation, who to his friends has had "such an air of the cold college—almost of the cold cloister," suddenly makes a grand exit shouting, "long, long live the Domvilles." Just before doing this, still blind to love, he commends Mrs. Peverel to marry his friend Humber. He is ready for London and the world.

The second act, at the villa of the dowager Mrs. Domville, banished all the sympathetic characters of the first act. Only Guy and Lord Devenish were retained. Guy has shed churchly black for the breeches, lace and wig of a man-about-town. He has learned very quickly to play cards and to drink; he is ready to marry his cousin, the dowager's daughter. Into this act James poured all the clichés of the boulevard theatres of Paris: the cousin turns out to be the illegitimate daughter of Lord Devenish and Mrs. Domville; she in turn is in love with a naval lieutenant. When Guy learns the truth, he aids in their elopement. In the midst of the act he indulges in a mock drinking scene borrowed from Émile Augier's L'Aventurière—in which the naval lieutenant and Guy pour glass after glass of port into the flower pots while pretending to make each other drunk. H. G. Wells pointed out that the characters came and went in this house "like rabbits in a warren." At the end, having found nothing but deceit around him, Guy again reverses himself. He has strayed from his true vocation. He must, after all, go into the Church.

The third act, even though it brought back the sympathetic Mrs. Peverel and her suitor, could not repair the damage. Lord Devenish rushes to Mrs. Peverel; if he can't marry off Guy to his illegitimate daughter, he may still save him for worldly things, and his own devices, by marrying him to Mrs. Peverel. Guy returns, and in another scene of great delicacy seems to be coming closer to an awareness of Mrs. Peverel's love. But Lord Devenish has left his gloves in the room; and the sight of these freezes Guy into a sense of all the world's treacheries. All hesitation is gone. He will say good-bye to everything. The final scene was exquisitely written:

GUY. I'm the *last*, my lord, of the Domvilles! (*Then, anticipating* DEVENISH'S *reply and speaking on his quick gesture of impatient despair*) You've been so good as to take a zealous interest in my future—and in that of my family: for which I owe you, and now ask you to accept, all *thanks*. But I beg you, still more solemnly, to let that prodigious zeal rest, from this moment, for ever! I listened to your accents for a day—I followed you where you led me. I looked at life as you showed it, and then I turned away my face. That's why I stand here again; for (*with intensely controlled emotion*) there are other things—there are partings. (*Then very gently to* Mrs. PEVEREL) Will my conveyance have come back?

MRS. PEVEREL. (*Listening an instant, and as if subjugated by his returning sanctity*) I think I hear it now.

GUY. Then I start this moment for Bristol. (*Sadly, kindly smiling*) Father Murray has had patience. I go with him to France, to take up my work in the Church! if the Church will *take* again an erring son!

MRS. PEVEREL. She'll take him.

LORD DEVENISH. And *you* give him?

MRS. PEVEREL. To *her!*

LORD DEVENISH. (*With high sarcasm, to* GUY) I hope you do justice to this lady's exemplary sacrifice!

GUY. (*Blank*) Sacrifice?

LORD DEVENISH. That of a sentiment consideration for her forbids me to name.

FRANK. She loves you, Guy!

LORD DEVENISH. He doesn't deserve to know it. (*Then smiling, gallant to* MRS. PEVEREL) If it were *me*, Madam! (*From the threshold*) Pity me!

MRS. PEVEREL. It was a dream, but the dream is past!

GUY. (*Gathering himself slowly from a deep, stupefied commotion*) The Church *takes* me! (*To* MRS. PEVEREL) Be kind to him. (*To* FRANK) Be good to her. (*At the door*) Be good to her.

FRANK. Mrs. Peverel—I shall *hope*!

MRS. PEVEREL. Wait!

I I

This was the play on which James had placed all his hopes and it had much in it that was literary and fine. But while the novelist was sitting at the Haymarket Theatre squirming over Wilde's play and the audience's enjoyment of it, curious things which had nothing to do with James's text occurred on the stage of the St. James's. In the first place there was the acting of Elliott as Lord Devenish; he played his devilishness with a villainy so obvious as to wither (Shaw said) "all sense and music out of James's lines with a diction I forbear to describe." Wells remarked that "he might have come out of Hogarth, but he has certainly no business to come into this play." This in itself would not have sufficed perhaps to alienate the audience, had not another distraction occurred in a curious and unexpected form. Mrs. Edward Saker, in the role of the dowager Mrs. Domville, appeared in what Shaw described as "a Falstaffian make-up." She wore not only an elaborate gown of the period, a voluminous skirt of black satin over a pannier crinoline of huge dimensions, but an enormous hat, one of those extravagant creations to which ladies were addicted in the late eighteenth century. It was tall, made of velvet and shaped like a muff; it towered on her head under nodding plumes. Her entrance with this piece of extravagant headgear came at a moment when the audience's patience had been tried by the fuss of the second act. The gallery, in which there had been a great deal of coughing and shuffling of feet, now began to titter. Mrs. Saker, struggling with her huge skirt, was unnerved. W. Graham Robertson, the designer, who had come with John Singer Sargent, later said that the dress was particularly good, but "it wanted wearing; the huge hoop, and great black hat perched upon a little frilled undercap should have been carried by one filled with the pride of them and consciousness of their beauty." Mrs. Saker at this moment had neither pride nor awareness of anything but discomfort. She tried to be as self-effacing as possible; but her costume filled a large area of the stage and her plumes waved with every motion she made. Illusion was gone. Alexander, unaccustomed to signs of discontent in his audience, displayed his nervousness in his acting. "Why does he open his mouth on one side like that?" Sargent whispered to Robertson. "It makes his face all crooked."

The drinking scene which followed the hat incident could provide—after this—none of the intended comedy. The actors were play-acting drunk, and Shaw was to recount many years afterwards, with unforgotten amazement, the surreptitious pouring of the drink into the flower pots. Alexander played this scene, Shaw said, "with the sobriety of desperation." James had once said of the Augier play he was imitating that its charm resided in "the delicacy with which the deepening tipsiness was indicated, its intellectual rather than physical manifestations, and in the midst of it, the fantastic conceit which made [the character] think that he was winding his fellow-drinker round his fingers." There was no suggestion in the way in which the scene was played in *Guy Domville* of any kind of "intellectual" drunkenness.

Thus the third act with its fine setting did little to restore stage verisimilitude. The unintended comedy had thoroughly demoralized the gallery; the doors with their genuine brass knobs, the solid shelves, the handsome grandfather clock—not to speak of Mrs.

Peverel all love, and Guy all renunciation—had lost their meaning. The last lines with their subtlety of phrasing and calculated
repetitions irritated the audience. There would be no romantic
ending. Moreover the audience's sympathies were no longer with
Guy or the actor who embodied him. The audience tended to
agree with Lord Devenish that Guy didn't deserve to know of Mrs.
Peverel's love—he seemed so insensitive to it. His vocation had
been insufficiently strong when it was a question of the family
name and a worldly marriage; and yet it became strong when
confronted with a deep and devoted love such as Mrs. Peverel's.

When Alexander delivered himself of what, in other circumstances, might have been a touching and deeply felt speech, "I'm
the *last*, my lord, of the Domvilles!" there floated out of the
darkness a strident voice from somewhere in the gallery:

"It's a bloody good thing y'are."

III

Henry James remained to the end of the Oscar Wilde play. He
listened to the final epigrams, heard the audience break into
prolonged applause and left the theatre with that applause ringing
in his ears. It was late evening. He walked down the short street
leading into St. James's Square. Oscar's play had been helpless,
crude, clumsy, feeble, vulgar—James later would throw all these
adjectives at it. And yet—it was almost unbelievable—the audience had liked it. This suddenly made him stop midway round the
Square. He feared to go on to hear about his own play. "How," he
asked himself, "*can* my piece do anything with a public with
whom *that* is a success?"

He entered the St. James's Theatre by the stage door. On stage
Alexander was backing away toward the exit, saying to Mrs. Peverel with some awkwardness in slowly measured accents, "Be kind
to him," and to Humber, "Be good to her." As H. G. Wells heard
it it sounded like "Be keynd, be keynd." Alexander had a long
face, but to Wells it seemed now, "with audible defeat before

him," the longest and most dismal face he had ever seen and the slowly closing door reduced the actor to "a strip, a line, of perpendicular gloom."

Backstage in these nervous moments no one said anything to James about the evening's accidents. The curtain came down and the panic-stricken author faced the nervous angry manager. Outside there was a great roar of applause. Alexander went out and took the curtain calls. He received the ovation to which he was accustomed. Then James's friends in the stalls began to call, "Author, author." The press reports of the evening agreed that a manager who knew the temper of the audience would have left well enough alone. But Alexander was unnerved. Perhaps Wells was right when he speculated that "a spasm of hate" for the writer who had given him such a play seized Alexander. Or Alexander may have hoped, by acceding to the call, to placate those troublesome voices that had jarred him so painfully at intervals during the play.

He brought James on, leading him by the hand. The novelist, having heard applause, came forward shyly, hesitantly; and at that moment the gallery exploded. Jeers, hisses, catcalls were followed by great waves of applause from that part of the audience which esteemed James and had recognized the better qualities of the play. The two audiences had declared war. The intellectual and artistic elite answered the howls of derision; the howls grew strong in defiance. This was an unusual kind of passion in an English theatre, where feelings were so seldom expressed. "All the forces of civilization in the house," Henry later wrote to his brother, "waged a battle of the most gallant, prolonged and sustained applause with the hoots and jeers and catcalls of the roughs, whose roars (like those of a cage of beasts at some infernal zoo) were only exacerbated by the conflict."

James faced this pandemonium; his dark beard accentuated the pallor of his face and his high bald dome. He showed, some of the witnesses said, a "scornful coolness"; others described it as a display of "quiet gallantry." At this moment various friends of his —Sargent among them—experienced a terrible desire to leap across the footlights, to lead James out of the zoo-cage in which he was for the moment trapped. Alexander shifted nervously from one position to another and followed with quick paces as the novelist fled. Two members of the cast, years later, said they had never forgotten the expression on James's face as he came into the wings. To Franklyn Dyall, who had a small part, and was just beginning his career, James seemed "green with dismay."

The brawl outside continued. Philip Burne-Jones was seen to turn in his box and applaud in the direction of the gallery. The gesture renewed the noise. James had once argued that certain plays should be hissed, since "the deceived spectator ought to hold in his hands some instrument of respectful but uncompromising disapproval." This was hardly "respectful"; moreover he had prescribed it for the play and not the author.

Alexander, feeling that the situation in the theatre had to be calmed, reappeared in front of the curtain. He held up his hand. English courtesy and discipline reasserted itself. The press reported him as saying slowly and with emotion that in his short career as actor-manager he had met with many favors at the hands of his audiences and "these discordant notes tonight have hurt me very much. I can only say that we have done our very best." He added that if he and his company had failed "we can only try to deserve your kindness" by doing better in the future.

A voice from the gallery said: " 'Tain't your fault, guv'nor, it's a rotten play."

The house lights came on. The well-dressed poured into the small lobby to wait for their carriages; the gallery emptied itself into the cold streets. H. G. Wells spoke to Shaw and they walked away from the theatre together. James escaped as soon as he could and made his way homeward. He had his answer. He had announced he would "chuck" the theatre if *Guy Domville* did not succeed. The theatre had "chucked him."

ELIZABETH ROBINS
From a photograph inscribed to Henry James, 1894

ST JAMES'S THEATRE

LESSEE & MANAGER
GEORGE ALEXANDER

Licensed by the Lord Chamberlain to Mr George Alexander, St. James's Theatre, King St., S.W.

On Saturday, January 5th, 1895,

WILL BE PRODUCED

A New and Original Three-Act Play,

BY

HENRY JAMES,

ENTITLED

GUY DOMVILLE

Guy Domville ...	...Mr	GEORGE ALEXANDER
Lord Devenish ...	...	Mr ELLIOT
Frank Humber ...		Mr HERBERT WARING
George Round ...	Lieutenant R.N.	... Mr H. V. ESMOND
Mrs Peverel ...	...	Miss MARION TERRY
Mrs Domville ...	...	Mrs EDWARD SAKER
Mary Brasier ...	...	Miss EVELYN MILLARD
Fanny	...	Miss IRENE VANBRUGH

PERIOD - - - 1780.

ACT I. .. .. THE GARDEN AT PORCHES.
ACT II. .. MRS. DOMVILLE'S RESIDENCE AT RICHMOND.
ACT III. .. .. AN INTERIOR AT PORCHES.

Preceded by a Comedy, in One Act, by JULIAN FIELD, entitled

"TOO HAPPY BY HALF"

Eric Verner	Mr H V ESMOND	Mary Verner ... Miss EVELYN MILLARD
Jack Fortescue	Mr ARTHUR ROYSTON	James ... Mr E. BENHAM
	Time	THE PRESENT DAY.

Stage Manager ... Mr H. H. VINCENT   Musical Director ... Mr WALTER SLAUGHTER

The Furniture by FRANK GILES & CO., High Street, Kensington   The Wigs by CLARKSON   The Dresses by Mesdames SAVAGE & PURDUE
and Mr J. OUTUNI & LAWRENCE.   The Incidental Music by WALTER SLAUGHTER   The Scenery by H. P. HALL.

House Manager ... ... Mr ROBERT V. SHONE

PRIVATE BOXES £1.11.6d to £4.4s
STALLS 10s. 6d. DRESS CIRCLE 7s.
UPPER BOXES NUMBERED & RESERVED (BONNETS ALLOWED) 4s.
NO FEES   PIT 2/6 GALLERY 1s.   NO FEES

BOX OFFICE OPEN DAILY FROM 10 TILL 5 O'CLOCK.
Seats can be Booked by Letter, Telegram, or Telephone No. 3905.

GUY DOMVILLE
The playbill

BOOK TWO

The Black Abyss
1895

POSTSCRIPTS

WE KNOW THAT HENRY JAMES WALKED HOME IN THE COLD DAMP
from St. James's to Kensington after he left the theatre on the
night of January 5, 1895. He later said that he had felt weary,
bruised, disgusted, sickened. "I swore to myself an oath never
again to have anything to do with a business which lets one into
such traps, abysses and heartbreak." The audience—that is the
gallery—had behaved "like a set of savages" pouncing on a gold
watch. James's choice of image was apt. To him *Guy Domville*
had been like a tightly built gleaming-golden piece of machinery,
an artifact of which he was extremely proud. The play had had
every advantage of production. And yet it had failed. In that
strange and necessary way in which we defend ourselves against
accidents and demons, James sought, in his anguish, causes outside
his art, outside himself. One couldn't hand a gold watch to a set of
savages and expect it to survive; one couldn't make a sow's ear out

of a silk purse. And yet he had been trying "heroically," as he sai
to convert the sow's ear into something fine, even exquisite. It w
time to purge himself of such heroisms.

From all that he wrote later it was clear he returned that nig
to De Vere Gardens in a deeper state of shock than he knew. H
had made mental allowance for possible failure; that could happe
to the best of dramatists. He had not allowed however for
display of violence against himself—he who had been an unobtr
sive figure in the London literary world for so many years. He ha
been hooted by a brutal mob as if he were some old-time crimina
led through the streets for execution. He felt numb; too numb ar
too indignant to experience the full pain of his hurt. He thoug
of his play as a bird winged by a huntsman, doomed to ear
death. These had been, he said, "the most horrible hours of n
life."

I

"Early next morning," Sir Edmund Gosse would write twenty-fi
years later,

I called at 34 De Vere Gardens, hardly daring to press the bell f
fear of the worst of news, so shattered with excitement had th
playwright been on the previous evening. I was astonished to fir
him perfectly calm; he had slept well and was breakfasting wi
appetite. The theatrical bubble in which he had lived a torment
existence for five years was wholly and finally broken, and h
returned, even in that earliest conversation, to the discussion
the work which he had so long and so sadly neglected, the art
direct prose narrative. I recall him saying to me, after the fiasco
Guy Domville, "At all events, I have escaped for ever from th
foul fiend Excision!" He vibrated [so Gosse remembered] with th
sense of release, and he began to enjoy, physically and intelle
tually, a freedom which had hitherto been foreign to his nature.

Memory has a way of telescoping fact, and Sir Edmund's rem
niscences must be retouched by documentary evidence. It is doub

ful whether Gosse called alone early the next morning. He had been invited to lunch, with at least three other guests: W. E. Norris, the Victorian novelist, who had come to London from Devon to see James's play; Julian Sturgis (brother of his friend Howard Sturgis) whom James had known as a boy, in the days when he visited the Russel Sturgises in Carlton Terrace; and Philip Burne-Jones, son of the painter and himself a skilful sketcher. The last was the young man who had shown such militancy the previous evening toward the ill-behaved gallery. James received his guests with melancholy politeness. He had planned the luncheon and he went through with it. "You would have been proud of your friend," he later told Margaret Brooke, Ranee of Sarawak. He was far from being "perfectly calm," as Gosse would claim; he was in a state of nervous exhaustion. But he put on a bold face. He confessed a day or two later to Norris that he had become aware, sitting at the table, how great was his weariness after five weeks of intensive rehearsal and the rude climax of the previous evening. He told Norris he would never forget "your kind, tender-embarrassed face when you came in to see me." His fatigue, he explained, made him "mingle but poorly in the fine, rich gossip of some of my guests." This suggests that James was silent much of the time, and that Gosse and the younger men bridged the awkwardness with anecdote.

James felt much improved the following day, after a better night's rest—sufficiently well to return to the theatre and sit in quiet anonymity in the gallery where the rumpus had occurred. The audience was well behaved; the production went smoothly. Alexander had made some further cuts, to which James reluctantly consented. Nothing occurred to disturb the players. At the end there was warm applause for the cast. James thus satisfied himself that the events of the first night were not altogether induced by what he had written. Alexander showed him an unsigned telegram received on the opening night, "With hearty wishes for a complete failure"—sent, he discovered, by two women from a near-by post office. The press carried reports that there had been an anti-Alexander "cabal"; certain individuals, it was said, were avenging a slighted young actress. Witnesses testified that the roughs had a leader and "refreshed themselves copiously between the acts." There had been a variety of motives in the behavior of the audience.

II

James's play had a good reception from the establishment critics, and he spoke with approval in particular of the notices of William Archer and Clement Scott. He made no mention however of Bernard Shaw's review, one of the best given the play. Was it good sense, Shaw wrote, to accuse James "of a want of grip of the realities of life because he gives us a hero who sacrificed his love to a strong and noble vocation for the Church?" And yet when some unmannerly playgoer, untouched by love or religion, howled at this, the intelligent spectators were asked to admit, "if you please, that Mr. James is no dramatist, on the general ground that 'the drama's laws the drama's patrons give.' Pray, which of its patrons?" queried Shaw. "The cultivated majority who, like myself and all the ablest of my colleagues, applauded Mr. James on Saturday, or the handful of rowdies who brawled at him?" He added: "It is the business of the dramatic critic to educate these dunces, not to echo them." James's dramatic authorship was valid when the right people were in the theatre. "Line after line comes with such a delicate turn and fall that I unhesitatingly challenge any of our popular dramatists to write a scene in verse with half the beauty of Mr. James's prose." Shaw likened the music in James's lines to an evening of Mozart after Verdi. *Guy Domville* was a story and not a mere situation—a story of fine sentiment and delicate manners. Wilde, Pinero, Jones had treated Alexander as if he were a tailor's dummy. James treated him, Shaw said, as if he were an artist.

Wells's review was written with his characteristic acuity. His one was that of the scientist. It was a question of a prognosis—and the prognosis was bad. The play had too many faults. The principal one was Alexander. "In the first act Mr. Alexander is a didactic puritan; in the second a fine generous blade; in the third he is that impossible, noble, iron-grey Mr. Alexander that we have seen before." This sounded as if it were written by a frequenter of the theatre rather than a novice. The play, said Wells, was a fine conception, weakly developed; it was beautifully written but too delicate for acting, "and whether that is the fault of player or playwright is a very pretty question." Everything pointed to "an early deathbed."

Arnold Bennett, writing as "Cécile," offered a conscientious and platitudinous notice, tailored for his feminine readers. The future author of *The Old Wives' Tale* found "fitful beauty" in James's work; he praised certain of the "exquisite scenes." The first act was "studded with gems of dialogue," of "too serene a beauty" to suit audiences accustomed to the "scintillating gauds" of Oscar Wilde and Henry Arthur Jones. The melodrama of the later acts however was hardly in keeping with the "unrivalled work which Mr. James has produced in fiction."

Thus the "new men" of the 1890's, each in his own way, rallied to the side of art—and of courtesy. The older reviewers were staunchly with James. A. B. Walkley brilliantly contrasted Wilde's new play with *Guy Domville*. Wilde's, he wrote, would not move the drama forward an inch, nor would it add to his reputation. James's play was "a defeat out of which it is possible for many victories to spring; in gathering the enemy's spears into his heart he has made a gap through which his successors will be able to pour in triumph."

James himself took no such heroic view of what he had done; but he came to see that he had, in spite of his stooping to conquer and his failure, struck a blow for literature and for a new drama. *Guy Domville* ran through its allotted month, the minimum time required to exhaust the credit of Alexander's loyal followers, and even a few days longer to include some profitable matinees Brighton. Then came a crowning bit of irony. Faced with failure Alexander had rushed into rehearsal a play by the very dramatis whose work was being compared with James's, whom James him self had used as a measure and augury for his own piece. *Th Importance of Being Earnest*, Wilde's comic masterpiece, settle in promptly at the St. James's for a promising run.

"There is nothing, fortunately, so dead as a dead play—unless be sometimes a living one," Henry wrote to his brother. "Osca Wilde's farce which followed *Guy Domville* is, I believe, a grea success—and with his two roaring successes running now at on he must be raking in the profits." *Guy Domville* had yielded Jam £275 in royalties, that is a little more than $1200, token of th prosperity that would have awaited him had he succeeded. On th closing night James said good-bye to the cast. "It has been a grea relief," he wrote to Elizabeth Robins, "to feel that one of the mos detestable incidents of my life has closed."

EMBARRASSMENT

JAMES WENT, FIVE DAYS AFTER "GUY DOMVILLE," TO PAY A PROM ised visit to the Archbishop of Canterbury, Edward Whit Benson, at the archiepiscopal residence, Addington, outside Lo don. The Archbishop had at various times expressed admiratio for James's work; on one occasion he had quoted from *Roderic Hudson* in a sermon. It must have been soothing to the injure playwright's self-esteem to be received in the ecclesiastical family circle with warmth and affection. In the great house James found two of the Archbishop's sons, Arthur Christopher, then a master at Eton, a prolific writer of verses and of Victorian "familiar" essays, and E. F. Benson, later to be a popular writer of light novels. Both remembered James's talk and recorded it. He said he had been, during his play-writing, in a dim water-world "sub-aqueous"—and had been "bewildered and hampered by the medium." Now, he said, he felt he had got his head, "such as it was," above the surface; he had at last "a new perspective and an unimpeded vision." This picture of himself as a drowning man suggests the depth of his melancholy; and equally suggestive was James's fascination, as he sat and conversed with the Archbishop over a cup of tea, with a little anecdote which the ecclesiastic told him. They had been talking about ghost stories. Both had agreed that the best had been told; that psychical research tended to wash ghosts clean of all mystery and horror. "Recorded and attested ghosts," James was to write, "are as little expressive, as little dramatic, above all as little continuous and conscious and responsive, as is consistent with their taking the trouble—and an immense trouble they find it, we gather—to appear at all." Having dismissed "certified ghosts," and lamented "a beautiful lost form," the Archbishop, in the waning light, spoke of an incident he had heard long ago, of a couple of small children in some out-of-the-way place to whom the spirits of certain "bad" servants were believed to have appeared; they had seemed to beckon, invite, solicit across dangerous places, such as the deep ditch of a sunken fence, so the children might destroy themselves. The Archbishop was vague, altogether without detail—but the ghostliness, the mystery, the terror was there; the terror of nightmare and the fright of innocence before the unknown. It was all dim, eerie, the very "shadow of a shadow." And it touched a raw nerve at this moment in the life of the novelist.

He had talked of his struggle in a dim water-world, as if he were drowning; he had suddenly been hurt by violent and uncontrollable forces. Henry James could indeed muse on a tale of horrible threats to children, the baleful influence of the extra-human that lies in wait for man in the very midst of serenity. In James's infancy there had been the *vastation* of his father, who, in the quiet of the domestic dining room, after a good meal, had been suddenly seized with a terror of the soul, as if some horrible goblin squatted in the room beside him. For months afterward the elder Henry's mind had been haunted by this vision. His experience had been personal, subjective, private; the son's ordeal was actual, physical, public. Yet the two episodes were related. Both represented the beast that lies in wait for men within the depths of life, the element of mystery and surprise—the nameless terror of nightmare.

Returning to De Vere Gardens Henry James scribbled in his notebook: "Note here the ghost-story told me at Addington (evening of Thursday 10th) by the Archbishop . . . the mere vague undetailed faint sketch of it." He then recorded the anecdote. Nearly three years would elapse however before he would be ready to write "The Turn of the Screw."

I

He had pronounced the detestable incident closed; but he could not stop the pain as easily as he could lower the curtain on his play. The behavior of the audience at the St. James's had struck at the very heart of his self-esteem, his pride of craft, his sovereignty as artist. He spoke of the theatre as an abyss—an abyss "of vulgarity and British platitude"—and also as "a black abyss." The theatre doubtless had been one kind of hell, and he was now out of it. He lived on however in his other, his private hell—wounded, sore, depressed. In one of his letters of this time he invoked Dante. He had been, he said, plunged into "the nethermost circle of the Inferno."

This then was James's journey through the wastes of the sym-

bolic sea of ice, the "heart of darkness" of which one of his
admirers would write. His personal letters after *Guy Domville*
were a cry of outrage and defiance. Later there came the nursing of
private grief, the search for balm, the rationalization and self-con-
solation that might ease his spirit. To his brother he wrote: "I no
sooner found myself in the presence of those yelling barbarians of
the first night and learned what could be the savagery of their
disappointment that one wasn't the *same* as everything else they
had ever seen than the dream and delusion of my having made a
successful appeal to the cosy, childlike, naïf, domestic British
imagination (which was what I had calculated), dropped from me
in the twinkling of an eye. I saw they couldn't care one straw for a
damned young last-century English Catholic, who lived in an
old-time Catholic world and acted, with every one else in the play,
from remote and romantic motives. The whole thing was for
them, remote, and all the intensity of one's ingenuity couldn't
make it anything else." He recognized however that the attitude of
the theatregoer toward a story in a play was different from his
attitude toward a story in a book.

Thus, with many nuances, he found explanations. But the one
to which he adhered above all, and which was the fundamental
truth, was that he was too refined and subtle a talent to reach the
"common man." This truth had been before him during all of his
dramatic years, and he could not say that the Comptons had not
warned him. Yet it had required a rebuff of the most violent kind
to bring it home, so deep had been his ambition, so profound his
determination to achieve stage glory—and the royalties that went
with success. "Produce a play," he wrote to William, "and you will
know, better than I can tell you, how such an ordeal—odious in its
essence!—is made tolerable and palatable by great success; and
how in many ways accordingly non-success may be tormenting and
tragic, a bitterness of every hour, ramifying into every throb of
one's consciousness." When he looked at his curious experience
through the light of his intellect he could see it with wry and

sardonic humor, charged with irony and paradox; and he wrote this into a series of stories about writers who are applauded, although their works are unread, or who try to "take the measure of the huge, flat foot of the public" but who succeed only in writing each time still another distinguished failure. Commenting on the deluge of mail which descended on him, James wrote to a friend that twenty-five years of "literary virtue and of remarkable prose never have brought me a five-and-twentieth of the letters that fifteen vulgar nights of the odious stage have caused to descend upon me." To the end of his days James was to wonder at this anomaly between achievement and the image—particularly the newspaper image—of the artist: at the audience-worship of the personality without the understanding of the *persona*. He was to see, a few months later, the massive Victorian funeral offered the votary of classicism in painting, Lord Leighton, and to muse on the elaborate mourning and the way in which Leighton's artistic relics were ignored; buried, the painter was quickly forgotten. James had once put Leighton into one of his stories ("The Private Life"), as an individual who was a superb performer in public and who ceased to exist the moment he had no audience. "So much beauty and so little passion," James mused. The public could recognize neither the presence of the one, nor the absence of the other.

II

He was in mourning for himself, for his dead self, who had floundered and struggled when the waters of disaster closed over his head. In his notebooks a year earlier, he had recorded the idea for a story:

I was turning over the drama, the tragedy, the general situation of disappointed ambition—and more particularly that of the artist, the man of letters: I mean of the ambition, the pride, the passion, the idea of greatness, that has been smothered and defeated by circumstances, by the opposition of life, of fate, of character, of weakness, of folly, of misfortune; and the drama that resides in—that may be bound up with—such a situation. I thought of the tragic consciousness, the living death, the helpless pity, the deep humiliation.

And then—"The idea of *death* both checked and caught me." He began now to toy anew with the story of this man, "the spectator of his own tragedy."

Pride, passion, pity, humiliation, "the living death." James's words help us to glimpse a few of the deeper feelings of the struggling artist, caught in mid-life, "smothered and defeated by circumstances"—some of these of his own making. He went on to think of this man, whose passional and sentient life is dead, as finding renewed life in some woman. James thus pushed away from himself the most painful part of his experience, and made a woman the repository of his anguish (as he would do in "The Beast in the Jungle"). "*She is his Dead Self,*" he wrote, underlining the words; "*he is alive in her and dead in himself.*" Having written out the note he finally abandoned the idea; he feared "there isn't much in it: it would take a deuce of a deal of following up." It would require more than this: it would require the fortitude to deal with his own failure.

Outside his notebooks, his letters reflect his heavy heart. "My youth is gone," he writes to the old friend of his Roman days long ago, Sarah Wister. "Life's nothing—unless heroic and sacrificial," he tells the Archbishop's son, Arthur Christopher Benson. "I pay the penalty of my magnificent imagination," he also writes, and twice he speaks, in a letter and in a novel, of having "the imagination of disaster." He remarks that "one outlives some of one's complications—if one doesn't live into too many others." He is weary of London; he feels as if he were homeless. He had had this experience after the death of his parents, and the end of the family house in Cambridge. In 1883 he had returned to London and found a house in St. John's Wood; he had felt suddenly a deep need for an anchorage. Then, thinking better of it, he had decided to remain in his bachelor's rooms in Piccadilly. Now his comfortable De Vere Gardens flat no longer seemed to suffice. He talked of finding "a much-needed bath of silence and solitude" in some rented house in the English countryside. His preoccupation with houses and children fills his writings at this moment: children, unwanted, unloved, displaced, seeking a hearth and love—these are the themes that figure in almost everything James wrote during the next five years.

He spoke of himself as unwanted a fortnight after the collapse of his play in a letter to his old friend William Dean Howells. Howells, with a certain prescience, had written before *Guy Domville*, to remind James that whatever the outcome of his theatrical ventures might be, he must remember that he was still primarily a novelist, possessed of a novelist's public that waited to read everything he wrote. In some such words (for the letter does not appear to have been preserved) Howells touched James's artist-sense and implied that the winds of the marketplace could not alter the record of James's achievement nor his ability to create—nor the devotion of his old friends, like Howells. In the midst of rehearsals James had read Howell's letter hastily. Now, taking it up to answer it, he found unexpected comfort in it.

You put your finger sympathetically on the place and spoke of what I wanted you to speak of. I *have* felt, for a long time past, that I have fallen upon evil days—every sign or symbol of one's being in the least *wanted*, anywhere or by any one, having so utterly failed. A new generation, that I know not, and mainly prize not, has taken universal possession. The sense of being utterly out of it weighed me down, and I asked myself what the future would be. All these melancholies were qualified indeed by one redeeming reflection—the sense of how little, for a good while past (for reasons very logical, but accidental and temporary), I had been producing. I *did* say to myself "Produce again—produce; produce better than ever, and all will yet be well."

"Every sign or symbol of one's being in the least *wanted,*

anywhere or by anyone." James spoke here not only of his recent history; one of his reasons for attempting plays had been his waning position in the magazines. In another part of his letter to Howells, James wrote: "Until the other month Henry Harper, here, made a friendly overture to me on the part of his magazine, no sign, no symbol of any sort, has come to me from any periodical whatever—and many visible demonstrations of their having, on the contrary, no use for me. I can't go into details—and they would make you turn pale! I'm utterly out of it *here*—and *Scribn*er, the *Century*, the *Cosmopolitan*, will have nothing to say to me—above all for fiction. The *Atlantic* and H[oughton] and M[ifflin] treat me like the dust beneath their feet; and the Macmillans, here, have cold-shouldered me out of all relation with them. All this I needn't say, is for your *segretissimo* ear." Howells had at least assured him about his "book-position." James had never in any event cared for the magazine world, he told his friend. "I hate the hurried little subordinate part that one plays in the catchpenny picture-book—and the negation of all literature that the insolence of the picture-book imposes."

The communion with his old-time editor had a tranquillizing effect. On the morning after writing this letter James roused himself and set down, with an air of finality, the following words in his notebook, as if to push all hurt out of his mind: "I take up my *own* old pen again—the pen of all my old unforgettable efforts and sacred struggles. To myself—today—I need say no more. Large and full and high the future still opens. It is now indeed that I may do the work of my life. And I will."

After this moment of resolution, he set down a row of crosses, as if to denote a contemplative pause. Then, "I have only to *face* my problems." Another row of crosses. Then, "But all that is of the ineffable—too deep and pure for any utterance. Shrouded in sacred silence let it rest."

THE YOUNG HEROES

DURING THE FIRST PHASE OF HIS WORK IN THE THEATRE, IN 1891 AND
1892, Henry James had written two tales whose pages are filled
with personal history. One was a story of an itinerant family on
the Continent—Americans as footloose as his own family had
been long ago—and the fate of their gifted son. The other was a
story of a rigid military family, whose tradition has been to supply
gallant soldiers for England's army. In the first story, "The Pupil,"
the young boy is ashamed of his down-at-heel parents who lead a
hand-to-mouth existence and expect the world to provide for
them. In the second, called "Owen Wingrave," the young Owen,
a few years older than the pupil, is in rebellion against his family's
militarism. He is determined to study the art of literature rather
than the art of war. The two young heroes have in common their
perception of the false values by which their families live; and both
die as a consequence of self-assertion. Women play a cruel role in
their deaths. Morgan Moreen dies at a moment when his mother
ceases to offer him the protection of her shoddy way of life. Owen
dies proving to a hard and demanding fiancée that he is not a
coward: he dies indeed in defense of his pacifism. The stories are
markedly different: the fundamental life-myth they embody is the
same.

I

James got his hint for "The Pupil" from his Florentine friend
and doctor, William Wilberforce Baldwin, a gifted healer who
had attended a generation of wayfaring Americans as they passed
through Italy. Even Baldwin's envious rival, Dr. Axel Munthe,
who practiced in Rome, admitted that Baldwin had "the inestima-
ble gift of inspiring confidence in his patients." He had, said
Munthe, "a striking personality, a fine forehead, extraordinary

penetrating and intelligent eyes, a remarkable facility for speaking, very winning manners." Baldwin had ministered to James after his attack of jaundice in Venice, in 1887. He had brought his carriage to the station when James, still shaky, arrived in Florence from the water-city, and conducted him to Fenimore's villa on Bellosguardo —for he had been Miss Woolson's doctor as well. Baldwin would have other distinguished patients, Mark Twain and Howells and, in the new century, Edith Wharton. James spoke of him as an "American physician of genius" and as "a charming and glowing little man." He had actually doctored three members of the James family: Henry and William and their sister Alice. Son of a New York State clergyman who had a large family, he had earned his way as a schoolteacher, studied medicine at Long Island Hospital, and after a brief period of practice in Connecticut had gone abroad to work with the great heart specialists in Vienna. His curiosity and eagerness to learn never left him. He returned to the United States every summer to keep himself up to date; and he knew the medicinal value of most spas on the Continent.

During Henry James's 1890 visit to Italy, Dr. Baldwin had proposed to him that they tour small out-of-the-way Etruscan towns, using rail and carriage as available, and walking to reach less accessible spots. Baldwin knew these places well; he was in the habit of setting up clinics for the peasants in the Abruzzi during the summer. Accompanied by an obese Falstaffian friend and language tutor of Baldwin's who acted as their guide, they visited Volterra, Montepulciano and Torrita di Siena, and certain villages in between. The little trip proved too hot and fatiguing for James, who had, of old, been a great long-distance walker. He came away from this adventure, nevertheless, with one of his finest tales. "Years ago, one summer day, in a very hot Italian railway-carriage, which stopped and dawdled everywhere, favouring conversation, a friend with whom I shared it, a doctor of medicine, who had come from a far country to settle in Florence, happened to speak to me of a wonderful American family. . . ." In his preface James went

on to describe this family to which, briefly, Baldwin had been
doctor. It was an itinerant family; it had jumped its hotel bills, "an
odd, adventurous, extravagant, band, of high but rather unauthen-
ticated pretension." They had a small boy, who was precocious
but who had a weak heart. The boy saw the prowling and precarious life of his parents and siblings "and measured and judged
them." Here, James wrote, was "more than enough for a summer's
day even in old Italy—here was a thumping windfall."

It was indeed a windfall and James wrote "The Pupil" at the
end of that summer of 1890 when he was back in London. He too
had been a precocious boy on the Continent; his father, though
not as nearly indigent or as much "a man of the world" as the
parent described by Baldwin, had dragged his family about from
place to place. Henry and his brothers had been "hotel children";
they had known the loneliness of strange places and the absence of
elders who had confided them to tutors and governesses. He had
memories too of anxieties provoked by money shortages, for there
had been a moment during the American depression of 1857
(when he was fourteen) which caused his parents to beat a
hurried retreat from a luxurious apartment in Paris to an economi-
cal residence at Boulogne-sur-mer. Out of this personal past and
Dr. Baldwin's anecdote, James wove his delicate tale of a sensitive
boy and his attachment to his tutor, the first of a series of tales
of the 1890's in which children suffer from parental neglect and
indifference and little boys die because they assert their claim to
live.

A poignant tale (we see the boy between the age of eleven and
fifteen), "The Pupil" was written with the technical virtuosity of
these years—it was told through a double vision: the boy's "troubled vision" of his family "as reflected in the vision," James
explained in his preface, "also troubled enough, of his devoted
friend" the tutor. Like the James family, the Moreens are a
country unto themselves, and "Ultramoreen" is a key word in their
humorous vocabulary. Little Morgan knows from the first that his

tutor, Pemberton, a graduate of Yale and sometime student at Oxford, will never be paid for his services; he attaches himself to the young man with the tenderness of a loved and neglected child who feels also guilty and ashamed at his family's improvidence and dishonesty. The tutor, on his side, becomes attached to his charge; he stays on, unpaid, in conflict between his personal needs and his feelings for Morgan—but not a little also because there is something irresponsible and shiftless in his own character; for we learn early that he spent all his resources, during a year on the Continent, in "a single full wave of experience." He too has a touch of the "Ultramoreen."

There is humor and pathos in the way in which James describes the life of the vagabond Moreens, first at Nice, then in Paris; their dash to a wintry and harsh Venice, their return to a further shabby life at Nice. Their false standards and values, their façade of arrogance and helplessness—"a houseful of Bohemians who wanted tremendously to be Philistines"—their belief in a providing world that doesn't provide, their petty luxuries and pretense to style: all this is shown as it affects the growing child. Quick of mind, Morgan can only be humiliated by his family. He is thoroughly aware of his mother's shameless use of Pemberton's love for him; if the tutor finds such happiness in the family, she reminds him, he needs no other reward, and she even borrows money from him. The ultimate parental decision to take advantage of the attachment and "unload" Morgan on the tutor, leads to a swift and complex ending. Pemberton had had a fantasy that the two might some day go off to lead a life together, away from the Moreen cares and improvisations. Morgan entered into this fantasy as if it were an "escape" story in a boys' magazine. Suddenly he discovers the power of reality over the imagined fiction. It is too sudden, too violent. Expecting to find Pemberton enthusiastic, he sees him wavering. In that "morning twilight of childhood" which Henry James so clearly understood, in which there was "nothing that at a given moment you could say a clever child didn't know," Morgan learns the terrible truth—and his life becomes a void. Betrayed by his parents, frightened by the glimpse of vacillation in the beloved tutor, not old enough to tolerate disillusion, he feels himself, in terror, alone. The panic is too much for his weak heart.

The tale, coming to James out of a hot Italian afternoon, from the case book of the gifted Baldwin, brilliantly re-imagined out of his own life, inaugurated the novelist's great decade of the short story. However for all its remarkable qualities it suffered a misadventure at the start. James had received a request for a series of tales from the new editor of the *Atlantic Monthly*, Horace Scudder, and he dispatched "The Pupil" promptly. Scudder had a sharp negative reaction, and for the first time in the history of his relations with the *Monthly*, one of James's stories was rejected. Scudder may have been worried by the possible hint of unconscious homosexuality in the attachment of tutor and boy. Yet there is no evidence that in the early 1890's—before the trial of Oscar Wilde —there was among readers or editors any such awareness of or alertness to deviation: friendship and affection between tutors and their charges were regarded as normal in the Victorian age. A more plausible theory is that the prosaic Scudder was worried that the *Atlantic*'s readers would resent a story about an American family which jumped its hotel bills and behaved with such deliberate mendacity. Americans were not supposed to do such things. James expressed his "shock of a perfectly honest surprise" at being turned down. He felt that the responsibility for the magazine's readers, when it was a question of "an old and honourable reputation," should be left to the author himself. *Longman's Magazine* accepted the tale in England and it appeared early in 1891; it was reprinted thereafter many times, and remains one of James's most popular stories.

I I

"Owen Wingrave" was written early in 1892, just after the death of Alice James. "Owen" is a Scottish name; it means "the young

soldier." The title of James's tale accordingly meant "The Young
Soldier Wins His Grave." James later said he got the idea for this
tale one day when he saw a young man in Kensington Gardens,
reading a book in one of the penny chairs; this had furnished him
with the image of his young pacifist. James's notebooks supply
another source. The idea had occurred to him during a reading of
the memoirs of Napoleon's General Marbot—a three-volume work
popular in England throughout the 1890's. Late in the century,
the flood tide of Napoleonic memoir-writing was at its height; old
diaries were being found; old memories were being searched. And
James's notebook entry begins with the words: "The idea of the
soldier—produced a little by the fascinated perusal of Marbot's
significant memoirs. The image, the type, the vision, the character,
as a transmitted, hereditary, mystical, almost supernatural force,
challenge, incentive, almost haunting, apparitional presence, in
the life and consciousness of a descendant—a descendant of totally different temperament and range of qualities, yet subjected to
a superstitious awe in relation to carrying out the tradition of
absolutely *military* valour—personal bravery and honour." James's
idea was to create a hero who was a soldier in every fibre, but who
had a horror of soldiering, not through cowardice, but through
hatred of war—"the blood, the carnage, the suffering." He would
make his hero perform a brave soldierly act even while defying
militarism. He would give him a "military temperament" and give
him the reward of gallantry, "winning it from the apparitional
ancestor."

This detailed note, at first glance, seems unrelated to the death
of James's sister; but the story he wrote during 1892, in its picture
of the dead weight of "family" and personal past as brought to
bear upon the living, reached very far back into the novelist's
experience; it stemmed from the time of late adolescence, from
the days of the Civil War when public opinion had told him he
must become a soldier while his own terror of violence and fractri-
cidal murder, his own will to peace and to poetry, had held him
back. The three volumes of Marbot's memoirs which James read

in their French original have survived in their expensive bindings
and they disclose in their marked pages what James felt when he
spoke of "fascinated perusal." Marbot was one of Napoleon's most
articulate generals; he was the second son of a soldier, and James
was always interested in second sons, like himself. Marbot had
written his memoirs in obedience to the Emperor's wish that he
"continue to write in defense of the glory of the French armies."
Now almost a century after the Napoleonic era, Marbot's family
had published the manuscript. The numerous page numbers pen
cilled in James's hand at the back of each volume refer us to
particular passages of violence and glory—the description of a
cavalry charge; the courage of the unknown; the battles of Auster
litz and Aspern; the loyal batmen; the coincidences of combat
Marbot coming to consciousness after being wounded and finding
himself naked in the snow, stripped of uniform and gear by those
who gave him up for dead; his constant references to his mother
the Emperor saying to Marbot, "Note that I do not give you an or
der; I merely express a wish"; Napoleon's "magic personality" and
its effect on the troops; the great cold at Vilna, the delight of the
bed after weeks in the open. One gets the impression from the sec
tions marked by James that he read the memoirs with a deep iden
tification and absorption but with confused feelings. He abhorred
violence, he respected courage. He was impressed, as his notebook
shows, with the sense of military tradition. The Marbots had all
been soldiers, and the sons of soldiers. General Marbot fights only
when it is a question of military combat; the battles with brigand
and looters, the summary executions, he leaves to others. He is
single-minded; he serves only the Emperor—only *la gloire*.

From the dates on the bindings and of publication, it is clear
that James bought at this time a large number of volumes about
the First Empire; some show signs of careful reading and contain
marked passages. In his library the novelist had, in addition to the
Marbot, the memoirs of Marshal Macdonald; Masson's book
about Napoleon and women and his volume of anecdotes about

the Emperor's private life; the reminiscences of General Bigarré, the aid to King Joseph (James seems to have read with particular interest Bigarré's account of his adventures among the Negroes); Arthur Lévy's *Napoléon Intime* of 1893; Barry O'Meara's earlier two-volume account of Napoleon on St. Helena. James also owned Lanfrey's five-volume life of Napoleon, as well as dozens of volumes of letters and biographies of figures in the Empire and after. Napoleon had cast a long shadow; and Henry James, who had seen the pageantry of the Second Empire and lived in a Paris in which memories of Napoleon remained vivid, was clearly attracted to him more as a man of action and a symbol of glory than as a soldier. In all probability his feelings for Napoleon were derived also from his close reading of Balzac; for it was in the pages of Balzac during his youth that James had found a supreme example of imagination resolved into action, the will to—and the egotism of—grandeur pushed to a denial of the impossible. We find in James's memoir of Wolcott Balestier written at this time the notion of the young man's having "Napoleonic propensities"—a "complete incapacity to recognize difficulties, his immediate adoption of his own or, in other words, of an original solution. It never could have occurred to him that there was not a way round an obstacle so long as a way was inventable, and the invented way, which in almost all cases was the one he embraced, always proved in fact the most amusing." This had charmed James in the young Balestier; it had dazzled him in Balzac. And it dazzled him in the records of the Empire he was reading at this moment. But he had no illusions about Bonaparte, for in "Owen Wingrave" (where the coach has "the stature of the great Napoleon"), Owen is said to believe him "a monster for whom language has no adequate name."

III

"Owen Wingrave" is thus rooted in James's experience and vision of a whole era and is linked also to the bloodshed—and glories—of the American Civil War. The actual story contains all the usual figures of James's family constellation; it reminds us in particular of the way in which he was under pressure as a young man to leave art alone, urged by his father, his practical mother and his elder brother, who advocated that he take a steady job in lieu of the hazards of publication. Henry had wanted simply to be "literary"; he had resisted the family pressure and achieved what it had regarded as impossible. He had thrown away his law books. He had refused to study science. He had quietly and determinedly locked himself in his room and written his tales and read novels while his brothers banged and shouted. So young Owen Wingrave goes into the park carrying the poems of Goethe when he should be studying the hard prose of Clausewitz.

In the tale, in a few tense pages devoid of his usual elaboration, James wrote the only "pacifist" story in all his fiction. Owen is a second son like himself; the older brother has been locked away, a mental case; and upon the second son falls the burden of upholding the family name. The name has a single historical virtue: that of the soldier. Aunt Jane Wingrave represents the traditions and the exploits of the British Army. She represents "the expansive property of the British name." She is a veritable grenadier. "If she was military it was because she sprang from a military house and because she wouldn't for the world have been anything but what the Wingraves had been." James adds: "She was almost vulgar about her ancestors."

Owen's father died of an Afghan sabre cut in a fight at close quarters. Owen's grandfather, Sir Philip, had survived to eighty, "a merciless old warrior." At Paramore, seat of the Wingraves, there is a haunted room, where one of the military ancestors killed a son who had been as rebellious as Owen. The drama of the tale itself fills but one evening. To Paramore have come Owen's "crammer," a man named Spencer Coyle, who is preparing him for military college; his best friend, also destined for the army; his intended, Kate, who never knew her father, for he was killed in a war. All attack young Wingrave. Sir Philip will cut him off without a penny. But his friend and his coach believe in more subtle modes of coercion, while to the sweetheart he is simply a "coward." She will not believe that he has already slept in the haunted room. Owen resists this terrible pressure. He would have war set down as a capital crime; he would hang cabinet ministers who declare it. The youth is handsome, original, talented; and we see him by James's indirect method largely through the eyes of his "persecutors." Owen has read his military lore—Caesar, Marlborough and Frederick; and he talks about the immeasurable misery of war; he knows about the widows, "bereavement and mourning and memory . . . the echoes of battles and bad news." His friend says that "he hates poor old Bonaparte worst of all." The coach rejoins, "Well, poor old Bonaparte *was* a brute. He was a frightful ruffian." And when Wingrave's friend questions whether he has "the military temperament" of his ancestors, Owen's rejoinder is "Damn the military temperament!"

We do not hear his quarrel with his sweetheart; but we know their voices were raised, and that he locks himself into the haunted room. There he is found in the eerie dawn, after strange noises have been heard by the actors in the drama. Owen lies on the floor, dressed as he had last been seen. In the original version of the tale James wrote "He looked like a young soldier on the battle-field." In the revision fifteen years later James changed this to "He was all the young soldier on the gained field." Thus he heightened the story's irony. The young pacifist has been a soldier in spite of himself: he has died for his own beliefs. But the victory has been won by tradition, and by family. One simply could not escape one's fate.

It is a vivid tale, and one of the most "deterministic" James ever wrote. He took small stock in it, for he had conceived of it as for the larger public—"a little subject for the *Graphic*—so I mustn't make it 'psychological'—they understand that no more than a donkey understands a violin." Nevertheless he had embodied in

"Owen Wingrave" the single theme which haunts his work throughout his middle years—that of the son, usually the second son, who must bear the responsibility for the family's traditions, who faces coercion by his "past" and who struggles to find a free life for himself.

IV

The two tales—of the unhappy pupil and of the young pacifist—were recollections of adolescence, and they were of a piece with the tragic experience of *Guy Domville*. It was as if James had to return constantly to a dream of second sons made guardians, in spite of themselves, of the family name. Owen Wingrave was supposed to be a soldier when he wanted to be a poet; young Domville wanted his monastery, but was told to go out into the world and have children; Nick Dormer (in *The Tragic Muse*) wanted to be a painter, but his family expected him to follow in his father's footsteps and be a politician. The young heroes were subjected not only to family pressure, but to a kind of inexorable weight of history. And resistance could be punishable by defeat—or even death. Nick Dormer lived, after defying his family, but the price would be the loneliness of art. Guy Domville too renounced "life" and would take vows in his monastery. The ivory tower, the religious cell—there one could live with the eternal, and avoid the passions and demands of flesh and family. But on those who did not withdraw, the young, the self-asserting, the verdict passed was death; and women were at hand to make certain the execution was carried out. Life had, indeed, stepped in to prove to James the truth of his fictions. He, a second son, had asserted himself by writing plays in defiance of his long-established reticences. He had left his ivory tower. His punishment had been inevitable. The world he had so strenuously wooed had told him it did not want him or his work. He had suffered a kind of spiritual death analogous to that of the young Owen, killed by irreversible forces, by the fates; or to that of Morgan Moreen for whom there seemed to be no escape, for whom "family" was more than an historical weight. It was a pressing humiliation, an eternal shame.

On January 15, 1895, James wrote to a friend that the theatre was an abyss of "vulgarity and platitude, and I suppose one ought to be glad of any accident which disengages one from it." Three weeks later he was planning a new play. Did he still see some glimmer of hope? Was there still a fantasy of recovery and conquest—and revenge? The impulse had a generous prompting. Ellen Terry, London's reigning actress, had attended the first night to see her sister play the lead in *Guy Domville*. She had witnessed James's humiliation. A woman of quick sympathies and openness of feeling, she invited James to call on her. In his notebook on February 6, 1895, he records that "I went yesterday, by appointment, to see Ellen Terry." Miss Terry asked him to write a one-act play for her; she was going to the United States on a tour with Sir Henry Irving, and she had a fancy to play an American woman. What better than a curtain-raiser from the pen of Henry James for his compatriots? Ever practical, and pushing aside all vows, he reread an old note, a sketch for a comedy he had wanted to write for Ada Rehan two years earlier. The idea of being played by Miss Terry—and in America!—was irresistible.

Strangest of all was the plot of the play he wanted to write—"an American woman as the beneficent intervening agent in the drama of an English social, an English family, crisis." He envisaged "a wild ostensible radical of an eldest son" and "a sympathetic and sensible younger brother." The younger brother, as usual in James, would be called upon to assume responsibility for an old house. Later James would eliminate the older brother altogether. The second son would be the radical and like Owen, like Guy, like Nick Dormer, he would be expected to sacrifice his feelings and ambitions for his family. He must forget his radicalism, cross party lines, become a Tory—a long leap for any radical Englishman to take. And all to retrieve an encumbered estate, a decaying old family house. This was James's newest fancy—almost as if he were rewriting *Guy Domville*. He was interested in the twist he would give to this personal myth. The young radiant American woman—this would be Miss Terry—would arrive at the house (first called by James "Summersoft" and later "Covering End"), convince the radical he must change parties, buy up the mortgages, maintain the family tradition. And she would be the fairy godmother. American democratic sentiment would support British conservatism: American dollars would bring about the triumph of Family. All would be saved—all but the hero's political integrity, a point James chose to overlook, as he had overlooked the Catholic "vocation" in Guy Domville's switch from the Church. This was his cheerful re-dreaming of the theme, his summoning of magical aids to pull him out of despair. Mrs. Gracedew is one of James's charming American heroines. One imagines her in the form and figure of Miss Terry offering the novelist, at this moment of crisis, the beneficent assurance that if the world did not value its play-writing son, she at least was prepared to do so. The play would be written that summer—and in the ensuing years would have a complex history.

DISCOVERIES

BY THE MIDDLE OF FEBRUARY, LITTLE MORE THAN A MONTH AFTER *Guy Domville*, Henry James had begun to dissociate the disaster from himself—"it is rapidly growing to seem to have belonged

to the history of someone else." This transference of the unbearable burden to other, to mythical, shoulders made it possible for
him to try to work again. "I have my head, thank God, full of
visions," he now wrote in his notebook. "One has never too many
—one has never enough. Ah, just to let one's self go—at last."

But he couldn't let himself go. Two forces contended within:
his intellect and his emotions. His intellect was as powerful and as
active as ever; indeed it now began to discover all kinds of solutions—artistic solutions. His emotions were blocked, defended,
confused, full of past and recent hurt. At this moment therefore
James begins to use the supremacy of his intellect. He concerns
himself more intimately with "method" than ever before. Rational
form and mind were thus interposed against the chaos of feeling.
If he allowed himself to feel too much he would have to surrender
to his despair, face imperious questions about his identity, his
goals, the struggle to *be*. His best, his "safest" identity was the
artist; there he was in full possession. This explains why at this
moment James conceived the idea of moving the architectonics of
the theatre into his De Vere Gardens study. For the first time he
began to elaborate scenarios for his novels. He had hitherto written them only for his plays.

Below the surface of his intellectual inquiry—or strategy—the
spiritual wound remained, deep and raw. We thus arrive at a great
human paradox involving the mystical forces of human survival.
At this moment of defeat Henry James seized the skills of his
"technique" as if they were a life-belt, and indulged in a vigorous
and mature inquiry into forms he had not hitherto questioned.
Simultaneously we have an emotional retreat—that retreat of
which man is capable in order to nurse and heal his spiritual as
well as physical wounds. One part of James remained in his study,
vigorously engaged in artistic inquiry, while the other took to its
sickbed. The Catholic "retreat" symbolizes this in religious experience; the biological process illustrates it in the physical world; and
we know how the evolutionary process, confronted with obstacles,

invents subterfuges, alterations, mutations. Or, in James's own
image, within the dim water-world of his inner being fancy and
dream took over in the service of his wounded ego—even while the
active novelist continued, in the world, to use his artistic tools
with greater skill than ever. In the materials of James's writing
and the forms he gave them, we can discern the life-in-death
health-in-sickness struggle. There was both progress and regression.
His mind moved forward—his feelings returned to childhood
hurts. Instinctively reaching for insights into his dilemma, James
recovered old buried memories. The technical progress is palpable:
we can study the form of his work. The regression is available to us
largely in the fabric of the novels and tales written between 1895
and 1900.

I

Howells had reminded James that he was in reality a novelist, not
a playwright; and the comfort James found in this was that he was
made suddenly to recognize that his failure in the drama was not
total. So, in the wake of his answer to his friend, and his first
jottings in the notebook, we come upon James's linking of his play
experiments to the novel. The entry in his notebook of February
14, 1895 shows him in the process of becoming aware that if he
had been, so to speak, a novelist turned playwright, he might think
now of these roles as reversed: he could be a playwright turning
back to the novel. On this day James begins by looking at his old
notes for the story that will become The Wings of the Dove. He
goes on to read a note that represents a first sketch for The Golden
Bowl. At this time of despair his imagination is already committing itself to his largest works. The note for The Golden Bowl
troubles him, for it contains too much of "the adulterine element." Harper's had asked for a light tale, and this wouldn't do.
"But may it not be simply a question of handling that? For God's
sake let me try: . . . I languish so to get at immediate creation."
And in that ruminative conversational fashion which is the great

charm of his notebooks, James suddenly has his moment of illumination. "*Voyons, voyons*: may I not instantly sit down to a little close clear full scenario of it?" The word *scenario* is "charged with memories and pains." Yet it touches a new chord of association. The healing pen traces these words: "Compensations and solutions seem to stand there with open arms for me—and something of the 'meaning' to come to me of past bitterness, of recent bitterness that otherwise has seemed a mere sickening, unflavoured draught." And then: "Has a *part* of all this wasted passion and squandered time (of the last five years) been simply the precious lesson, taught me in that roundabout and devious, that cruelly expensive, way *of the singular value for a narrative plan too* of the (I don't know *what* adequately to call it) divine principle of the Scenario?" If this was so, he was ready, he told himself, to bless the pangs and pains and miseries of his tragic experience.

IF there has lurked in the central core of it this exquisite truth—I almost hold my breath with suspense as I try to formulate it: so much, so *much* hangs radiantly there as depending on it—this exquisite truth that what I call the divine principle in question is a key that, working in the same *general* way fits the complicated chambers of *both* the dramatic and the narrative lock . . . why my infinite little loss is converted into an almost infinite little gain.

This was "a portentous little discovery, the discovery, probably, of a truth of real value even if I exaggerate, as I daresay I do, its *portée*, its magicality."

II

What happened can be read in Henry James's writings from this point on. The image of the key and the lock was apt: and it applied to his life as well. He was closing a door behind him. He was opening a door on his future. He would never again write the kind of novel he had written before his dramatic years. The stage had given him new technical skills; these he would now use in his fiction. A story could be told as if it were a play; characters could be developed as they develop on the stage; a novel could be given the skeletal structure of drama. The novel in England and America had been an easy, rambling, tell-the-story-as-you-go creation; novelists had meandered, sermonized, disgressed and long enjoyed the fluidity of first-person story-telling; they had taken arbitrary courses ever since the days of Richardson and Fielding. Henry James now saw that he could launch an action and then let it evolve with the logic of a well-made scenic design. Beginning with *The Spoils of Poynton,* written during the ensuing months, there emerged a new and complex Henry James of the novel. His work required also a new and complex reader: one who had to be aware he was "following," not simply reading, a story. In earlier years a brief notation had sufficed in James's working journals to record ideas for tales; now we observe him setting down detailed and seemingly mechanical scenarios, even for short stories. "What then is it," he asks himself as he works on *The Spoils of Poynton,* "that the rest of my little second act, as I call it, must do?" And he also says: "What I feel more and more that I must arrive at, with these things, is the adequate and regular practice of some such economy of clear summarization as will *give* me from point to point, each of my steps, stages, tints, shades, every main joint and hinge, in its place, of my subject—give me, in a word, my clear order and expressed sequence. I can then *take* from the table, successively, each fitted or fitting piece of my little mosaic."

James did not achieve at once a full-blown dramatic method for his fiction. He proceeded by trial and error, to the exasperation of his readers and the bewilderment of his critics. His art had been the art of lucid narrative; he had possessed the closely observed life of the society of his time; he had forged for literature the American–European myth. From this point on, he entered the company of the great artists who, in their late years, find themselves possessed of unsuspected energies and resources. So Michelangelo, long ago, could work with undiminished vigor into old age; and Shakespeare, who died much younger, freed himself to write

The Tempest. In music Beethoven wrote his greatest quartets at the end, and Bach, after a lifetime of labor, planned "The Art of the Fugue." In the years after James, Yeats would shed the earlier trappings of his poetry, and remake his art into the maturity of his life. Examples of such growth are rare in the annals of the greatest art. In the art of the novel, Henry James moved on to new and difficult experiments at the very moment when other novelists have found their talent spent, "written out." The American novelist's quest for "compensations and solutions," his desire to assuage and heal his injured spirit with the awareness of his unimpaired artistic vitality, led him to seek for new modes of expression at a time when others lapse into staleness and withdrawal. "Oh yes," James was to recognize, "the weary, woeful time has done something for me, has had in the depths of all its wasted piety and passion, an intense little lesson and direction."

He experimented with systematic scenic alternation; with telling a story wholly in dialogue; with devices by which he left out certain scenes and supplied material through retrospective action. He tried to create "informing" characters as aids to narrative; and he arrived at the ultimate integration in his work of "picture" and "scene." Above all he grew watchful, as if he were a lens, over "point of view." He had begun long ago by thinking of story-telling as a form of painting; he now merged painting with drama. On the surface some of the later novels seem the very opposite of dramatic; the situation appears indeed to be static, for James, in his great elaboration, slowed his action. And often we are placed in the minds of his supersubtle observers to the exclusion of much of the "normal" detail of the conventional novel. It was a case of the novelist skilfully withholding information rather than giving it; or making it available piecemeal, doling it out and asking the reader to keep close track of it. In his earlier novels James had emulated the richness of Balzac by creating a large background and describing an entire setting. Now only relevant stage "properties" are described. No chair is mentioned if a character is not to sit down;

a mirror is on the wall only because we see the heroine looking a herself in it. There exists a frugal economy of pictorial substanc in these novels; and all characters are used "functionally." Wit all this, perhaps to compensate for economy of situation, closenes of scene and sparseness of stage "properties," James furnished hi novels with an extravagance of image and a largeness of metapho a general and ever-increasing embroidery of style, infusing larg amounts of poetry into his pages. In his late prefaces the recurrin motif is "dramatise, dramatise." He was to be endlessly delighte with "the charm of the scenic consistency," with "the blest opera tion of my Dramatic principle, my law of successive Aspects," an with those "scenic conditions which are as near an approach to th dramatic as the novel may permit itself."

III

He had been unable to meet the conditions of the stage. Now h imported the stage into his novels. Here he had no need o managers, actors or stage properties. He had abandoned all hop of box-office earnings; but he had gained instead an artist's visio of what his narrative fiction might be if he had a plan, a design, method. His protagonists were to be shown at crucial moments i their lives as in Ibsen, caught in the workings of their destinies. H could at last create an "organic" novel, so that everything in hi story was related to everything else, as the organs are in the huma body. He gave to his fictions an intricate cellular structure. Eac experiment justified itself and required a separate solution. He ha learned also that he need be neither a "realist" nor a "naturalist" the new symbolism, especially as Ibsen and Maeterlinck used it o the stage, gave him a freedom from material things and a liberty t imagine: if what he created was real to him it could be real t others, though not necessarily to some of the critical fraternity an those who wanted him to go on doing what he had done before His final novels were a synthesis of all that he had ever learne about his art, and he wove into this fabric the complex civilizatio of his mind, his vision of essences.

Almost fifteen years later, after these last novels were written, and he was still hoping to write others, he could speak of the sense "divine and beautiful, of hooking on again to the sacred years of the old De Vere Gardens time, the years of the whole theatric dream and the 'working out' sessions, all ineffable and uneffaceable, that went with that, and that still live again, somehow (indeed I *know* how!) in their ashes." For Henry James the years devoted to the writing of plays were to become, after a long period, "the strange sacred time"—strange because of the suffering, the pain, the irony of technical resource mastered in the teeth of failure; sacred, because there resided in this the mystery and sanctity and passion of his imagination that enabled him to triumph again and again over "the sacred mystery of structure." The word "sacred" is constantly on his lips. In the end, Henry James's dramatic years would be "the sacred years." But in another part of his being, in that part which masked a continuing despair, these might also have been called "the treacherous years," for they had harbored within them false prospects, false hopes, cruel deceptions, and a host of private demons.

IN IRELAND

EARLY IN MARCH OF 1895—FIVE WEEKS AFTER THE CLOSING OF HI
play—Henry James went to Ireland. He had little heart for visits
but he had promised his old friends, the Wolseleys, who wer
living in great state in Dublin, that he would spend a few day
with them. Lord Wolseley was commander-in-chief of the Englis
forces, the army of "occupation," as James ironically remarked
And then the novelist had found, in his *Guy Domville* mail,
friendly note from the second Lord Houghton, the Lord Lieuten
ant of Ireland, inviting him to spend a week at the viceregal court
The first Lord Houghton, the Viceroy's father, had been th
"world-wrinkled" Victorian, the "bird of paradox," who had be
friended James long ago, when the American was a comparativ
stranger in London. Now the son, emulating his father, made th
timely gesture to the rejected playwright. Henry appears to hav
felt that it would be graceless to decline; and he welcomed th
opportunity at the same time of keeping his promise to th
Wolseleys. He crossed to Dublin on March 9. The "unwanted
novelist was still very much *persona grata* in the high world. H
was to be guest both of State and Army in the embattled land o
his forefathers.

I

James had visited Ireland twice before. In 1883 he had stopped i
Cork and Dublin after a trans-Atlantic crossing. These cities wer
filled at that moment with soldiers and forebodings of violence an
he had cut short his stay. Moreover he had been in no mood fo
touring in that year of his mother's death. Then, almost a decad
later, after a bad influenza, he had recuperated in the early sun
mer of 1891 at Kingstown, near Dublin. Ireland was best known t
him in the continuing Home Rule struggle in Parliament, in th

recent drama of Parnell, which he and his sister had followed with deep feeling, and in fairy tale memories out of his childhood. The senior Henry James had made much in old bedtime stories of his visit as a young man to the County Cavan village from which the first William James had emigrated to America. He had taken with him the family Negro servant in Albany, Billy Taylor; and he had arrived, as James put it, "a gilded youth," to create a sensation among the villagers. There had been other elements in the story—whisky abundantly poured out by the local doctor and lawyer, and a girl named Barbara who ate gooseberries in a garden "with a charm that was in itself of the nature of a brogue." All these memories belonged to the lore of Henry James's childhood. With a strong sense of the "Irishism" of his family, Henry now set foot on the ancestral soil, but with less exuberance than his father and with a skeptical eye.

The visit proved from the first "explosive." James intended nothing more violent by the word than the fact that it represented an extraordinary variation from his life of "little slow contracted literary habits and small decorous London observances." As prelude he went first to stay with Lord Houghton's private secretary, Herbert Jekyll—"the kind and clever Jekyll"—in his lodge in Phoenix Park, before going to the great formalities of the Castle. Then his brief taste of viceregal life began. In all of James's letters describing the visit there is a strong feeling of shock—"the sense of the lavish extravagance of the castle, with the beggary and squalor of Ireland at the very gates." The novelist however seems to have made no allowance for Lord Houghton's good will and his terrible difficulties in his office—"the most thankless," John Morley was to say, "that any human being in any imaginable community could undertake." The viceregal court was boycotted by the Irish aristocracy, the gentry and the landlords, since Houghton was the appointee of a Home Rule government and had been close to Gladstone during the writing of the first Home Rule bill. In his isolation, Houghton sought to enliven his court by inviting large

parties from England. James mocked the *bleu-ciel* coats lined ﹏
azure of the eight aides of the Viceroy. He promptly develope﹏
lumbago and found it a weariness to have to stand all evenir﹏
"on one's hind legs" during the four balls given by the Viceroy ﹏
the six days of his stay. The young Lord Houghton was attractiv﹏
intelligent, artistic; a widower with three daughters, he was co﹏
stantly under the hopeful gaze of dowagers with available daug﹏
ters. He had lately inherited great estates from his uncle Lo﹏
Crewe (and was indeed to become himself in the fullness of tim﹏
the Marquess of Crewe). With his ample resources, he passed h﹏
uncomfortable time in Ireland in bestowing the most luxuriou﹏
kind of hospitality. James clearly squirmed at this "grandeur in ﹏
void." He described the Castle as "tarnished and ghost-haunted﹏
and he considered Lord Houghton to be leading "a strange an﹏
monstrous life of demoralization and frivolity." He experienced ﹏
haunting discomfort" and spoke of his visit as "a gorgeous bore﹏
To some friends he was even more candid: the visit had been "a﹏
unmitigated hell," "a weariness alike to flesh and spirit," "a Purg﹏
torio." He was clearly moved by "the tragic shabbiness of th﹏
sinister country." It was all too much for the grandson of th﹏
County Cavan William James. With great relief he bade farewe﹏
on the sixth day to the well-meaning Viceroy, and drove to th﹏
Royal Hospital in another part of the city for his stay with th﹏
Wolseleys.

11

The transition from hollow viceregal splendor to the militar﹏
alertness of the Wolseley establishment was a welcome relie﹏
Lady Wolseley gave James the run of the Sèvres room in th﹏
mornings, and he described the inkpot on the desk as the large﹏
he had ever used, overflowing "like the Wolseley welcome an﹏
their winecups." He seems however to have made little use of th﹏
inkpot, for he found the fine clean-cut young military me﹏
"charming and wholesome" in their soldierly deportment, e﹏

remely attractive. He liked being in "an intensely military little
world of aides-de-camp, dragoons and hussars." There were amiable colonels to take him on tours; and he visited the old red-coated
cocked-hatted Irish pensioners of the English armies. He was full
of admiration for the place, built by Charles II, and in particular
the great rococo hall, "one of the finest great halls in the British
Islands," where Lady Wolseley staged a beautiful costume ball.
She allowed James to come in evening dress and he proved the
only black-coated figure there. The women came on this occasion
—it had been Lady Wolseley's whim—dressed like ladies in the
paintings of Sir Joshua Reynolds, Gainsborough and Romney. The
men were in uniform, or court dress, or "the prettiest of all the
fopperies of the English foppish class," evening hunt dress. James
spent ten delightful days in these surroundings, watching the
sentinel-mounting and a great deal of military ritual.

For a "man of peace" (as he constantly reminded Wolseley)
James was happier among soldiers than among courtiers. But then
he had known the Wolseleys for many years, indeed since his first
dinings-out in London when he had been made welcome at their
great house in Portman Square. For an Englishwoman, Lady
Wolseley seemed to him to have the best attributes of an American woman; she, the former Louisa Erskine, was attractive in her
younger years, dark-haired and dark-eyed, and from the first James
became, as he said, "quite thick" with her. The more than a
hundred letters written to her during four decades show how
much he liked her and her expertise in old houses and old things;
he had a connoisseur's eye for antiques and furnishings. The
Queen Anne bric-à-brac at the Wolseleys long ago had been
abundant "to a degree that quite flattens one out."

As for her husband, he was one of Victoria's bravest and most
renowned soldiers. James liked his eye of steel—the one that
remained, for he had lost the other in the Crimea. He liked
Wolseley's rosy dimples, his simplicity, his belief in "glory"; he
admired his record in all the colonial wars of the era. Badly

wounded in the Crimea, Wolseley became a captain at twenty; h
had fought in the Burmese war, had been at Lucknow and i
China; he had gone to the relief of the ill-fated Gordon a
Khartoum. Stationed at Ottawa, he had handled the Red Rive
rebellion in Manitoba and had crossed into the United States
cast an expert British eye on the Civil War. Quietly he ha
slipped through the embattled North to the Confederacy to mee
Stonewall Jackson ("a glorious fellow," said Wolseley) and t
have a long talk with Robert E. Lee ("an English gentleman"
He also admired Lincoln, and had praise for Grant. His exploits i
the Ashantee campaign were legendary, and on his return t
civilian life, he had been a great leader in the War Office fo
reform of the British Army. James found "an extraordinary char
in his unquenched youth." Wolseley on his side delighted i
James's conversation. Their esteem was mutual.

A decade later, when Wolseley had been named Field Marsh
and Viscount, he wrote his *Story of a Soldier's Life*. James rea
these two stout volumes with the same fascination he had foun
in the memoirs of General Marbot, and his pencil again marke
salient passages describing personal heroism and the glory of arm
The Field Marshal, whom James judged "a singularly and st
diously delightful person" and a supreme example of the "cult
vated British soldier," believed in the glory of arms as in '
national religion." James marked the passage, "A nation withou
glory is like a man without courage, a woman without virtue . .
glory to a nation is what sunlight is to all human beings." He als
marked the passage in which Wolseley recalled his first cavalr
charge: "You are for the time being lifted up from and out of a
petty thoughts of self and for the moment your whole existenc
soul and body, seems to revel in a true sense of glory." Th
novelist wrote the Field Marshal a long and enthusiastic lette
"It's a beautiful, rich, *natural* book—and happy the man who
life and genius have been such that he has only to *talk*, ver
ciously, and let memory and his blessed temperament float hi

on, in order to make one live so with great things and breathe so the air of the high places (of character and fortitude)." James described himself, again not without a touch of irony, as "a poor worm of peace" and regretted that he had not extracted more reminiscence from Wolseley during their many meetings. "However men of genius never can explain their genius, and you have clearly been a soldier and a paladin, and understood that mystery very much in the same manner as Paderewski plays or as Mr. Treves removes appendices." James added that "what, as a dabbler in the spectacle of life, I think I most envy you, is your infinite acquaintance, from the first, with superlative *men*, and your having been able so to gather them in, and make them pass before you, for you to handle and use them. They move through your book, all these forms of resolution and sacrifice, in a long, vivid, mostly tragical procession."

It was this kind of masculinity, the masculinity of heroism and glory rather than the masculinity of the barracks and the smoking room, that James cherished. He had no stomach for the violence of Kipling, but he had a deep passion for the probity of a soldier such as Wolseley. Thus he could write, at the end of his stay in Dublin—of that part of it passed at the Royal Hospital—that "the military *milieu* and type were very amusing and suggestive to me."

For the rest, he was completely clear about his stay at the Castle: "I was not made for vice-regal 'courts,' especially in countries distraught with social hatreds."

A SQUALID TRAGEDY

THE OSCAR WILDE CASE BURST UPON LONDON A FEW DAYS AFTER Henry James's return from Ireland with a kind of moral violence, that of a subject long repressed and now suddenly brought into the open. From the first the novelist characterized it to his friends as "a very squalid tragedy, but still a tragedy." The brilliant maker of epigrams, the wit of London society, the reigning playwright, had fallen from his high estate. He was lodged first in Holloway jail on a charge of homosexual offenses and later sentenced to serve two years at hard labor. Oscar's two successful plays were immediately pulled from the boards; *The Importance of Being Earnest* was killed by the outcry of an outraged Victorian society, and George Alexander, for the second time in two months, found himself without a play. James's disaster in his theatre had been almost private by comparison.

Two days after Wilde was committed for trial, James wrote to Gosse that he found the affair "hideously, atrociously dramatic and really interesting" but added that its interest was qualified by "a sickening horribility." It was, he wrote, "the squalid gratuitousness of it all—of the mere exposure—that blurs the spectacle. But the *fall*—from nearly twenty years of a really unique kind of 'brilliant' conspicuity (wit, 'art,' conversation—'one of our two or three dramatists, etc.') to that sordid prison cell and this gulf of obscenity over which the ghoulish public hangs and gloats—it is beyond any utterance of irony or any pang of compassion. He was never in the smallest degree interesting to me—but this hideous human history has made him so—in a manner."

James sealed this letter. Then he had a further thought. He scrawled across the back of the envelope, in French, that it was both a pity and a blessing that John Addington Symonds was no longer alive. "*Quel dommage—mais quel Bonheur—que J.A.S. ne soit plus de ce monde.*"

I

The allusion to John Addington Symonds would have been lost upon most Victorians had they read James's words on the flap of the envelope. It had a particular meaning for Gosse. Both had known for some years that Symonds had been a crusading homosexual, eager but unable to proclaim from the housetops the ecstasy he felt in love between men. He would have been the André Gide of his time and made the world his confessional—had the time been more propitious. Erratic, disturbed, tubercular, he had wandered in search of his health as D. H. Lawrence would do thirty years later. He might be described today as the D. H. Lawrence of homosexuality whom circumstance, and the climate of his time, prevented from writing a *Lord Chatterley's Lover*. Wilde, in an impulsive and self-destructive way, brought his tragedy on himself by denying the truth and suing for libel when he was called a sodomite. Symonds, wavering between caution and the need to protect his wife and daughters, carried on a subterranean crusade on behalf of inversion, using the Greeks, and the example of the *Symposium*, to discuss the subject most intimate to him. He also circulated privately-printed pamphlets and wrote passionate poems about what was called in those years "the love that dare not speak its name."

Gosse had been in Symonds's confidence since the mid-1870's. Symonds had, at the beginning, made cautious epistolary overtures to him, saying he discerned in his writings a "tender sympathy with the beauty of men as well as women." Symonds's biographer says Gosse reacted with some "alarm," and Symonds retreated with the explanation that his Greek poems were "distinctly archaeological." Some time would elapse before Symonds would make a complete avowal to him. Indeed it was not until fifteen years later, in 1890, that Symonds returned to the charge in a fully open manner and Gosse, now a man of the world and a power in literary London (and much less alarmed by such matters), wrote an "understanding" reply which has been grossly misinterpreted as an admission by him of his own homosexuality. He was to write a similar "understanding" reply to Gide a quarter of a century later, and the two letters, read side by side, testify essentially to Gosse's need to ingratiate himself with his fellow-writers rather than to cultivate the confessional mode. Gosse did say to Symonds in this letter that there was an "obstinate twist" in his life, but the fuller text of the letter shows that he was alluding not to inversion but to his "cowardice" in not taking originally a large-minded and generous view of Symonds's "problem."

James seems to have met Symonds on only one occasion, at lunch early in 1877 with Andrew Lang. He reported to his brother that he found him "a mild, cultured man, with the Oxford perfume, who invited me to visit him at Clifton." James never accepted the invitation; and shortly thereafter Symonds went to live in Switzerland. So far as we know they exchanged letters only once. This was when James's essay on Venice appeared in the *Century* in 1882. The novelist sent a copy to Symonds "because it was a constructive way of expressing the good-will I felt for you in consequence of what you have written about the land of Italy— and of intimating to you, somewhat dumbly, that I am an attentive and sympathetic reader. I nourish for the said Italy an unspeakably tender passion, and your pages always seemed to say to me that you were one of a small number of people who love it as much as I do—in addition to your knowing it immeasurably better." James added that "it seemed to me that the victims of a common passion should sometimes exchange a look, and I sent you off the magazine at a venture."

Symonds was concerned with a different level of "common passion." And Henry never knew how critical Symonds was of what he called "the laborious beetle-flight of Henry James." The English writer's proselytizing letters—his attempts to engage friends and strangers in a kind of continuing symposium on homo-eroticism—is now a matter of record. James was aware that Symonds corresponded with his old Newport friend, T. S. Perry, and he probably would have been amused to learn that Symonds had also challenged James's old friend of his Paris time, the American mathematician-philosopher, C. S. Peirce, finding him "a fierce and Quixotic ally, who goes far beyond my expectations in hopes of regenerating opinion on these topics." As is known, Symonds singled out Walt Whitman above all as a potential ally, and cross-examined him particularly on the subject of *Calamus*. The elderly poet grew increasingly impatient; he responded to the praise but not to the verbal embrace; and in his final rejoinder summarily informed Symonds that he had fathered six illegitimate children—as if to set at rest once and for all any question about his heterosexuality.

II

Early in their friendship Gosse told James the history of Symonds's unhappy marriage without apparently divulging that Symonds had sought a wife in an attempt to escape from his homosexuality—if indeed Gosse at that time, in the early 1880's, himself knew all the details. James's notebook entry of 26 March 1884, a month after he had corresponded with Symonds, substantially foreshadows his tale of "The Author of Beltraffio" as he set it down shortly afterwards—"the opposition between the narrow, cold, Calvinistic wife, a rigid moralist; and the husband impregnated—even to morbidness—with the spirit of Italy, the love of beauty, of art, the aesthetic view of life, and aggravated, made extravagant and perverse, by the sense of his wife's disapproval." The delicately told yet lurid little tale culminates in a violent Medea-like action: the mother prefers her child dead rather than have him survive to live with a pagan-spirited father. "I am told, on all sides here," Henry confessed to his brother William February 15, 1885, "that my 'Author of Beltraffio' is a living and scandalous portrait of J. A. Symonds and his wife, whom I have never seen." Gosse told James, in praising the tale, that he had shown great insight into the secret of Symonds's character and the novelist promptly asked to be told what this secret was. "Perhaps I *have* divined the innermost cause of J.A.S.'s discomfort—but I don't think I seize on page 571, exactly the allusion you refer to." Page 571 of the serialization of the story (in the *English Illustrated Magazine*) has this significant passage about James's fictional author of "Beltraffio": "I saw that in his books he had only said half of his thought, and what he had kept back—from motives that I deplored when I learnt them later—was the richer part. It was his fortune to shock a great many people, but there was not a grain of bravado in his pages."* This might not altogether fit Symonds, but it was certainly true that he would have liked to say publicly much that he spoke only in private.

In writing to Gosse about his glimpse into the "innermost cause" of Symonds's "discomfort," James said he was "devoured with curiosity as to this revelation. Even a postcard (in covert words) would relieve the suspense of the perhaps-already-too-indiscreet H.J." We know James ultimately was made a party to Gosse's intimate knowledge and even shown some of Symonds's papers.

It was Symonds's privately-printed pamphlet, *A Problem in Modern Ethics*, of 1891 which prompted much private discussion and when Gosse showed the booklet to Henry James the novelist thanked him for "bringing me those marvellous outpourings." He added:

J.A.S. is truly, I gather, a candid and consistent creature, and the exhibition is infinitely remarkable. It's, on the whole, I think, a queer place to plant the standard of duty, but he does it with extraordinary gallantry. If he has, or gathers, a band of the emu-

. . . .

* It is interesting to read the same passage in the New York Edition as James revised it almost a quarter of a century later when he had for years possessed the full personal history of Symonds: "It came to me thus that in his books he had uttered but half his thought, and that what he had kept back—from motives I deplored when I made them out later—was the finer, and braver part. It was his fate to make a great many still more 'prepared' people than me not inconsiderably wince; but there was no grain of bravado in his ripest things."

lous, we may look for some capital sport. But I don't wonder that
some of his friends and relations are haunted with a vague malaise.
I think one ought to wish him more *humour*—it is really *the*
saving salt. But the great reformers never have it—and he is the
Gladstone of the affair.

Perhaps to exemplify the humor of which he spoke, James signed
the letter "yours—if I may safely say so!—ever H.J."

III

Symonds died in 1893, and when Gosse wrote to give James the
news the novelist responded warmly in tribute to the "poor much-
living much-doing, passionately out-giving man." He had never
had a clear vision of him, he said, but he felt the news as a pang;
yet the end had perhaps come at the right time. Symonds had
done his work and was spared living into feverish overproduction
and repetition. There had been an "achieved maturity"—"the full
life stopped and rounded, as it were, by a kind of heroic maxi-
mum." When Horatio Brown's biography of Symonds appeared
early in 1895 James read the two volumes promptly. The memoir
is discreet and measured. James marked a few passages in it—one
relating to an early trance described by Symonds; another to the
effects of chloroform upon him; and one passage in which Brown
described how Symonds abandoned speculation, inquiry and anal-
ysis in a metaphysical sense and concentrated "on man, on human
life," so that he had discovered the sensuous and sentient existence
of the artist.

Just before leaving for Ireland James had been urged by his
Venetian friend, Mrs. Curtis, to write an appreciation of Symonds.
She felt the English reviewers had not done justice to him and
suggested that the Brown biography could serve Henry as the basis
for an essay-review. James replied he was too busy; moreover "the
job would be quite too difficult," indeed the difficulty was "insur-
mountable." There was, wrote James, an entire side of Symonds's
life which was "strangely morbid and hysterical and which towards

the end of his life coloured all his work and utterance. To write of
him without dealing with it, or at least looking at it, would be an
affectation; and yet to deal with it either ironically or explicitly
would be a Problem—a problem beyond me." James thus subtly
injected Symonds's own term for homosexuality. He praised Symonds's gifts; yet there were things in the man and his work he
could not understand, "a need of taking the public into his *intimis-
sima* confidence which seems to me to have been almost insane."

While the Oscar Wilde case was in progress Gosse sent to
James a large bundle of Symonds's letters. As on the occasion of
his reading of A *Problem* the novelist referred to these as "the
fond outpourings of poor J.A.S." His attitude toward Symonds
suggests that James passed no moral judgment on his homosexuality or his passionate crusade. What seems to have bothered him
was Symonds's desire for public display in matters James deemed
wholly private. Both in his friendships up to this time and in his
correspondence, James seemed to maintain the "distance" he had
always kept from questions of sex. A kind of cool formality intervened—and almost a touch of condescension toward his more
involved friends. The words "fond outpourings" had in them a
note of irony, tolerance, patronage. Symonds must have sensed
this in James: for although he expressed pleasure at his writings
about Venice, he complained to Horatio Brown of James's "real
critical obtuseness," singling out his essays on Maupassant and on
Pierre Loti. The choice was significant; in both these essays James
criticized the eroticism of the writers and in his paper on Maupassant accused the French story-teller of dwelling too exclusively on
the physical and the sensual, leaving out the reflective and medita-
tive side of man.

IV

This "distance" from people and from passion enabled Henry
James to be both cool and compassionate to Wilde as well. In the
letter he wrote to Gosse about Symonds's "outpourings" James

also said he thought he saw a gleam of hope for "the wretched Wilde" in "the fearful exposure of his (of the prosecution's) little beasts of witnesses. What a nest of almost infant blackmailers!" On April 26 he wrote to his brother, "you ask of Oscar Wilde. His fall is hideously tragic—and the squalid violence of it gives him an interest (of misery) that he never had for me—in any degree—before. Strange to say I think he may have a 'future'—of a sort—by reaction—when he comes out of prison—if he survives the horrible sentence of hard labour that he will probably get. His trial begins today—however—and it is too soon to say. But there are debts in London, and a certain general shudder as to what, with regard to some other people, may possibly come to light." To Paul Bourget he wrote, once the sentence had been pronounced, that he considered it "cruel." Solitary confinement, he said, rather than hard labor, would have been more humane. Later that year James was approached to sign a petition drawn up by the American poet, Stuart Merrill, and circulated on behalf of Wilde among French and English writers. The overture was made through Jonathan Sturges, who was then—as often—in a London nursing home. This was in November of 1895, when Wilde had been in prison six months. To Merrill, Sturges wrote: "James says that the petition would not have the slightest effect on the *authorities* here who have the matter in charge, and in whose nostrils the very name of Zola and even of Bourget is a stench, and that the document would only exist as a manifesto of personal loyalty to Oscar by his friends, of which he was never one." In a letter to Francis Vielé-Griffin, the Franco-American poet, Sturges further reported that James was convinced that given the public attitude toward the case, Wilde would best be helped not by petitions or publicity but by quiet and authoritative pressure on the Home Office.

To what extent James himself intervened behind the scenes we do not know. But he did discuss the Wilde case with a Member of Parliament (probably R. B. Haldane) who, during the short-lived Rosebery Government, sat on the Commission for Penal

Reform and visited Wilde in jail. On November 10, 1895 James wrote to Alphonse Daudet that he had had news from this man that Wilde was *"dans un état d'abattement complet, physique et moral"*; that Wilde had lately been ill in the infirmary, and that some easing of conditions for him might occur. He said also his political friend had discerned in Wilde no will to resistance, no faculty for recuperation. If he had this faculty, James added, "what masterpiece might he yet produce!"

THE TWO ROMANCERS

IN JUNE 1893, WHEN HE HAD BEEN ACTIVELY CORRESPONDING WITH Robert Louis Stevenson, Henry James had written to him of his recent trip to the Continent, "I saw Daudet who appears to be returning from the jaws of slow death—getting over creeping paralysis. Meredith I saw three months ago—with his charming *accueil*, his impenetrable shining scales, and the (to me) general mystery of his perversity. That perversity is flowering, I believe, into two soon-to-be-published serials."

When James coupled Alphonse Daudet and George Meredith in his little budget of news for the South Seas, he little dreamed that two years later he would be present at—would indeed be an agent in—a memorable meeting of the two romancers. Daudet was fixed for him irrevocably in Paris; Meredith in his cottage at Box Hill, near Dorking, in Surrey. Both were crippled by similar forms of paralysis, and moved about with difficulty. Daudet made no pretension to understanding England and the English. Meredith's main fault, to James, was "that he thinks he is French, which he isn't." James was instrumental in bringing together the Provençal Gaul and the English "Gaul"—in a touching little comedy that played itself out that spring, in the very midst of the Oscar Wilde headlines in London.

I

Of the generation of French writers whose members he had met when he had first settled in Europe, Henry James had come closest to Alphonse Daudet. Maupassant had been a mere acquaintance, in the days of Flaubert's *cénacle*. Zola had fascinated, but also bored; and he knew him only casually, had seen something of him in Paris and more recently in England. Edmond de Goncourt had received him at Auteuil, where they had gossiped politely. But between Daudet and James a warmer chord had been struck; part of this went back to their common attachment to Turgenev. A greater part resided in Daudet's meridional expansiveness and his vivid and pictorial style, which James genuinely admired. "He cannot put three words together, that I don't more or less adore them," James wrote. On his side, the French novelist had a marked respect for James, not least for his command of the French tongue. "*S'il se tire de sa langue comme de la nôtre, c'est un rude lapin,*" he had written to the English journalist Theodore Child. "What a dear little note from Alphonse," James wrote to Child. "My heart warms to him and I am most grateful to him for the rank he assigns to me in the animal kingdom." His heart continued to warm toward the French writer, sufficiently for him to have translated in 1889 the last of the *Tartarin* series, the only sustained work of such nature James ever did. Friendship—and the fat fee given him by Harper, £350—induced him to go to Paris to do the work at high speed from Daudet's galley-proofs.

Even before that time he had been a welcome visitor in the Daudet home, Rue de Bellechasse, in the Faubourg St. Germain. He had been struck at the time of his translation by the novelist's courage in face of his creeping paralysis, the fruit of indiscretions in his bohemian days. And he had noted half bewildered but not without a touch of awe, that Daudet, in the naturalistic mode, studied his own symptoms, intending to make capital of them in a novel he would have called (had he ever written it) *La Douleur*. In James's correspondence with Child, Daudet figures as "the little thing," an affectionate reference to his smallness of stature and charm of manner (an allusion, also, to Daudet's autobiographical novel, *Le Petit Chose*). The French novelist had large dark liquid eyes and a vivid bearded countenance; it revealed his ill health and suffering, but it was endlessly lively, endlessly alert. The last thing James expected was that Daudet, with all his infirmities, would want to travel. In the midst of the Oscar Wilde excitement, however, and at a moment when James was nursing a sore throat which confined him to De Vere Gardens during Easter of 1895, came a letter from Paris. "The little thing" wanted to pay a spring visit to London, doubtless in emulation of Zola's recent trip. He planned to bring his wife, his sons Léon and Lucien, his young daughter Edmée. There would also be Victor Hugo's grandson and his wife. Would James dig up some comfortable rooms for all seven of them? "I will probably inflict a thousand nuisances on you," Daudet had written—"*je compte bien vous infliger mille ennuis*"—and Henry remarked to his brother, "he will doubtless be as good as his word." But if it was a bother, it was also amusing. James promptly arranged an intimate dinner in Daudet's honor at the Reform Club, took a suite of rooms for him at Brown's, sent off letters to the Gallic invaders offering advice and guidance and arranged to take Daudet to visit George Meredith at Dorking.

II

For Meredith, James had an affection even more profound and more intimate than for Daudet. He had met him long ago, in 1878, and admired the man rather than the novelist. He liked his wit, his paradox, his faculty in conversation for piling fantasy upon fantasy to some ultimate absurdity, until it all collapsed amid his own hearty laughter. James said, on meeting him, that if Meredith did not live in the country he would have tried to see much more of him. But as it was, he went periodically to Dorking and spent long hours with his distinguished *confrère*. "He is brilliantly intelligent and the wreck of a prodigious wit," James wrote of him in 1888. "He is much the wittiest Englishman, and the most framed for conversation, that I have ever known—for playing with intellectual fire."

The "intellectual fire" is suggested in James's notebooks, where he recorded two ideas furnished by his talk with Meredith. One evolved into the tale "The Great Condition," written in 1899, which tells of a man who becomes worried about the past of the woman he is to marry. The woman replies, "Give me six months. If you want to know it *then*—I promise I will tell you." James turned this into a story in which the fiancé breaks off his engagement and another man wins the woman who, we gather, has no secret to tell. An earlier idea, of 1894, which much appealed to James, he was however unable to write; perhaps because there was too much sex involved in it. "Note at first leisure the idea suggested to me by George Meredith's amusing picture—the other night—of the bewilderment of A.M. in the presence of the immense pretensions to 'conquest' (to 'having repeatedly overthrown Venus herself') of A.A." A.M. was probably Admiral Maxse, who had fought in the Crimea, an intimate of Meredith's, and A.A. we may hazard a guess was Alfred Austin, soon to be named poet laureate. James had the idea that the man who boasted about his conquests of Venus was in reality a fraud; and that the man who kept quiet and was bewildered by the boasting had himself had great successes in the bedroom. He toyed with the story in the days after Miss Woolson's death in Venice, but never wrote it. The notebook entries suggest that Meredith's anecdotes were unusually "racy." In 1892 we find James speaking in a letter of "the great once-dazzling George Meredith, whom I like, and whom, today, one can't but be tender to in his physical eclipse—overtaken by slow (very gradual) paralysis." He likened him to "the movement of the frames of the fireworks without all the coloured lights." Meredith was "a very honourable disinterested figure in his old age and very superior to any other here, in his scorn of the beefy British public and all its vulgarities and brutalities."

III

On May 6, 1895 Henry James met the Daudet party and their Hugo companions at Victoria Station and conducted them to Brown's. Daudet was insatiable in his desire for sightseeing; when he could not stagger into places on his own legs, he arranged to be carried in a bath chair. In this condition, he visited Westminster Abbey and was given tea in the Westminster Deanery. James remarked that the French novelist was surprised to find in the Abbey statues of actors—John Kemble, Mrs. Siddons. "In France," James noted, "the drama is primarily the Author . . . the actors are kept more in their places." Madame Daudet was counselled by James as to the proper hour to observe London society in Hyde Park. He enjoyed talking to the sons, although he strongly disliked the twenty-seven-year-old Léon Daudet, a gifted stylist and vigorous polemicist, also a notorious royalist and anti-Semite. James privately predicted that Léon would some day "swing," a shrewd judgment. Léon Daudet died a less violent death but led a turbulent life. For the younger son, Lucien, then seventeen, James had much sympathy. Madame Daudet impressed him as worldly and amusing; she was "rotund and romantic . . . had very good clothes and golden bronze hair"; he enjoyed her comments on the way Englishwomen dressed—or rather failed to dress. There were times when James lost patience with his visitors, particularly with Alphonse's "mania for being interviewed and all *à propos* of three weeks at Brown's hotel." On one day of the British spring, which that year was rainless and mild, James took his French celebrities to Oxford; on another to Windsor. Daudet was tired and contented himself with looking at Windsor Castle from his carriage.

They drove past A. C. Benson's picturesque cottage at Eton, where James left a card, and later apologized for not arranging a visit for his guests. "*Ah, si vous saviez comme ces petits coins d'Angleterre m'amusent*," Daudet told James.

The dinner at the Reform Club was staged by Henry with his customary care and we gather with some trepidation, for he wrote to Gosse that his guest had "a malady of the bladder, which makes him desire strange precautions—and I see—I foresee singular complications—the flow of something more than either soul or champagne at dinner." But the occasion seems to have gone well, and James mustered a dozen French-speaking notables in London (for Daudet spoke little English)—among them John Morley, George du Maurier, Arthur Balfour, Sir Lawrence Alma-Tadema, Sir Edward Burne-Jones, Admiral Maxse, the old dilettante Hamilton Aïdé and Gosse. Gosse in his recollections of Daudet seems to be referring to this occasion when he describes how the French novelist struggled up a short flight of stairs and, once seated at table, "a sort of youth reblossomed in him." Daudet was silent at first, almost motionless, and then head, arms, chest "would vibrate with electrical movements, the long white fingers would twitch in his beard, and then from the lips a tide of speech would spout—a flood of coloured words." Over dessert he began to talk of the melon harvest at Nîmes. "In a moment," Gosse remembered, "we saw before us the masses of golden-yellow and crimson and sea-green fruit in the little white market-place, with the incomparable light of a Provençal harvest morning bathing it all in crystal. Every word seemed the freshest and the most inevitable that a man could possibly use in painting such a scene, and there was not a superfluous epithet."

Léon Daudet was to record long after that "every day Henry James came to fetch us for a walk, a tea, a lunch, a dinner at the Club," and he described the American novelist as having "a noble and complete nature, a spirit marvelously lucid. His knowledge, he said, was wide, "his taste was sure and perfect; and joined to this an ironic gift, of a benevolent kind." James seemed to Léon Daudet like a doctor or a judge who "inspired serenity and confidence." There were days when the novelist and his illustrious visitor simply sat at the window of Brown's and watched the life of the street below. "What an air of pride these English soldiers have!" Daudet remarked, looking at a military figure walking down the street. "How well-set they are for marching on parade in their fine-figured strut." James rejoined, "My dear Daudet, they have to be thus, they have to take account of the young and pretty servant girls looking at them from the windows." The journalists often spoke of Daudet's emaciated and exquisite features as "Christ-like" and James said, "I felt as if I should go mad if I even once more, let alone twenty times more, heard Daudet personally compared (more especially facially compared, eyeglass and all) to Jesus Christ." We get another view of these moments in James's letter to Lady Wolseley, after the Daudets were gone: "They clung to me like a litter of pups to an experienced mamma. They were very amiable, very uninformed, very bewildered, very observant and perceptive, on the whole, and very overwhelming."

IV

The meeting of Daudet and Meredith occurred on May 16, bringing together three novelists of widely different talents—the loquacious Daudet, with the sun of southern France in his talk, Meredith, the poet-novelist of England, and the trans-Atlantic James, who stood aside as intermediary and left the foreground to the other two. Daudet and his son Léon made the trip by train from Charing Cross to Dorking accompanied by James. With great effort Daudet climbed from the train and almost fell into the arms of the tall, white-bearded, white-haired Meredith. The dark-eyed meridional and the blue-eyed Briton embraced. Henry described the scene to his brother William: "Strangely and grotesquely pathetic was the meeting between the French and the English romancer—*coram publico*, on the railway platform each staggering and stumbling, with the same uncontrollable paralysis into the arms of the other so that they almost rolled over together on the line beneath the wheels of the train." Meredith leaned on the arm of Admiral Maxse; Daudet was supported by Léon. The little party slowly got into the carriage and drove to Flint Cottage where Meredith was giving dinner to his guests, who would then take a train back to London. Daudet himself evoked the meeting in a letter he wrote that evening—"the ironic fraternity, two novelists dragging a wing, like two wounded seagulls, maimed, birds of tempest, punished for having affronted the gods."*

For other recollections of the occasion we must rely on Léon Daudet's doubtless embellished memoirs; but it seems clear that Meredith professed his love for Daudet—"*Laissez-moi dire que je vous aime*"—and told him that he had set aside some bottles of Votes-Rôties ten years before in the hope of such an occasion. Léon remembered that the wines were remarkable and that "Meredith's commentary surpassed them in colour and richness." Daudet was delighted to see on the table Mistral's *Mirèio* and *Calendau*. The English poet-novelist read aloud the *Poème du Rhône*; certain of the passages in the Provençal, Meredith could not decipher. "I live here in the midst of Scythians, you understand, don't you, Daudet," Meredith said. And later he remarked to his guest, "How lively you are," and as if to explain his appreciation of this liveliness he added, "You know I'm not really English; I'm a Gaul." When the name of Wilde came up, Meredith was quoted by the younger Daudet as saying, "a mixture of Apollo and a monster." To James, Daudet was "very appealing and pathetic in his advanced and yet combatted infirmity—wasted and worn, saturated with morphine and chloral." "*Depuis dix ans*," Daudet told him, "*je n'ai que le sommeil artificiel.*" A few days after the visit to Box Hill, Meredith came to London to dine with Daudet; and he returned again, in spite of his infirmities, to go with James to Victoria Station at the end of May to bid farewell to the

. . . .

* "*C'est une sensation de fraternelle ironie, ces deux romanciers qui trainent l'aile comme deux goelands blessés, estropiés, ces oiseaux de tempête, punis pour avoir voulu affronter les dieux.*"

visitors. It is recorded that the two invalids clasped hands through the window as the train began to move—and with their muscular infirmities disengaged them with difficulty.

Daudet was expansive to the last. Within a day of his return to Paris he wrote James that he had had great admiration for the subtleties of his talent and the profundity of his spirit; but that now after spending three weeks near to him "during which I looked at you closely, I want tó give you all my friendship and I demand all yours. Let's have not another word on the subject."*

"That is charming," Henry commented to William, "and genuine, I think, and I am sincerely touched, but it is a rather formidable order to meet. However, he inspired great kindness." He answered Daudet tactfully. "I will best show you how touched I am by receiving your words in affectionate silence." The Daudets had made James promise he would some day visit them at Champrosay. The promise was never kept, for James did not go abroad for several years, and in 1897 Daudet died suddenly one evening while dining with his family. In a brief tribute James pronounced one of his characteristic eulogies. Daudet had been "as warm as the south wall of a garden or as the flushed fruit that grows there," and of all consummate artists he had been the most "natural." He was at the opposite pole from Flaubert in this respect. Flaubert, with "a kind of grand, measured distance from his canvas—paced as if for a duel—seemed to attack his subject with a brush twenty feet long." Daudet's charm lay in his agitation, and his nerves. "His style is a matter of talking, gesticulating, imitating—of impressionism carried to the last point." And James also said, "The sun in his blood had never burnt out."

. . . .

* "Je ne veux vous dire aujourd'hui qu'une chose: avant d'aller à Londres j'avais pour votre talent subtil, la profondeur de votre esprit, une sympathie très-grande; maintenant, après ces trois semaines vécues en commun, pendant lesquelles je vous ai bien regardé, c'est toute mon amitié que je vous donne et toute la vôtre que je vous demande. Ainsi, plus un mot là-dessus!"

THE FIGURE IN THE CARPET

AFTER THE DAUDETS LEFT, HENRY JAMES HAD A VIOLENT ATTACK OF the gout—his foot was "like the Dome of St. Paul's." To Dr. Baldwin he wrote of his "fruitless six months, with gout, sore throats, a futile month's visit to Ireland, interruptions innumerable, and just lately, to finish, the whole Alphonse Daudet family." He would not be going to Italy this year, he told Baldwin, and referring to a recent earthquake there he added, "Our earthquake, here, has been social—human—sexual (if that be the word when it's all one sex). You probably followed in some degree the Oscar Wilde horrors."

There had been also his personal earthquake. The passage of six months since *Guy Domville* had not diminished his uneasiness and his melancholy. He was now face to face with a long summer and did not know where to turn. He had done very little work, had written only one tale published in the *Yellow Book* ("The Next Time"), and he was having difficulty getting on with a novel. He had never felt so much at loose ends. His decision not to go to the Continent could have been foreseen; he had found too many American tourists in Italy and Switzerland during the previous spring and summer, when he had made his doleful journey to help Miss Woolson's relatives close up her apartment in Venice. The death of Fenimore had blunted his desire to go abroad. He talked much of abandoning London for the English countryside but shrank from doing so. He would have to face solitude and work, and he had no appetite for either. Instead he involved himself with passing Americans. "There is a compatriot for every day in the week," he said. John La Farge appeared, after the failure of a show of his South Sea watercolors in Paris. He revived old memories, but seemed "Americanly innocent." And he was thoughtless. He sent three French ladies to James, to be guided through

London. "What does he expect me to do with them?" James wailed to Henrietta Reubell. Then Mrs. Gardner came; for a few days he played out his usual comedy of pretending he was her most abject courtier, but her queenliness no longer amused him. He left her with one of his usual flourishes, after taking her to a couple of art exhibitions. Life, he told her, was too "complicated and conflicting." With characteristic irony he added, "you are a great simplifier—I wish you would simplify *me!*" Nothing seemed simple now. London was "a seething hell." His impatience and anger finally exploded in his notebook—"the deluge of people, the insane movement for movement, the ruin of thought, of life, the negation of work, of literature, the swelling, roaring crowds, the 'where are you going?,' the age of Mrs. Jack, the figure of Mrs. Jack, the American, the nightmare—the individual consciousness —the mad, ghastly climax or denouement."

And he added: "The Americans looming up—dim, vast, portentous—in their millions—like gathering waves—the barbarians of the Roman Empire."

I

He lingered until late July amid the visiting "barbarians" and then suddenly bolted—to Torquay in Devonshire where he had spent a few days the previous year. A winter resort, Torquay offered him general quiet and pleasant southern warmth. He obtained a fine suite in the Osborne Hotel on Hesketh Crescent, with a large sitting room and a balcony. A six-foot chambermaid prepared his hot bath every morning. He took bicycle lessons and boasted of his black and yellow bruises. He paid calls on W. E. Norris, who lived in a large villa on a near-by hilltop and who had shown James much sympathy at the time of *Guy Domville*; he would not be utterly lonely at Torquay. He described Norris as "the mildest, kindest, cleanest of novelists and of gentlemen—tremendously old-fashioned at 45," and "the gentlest and sweetest of men, one quite loves him." Norris apparently felt the same about James.

They ran out of conversational subjects during the first quarter of an hour every time they met. This did not trouble Henry. Norris was "accepting"—and James needed this more than anything else.

"Peace wraps me round," he wrote to Miss Reubell after settling into his hotel. He liked the view; the sea had a lovely Italian blueness. And the tranquillity—"not a cat in the house!" So it seemed, at least for three weeks. During this time he completed the little one-act play about "Mrs. Gracedew" he had promised to Ellen Terry. Then, perhaps because life was too tranquil, perhaps because he still had stage-fever, he went back to London. He spoke to one of his correspondents of having to go "for two or three compulsory weeks."

The principal reason for this foray seems to have been a desire to see Miss Terry personally about the play. Whether he was able to talk it over with her in detail we do not know. It seems hardly likely. She had just finished a long run in one of Sir Henry Irving's productions. The company was about to sail for an extended American tour. And the fact that she gave Henry James a rendezvous in her box at a play suggests that she was squeezing him into a very crowded schedule. We know of the rendezvous because James had promised to go to the theatre with Mrs. Henry White, wife of the American diplomat, and he informed her that Miss Terry "who goes abroad on Sunday and has only that moment" wanted to talk to him during the intermission "about a small change in something I have done for her." Miss Terry wrote him that she liked the play and he replied, "You are indeed the Gentle Reader, you read with imagination . . . I want to write you another (already!) one-act play—yearn after such." The actress paid him £100 and apparently told him she would not produce the one-acter in America—she was scheduled to play *Madame Sans-Gêne*. She seems to have promised production on her return. "It will seem a long year—but art *is* long, ah me!" James replied. "At all events, if the Americans are not to have the Gem, do excruciate them with a suspicion of what they lose." This was his final gesture to the theatre which proved as fickle as ever. Miss Terry never produced *Summersoft*, and two years later he would make a short story of it.

If the actress was the principal reason for James's return to London from Torquay, there was also another which few of his friends knew. A diary entry in the journals of Clara Benedict, Miss Woolson's sister, tells us that "Mr. James said he would come up from Torquay and be with us the week before we sailed." He was as good as his word. He had been loyal to Mrs. Benedict and her daughter just a year before—had gone to Venice in the spring of 1894 to be with them. Now, after a twelvemonth, he still seemed to feel some sense of duty or obligation, some need for common kindness, and also piety to Fenimore's memory. He took the Benedicts to dinner at the Indian Exhibition to which all London was flocking. They dined also in Mayfair and he saw them off to America. How he felt about them we know from his saying to Dr. Baldwin that the United States had "swallowed them up—and will keep them I suppose—till it heaves them forth again." To another friend of Fenimore's—Francis Boott—he characterized Mrs. Benedict as "very considerably mad," and spoke of her and Miss Woolson's niece as "very futile and foolish, poor things." Nevertheless some feeling of guilt and of attachment to Fenimore's memory had caused him, and would cause him in future years, to show an excess of generosity to the Benedicts.

After they sailed, James was free to return to Torquay. Instead he remained entangled with visitors and London society. He saw the Kiplings, on the eve of their return to America. The poet was "strangely ungrowing." He spent a Sunday in the country with the Humphry Wards. He entertained Graham Balfour, who brought him news of Fanny Stevenson in San Francisco. He spent some time with Mrs. Mason, one of the favorite riding companions of his old Roman days. Count Primoli, the Bonaparte dilettante, turned up from Rome with his usual stories about the Princess Mathilde, and in his company was the young Prince Karageorgev ich (who was a member of the Yugoslavian dynasty). James described the Prince as "not a bit of a personality, an individual—only a well-directed little faintly-perfumed spray of fluid, of distilled amenity." He entertained Barrett Wendell of Harvard and complained to William when the professor sent him his book on Shakespeare. "Besides being critically very thin and even common," he wrote, "it is surely not written as the Professor of English of Harvard should write. It has made me unhappy." Part of that unhappiness consisted in his having to write Wendell "with anguish, a mendacious letter of thanks." Still complaining of being "confined to the torrid town," he went off to spend a week-end with George du Maurier at Folkestone. *Trilby* was breaking records as a best-seller, and would be a roaring success as a play. The quiet and gentle du Maurier, a professional artist but an amateur writer, was having the very kind of success James needed. Yet he found du Maurier depressed "in spite of the chink —what say I, the 'chink'—the deafening roar—of sordid gold flowing in to him." Returning to London James wrote to Gosse: "I came back feeling an even worse failure than usual."

11

It was by now early September. James made arrangements for the installation of electric light in his De Vere Gardens flat. As painters, paper-hangers and electricians took over, he left once more for Torquay. It was a good time to be away. Moreover his Devonshire retreat promised to be very sociable. The Paul Bourgets, passing through London, had once again decided to join him for a month. There had been their famous sojourn together in Siena in 1892; and then the previous year they had lived side by side in Oxford and taken long walks in the college gardens. They were much less demanding than the Daudets. James always found the French novelist a great conversational asset, an "intellectual and colloquial luxury." The pair clung to James; he in turn clung to Norris. "Bourget's mind is, in the real solitude in which I live, beneath what has been so much social chatter, a flowering oasis in conversational sands." Henry wrote thus to William, adding, "he is more or less spoiled by a success that (in its extreme abundance), I don't wholly account for."

Writing to Francis Boott he described Norris's hilltop villa in terms of Italy. It had a lovely view and Norris lived with an only daughter "exactly as you used to do at Bellosguardo." Torquay was "all dusty roads and villa walls . . . Norris is a dear like you, and passionately fond of music, like you. His daughter too, is Lizzie's age: the age Lizzie was (23!) but there the resemblance ends. She doesn't care a straw for 'art'—or only for the art of foxhunting. She is a pure amazon—one of those frequent English types who is exclusively horsey and yet not a bit 'fast.'" Norris played golf every morning, during the hours James was writing. The English novelist wrote "at the inconceivable hour of three till five. Then he potters in his garden; then, at six, I, finishing my longish and solitary walk, drop in, or rather climb up, and have tea with him. At eight he dines *tête-à-tête* with his daughter, both infinitely dressed—and after dinner he plays the piano. So you see it's all much like you." As for Norris's books, "ah, his books—nothing would induce me to tell you what I think of them! Seriously, I don't think anything at all." If Norris supplied some deeply felt want in James's life, the American novelist seems also to have given the English writer a great deal of friendliness. Norris once spoke of "my rather absurd old-man's fad for hearing from all the people I care for at Christmas." During James's late years, no matter where he was, a long Yule letter was invariably dispatched to Torquay.

III

James had promised Heinemann two novels during the coming year; and he was supposed to write three tales for the *Atlantic Monthly*. He felt a certain pressure not only to fulfill these agreements, but to begin earning money again. His vain theatrical xperiments, he wrote William, had brought him "to the verge of bankruptcy." Once again he communed with himself in his note-books. "I am face to face with several little alternatives of work. . . I must thresh out my solutions, must settle down to my jobs." Then, impatiently, he told himself, "It's idiotic, by the way, to waste time in writing such a remark as that! As if I didn't feel in all such matters infinitely more than I can ever utter." He had lost sight of "the necessary smallness, necessary singleness of the sub-ject. I've been too proud to take the very simple thing. I've almost always taken the thing requiring developments. Now, when I embark on developments I'm lost, for they are my temptation and my joy. I'm too afraid to be *banal*. I needn't be afraid, for my danger is small."

The danger was small, but he was caught now in the complexi-ies of his troubled imagination as well as his desire for experi-ment. By telling his stories in short dramatic scenes, he required more words than had been necessary in his *laisser-aller* days. Even when he tried subjects that were small, the process of dramatizing them required a larger statement. His goal was 8,000 to 10,000 words; and now he nearly always ended with 18,000 or 20,000. He had started a story for the *Atlantic* about a squabble between a mother and son over some antiques. At 25,000 it was not yet complete. He set it aside and began what seemed to him another small tale which he called "The Awkward Age." It too resisted compression. When it reached 15,000, he wrote to the editor, "I must try again for you on a tinier subject—though I thought this was tiny." And he confessed that "I can't do the very little thing any more, and the process—the endeavour—is most expensive—it is so long and complicated." He attempted a new story inspired by having seen while riding on top of a London bus an attractive woman's face disfigured by a pair of abnormally large spectacles. It took him almost a month to write "Glasses," and then he ruefully informed the *Atlantic* it had exceeded 15,000. Apologetically he asked the editor whether he would serialize it in two instalments.

"The thing is so highly finished . . . that it is a double pity it's so
ill-starred. Of course, however, you may say 'Who in the world
cares for high finish?' " The editor, Horace Scudder, liked the tale
and ran it in a single issue. James was elated. "Ask *anything* of me
then—I won't refuse it!" Scudder offered to take the overblown
story about the squabble over a houseful of antiques as a three- or
four-instalment novel of about 35,000. James promptly bargained
for 5,000 words more; and by the time he finished it, it had
become a 75,000-word novel, published in the magazine in seven
instalments as "The Old Things." In book form it would be called
The Spoils of Poynton.

What had happened to the author who could, with his turning
hand, produce tale after tale, sometimes one or two a week? We
may surmise that at this stage, given his mood and his despair, he
resisted writing altogether. His notebooks show him setting down
over-elaborate outlines, even for short things. In the old days he
wasted no time on such preliminaries. He still possessed the art of
brevity in spite of his new techniques; but the combination of
psychological hindrance and his quest for original forms was proving too much for him. And then the substance of his tales—the
four he would complete in 1895—showed a state that he himself
called "embarrassment." These are the tales that are to be found
in the volume entitled *Embarrassments* published early in 1896.
One feels that at this moment James wanted simply to be left
alone; to have the consoling company of Norris; to ride his bicycle
and brood on his problems or dawdle on The Crescent. Instead he
had to keep at his work, to refill his empty purse. A fantasy he set
down in his notebook clearly suggests this. He begins by recalling
that old Mrs. Procter long ago had described how pleasant it was
simply to sit by her fire and read a book. He would write a tale
about an "old party" who finds delight in simple elderly pastimes
—"a quiet walk, a quiet read, the civil visit of a friend or the
luxury of some quite ordinary *relation*." In his fantasy however the
"old party" is ousted from his fireside by his estranged wife who

now turns up. "I see it all, I feel for him." The old party disappears, he "vanishes away, leaving the wife in possession." She takes over his quiet, his fireside, his book. "I see *her*—having exterminated him—given up to the same happy stillness as *he* was. She is in his chair, by his lamp, at his table, she expresses just the same quiet little joy that he did." The theme is very much like that of "The Altar of the Dead," written a year before, in which a woman invades and takes over a man's private altar consecrated to his dead—and uses it to mourn the very individual he hated. The tale of the altar had reflected his feeling that Miss Woolson, by her suicide, had ravished his inner quiet. In killing herself, Miss Woolson had made him feel that in some strange way she had "exterminated" him—certainly she had obliterated the quiet of his common day. He did not write this tale of the "old party," but instead wrote another, about an author and an unfathomable secret.

IV

James's re-exposure to the Benedicts in London had reawakened old Bellosguardo recollections and the painful memory of Miss Woolson's death in Venice. There was every reason for believing that she had killed herself in a moment of high fever during influenza; but James knew also that she had long been lonely, unhappy, depressed, had often hinted at suicide and in those last weeks had wandered aimlessly about in desolate Venice at the Christmastide, lost in her memories. James had felt personally involved; and somehow he blamed himself: some intuition told him that he had taken her affection too much for granted, and accepted it without true reciprocity. Miss Woolson had, long before, written a story about a woman writer like herself, who takes her work to a successful literary man. Dissatisfied with it, he tries to edit it, only to discover that it contains an "especial figure in a carpet," which unravels when he tampers with the copy. Whether James remembered that image, or found it elsewhere, he now planned a tale called "The Figure in the Carpet" and wrote it shortly after his return to town, under the new electric lights in De Vere Gardens.

It is one of James's artificial comedies of authorship. A young critic has reviewed the latest novel of Hugh Vereker and at a country house he hears Vereker call his review "the usual twaddle." Later Vereker discovers the identity of the critic, and is contrite; he explains to the young man that no one has understood his work nor discerned its secret—its "figure in the carpet." He speaks of this as his "general intention." It is not really a secret at all; Vereker has not tried to conceal anything; it is simply something in his work everyone has overlooked. It resides in "the order, the form, the texture" of his novels. Pressed further by the young critic, the novelist says that what nobody had ever mentioned in his writings was "the organ of life." Placed in the context of James's total work it is not difficult to suggest what James was thinking of when he wrote this tale. We have his pronouncements, often reiterated, that it was art that *made* life. Consequently we may say that the "organ of life" is art. "Who in the world cares for high finish?"—his words to the *Atlantic* editor—had expressed this. The order, form, and texture of a work constituted the art with which it was written. And very few paid attention to James's art. Vereker wryly observes to the young reviewer, "It's quite with you rising young men that I feel most what a failure I am."

The unnamed young critic tells all this to a fellow-critic, George Corvick, who takes it very seriously and begins a systematic search for the author's secret. He also tells his fiancée, Gwendolen Erme, who at nineteen had written a three-decker novel James whimsically called "Deep Down." Things have not gone well between Corvick and Gwendolen, but now in their common pursuit of Vereker's "exquisite scheme" they find true common ground. Art proves a more powerful force than life in the wooing. Corvick finally makes his discovery; he journeys halfway across the world to consult Vereker, who confirms it. And Gwendolen now marries him.

The marriage is short-lived. Corvick dies in an accident during his honeymoon. Later Vereker dies; and after him his wife. Only Corvick's widow now knows the secret and the curious little narrator asks her bluntly for it. She is just as blunt: "I mean to keep it to myself," and with this knowledge she writes a better novel, called "Overmastered." When the narrator pursues her with his questions about the "figure" she tells him, "It's my *life*." Like the narrator in "The Aspern Papers," the busy and curious little man wonders whether he shouldn't try to marry her—the figure in the carpet seems traceable and describable "only for husbands and wives—for lovers supremely united." However, she marries a third-rate critic; and when, after a time, she dies, the narrator discovers that she never told this husband Vereker's secret. He is left with an unsolved mystery—"I was shut up in my obsession for ever—my gaolers had gone off with the key."

We have a convergence in this tale of the two themes that constituted James's "embarrassment." The first, the more obvious one, was his sense of being a misunderstood author; of his having offered the world art—his own figure in his Persian carpet—and been rebuffed. No one had really understood what he wanted to do. The *Guy Domville* audience had behaved like a set of savages with a gold watch. The second theme was the burden of Miss Woolson's unfathomed secret. Had it been a secret of human relations, a defect in his own "system" of friendship? He was left shut up in his obsession—forever! How deeply this troubled him we may judge by the tale "The Way It Came" (later renamed "The Friends of the Friends") which immediately followed the story of Hugh Vereker. In the tradition of Defoe, it is a tale of a man who will never know whether he talked to a woman just before or after her death. His fiancée, who narrates the story, is also left in eternal doubt. Did her fiancé have a tryst with a living woman or with a ghost? As she kneels by the bedside of the dead woman, her thought is that "Death had made her, had kept her beautiful; but I felt above all, that it had made her, had kept her, silent." Again James's image is that of a key—"it had turned the key on something I was concerned to know."

From this moment on—and for the next five years—his stories would be about little girls and young female adults who want to know—who try to probe the secrets of the world around them, but who do not possess enough facts for their inductions and deductions. The ultimate work, *The Sacred Fount*, with its obsessed narrator, is implicit in the obsessed narration of "The Figure in the Carpet." And in all these tales James seems to have worked toward a single conclusion: the facts of life were crude and raw; art colored and gilded them, and suffused them with eternal truth. The human imagination brings life into existence.

v

James remained at Torquay for two months while his apartment was renovated. During the last days of his stay, his young friend Jonathan Sturges came to be with him. The Bourgets by this time had left. Sturges, usually cheerful, sardonic, a veritable "little demon," was downcast and deeply unhappy. James believed he had fallen in love with some woman in France, and for the first time had had to face the fact that in his crippled helpless state he could not hope for love as other men. In this mood, one evening, Sturges began to tell James about a little incident that had occurred the year before in Paris. He had met Howells one day in Whistler's garden in the Rue du Bac. Howells was full of sad emotion. He had just arrived. Paris was beautiful. And he had to leave, recalled to America because his father was dying. In the garden setting Howells had said to young Sturges: "Oh, you are young, you are young—be glad of it: be glad of it and *live*. Live all you can: it's a mistake not to. It doesn't so much matter what you do—but live. This place makes it all come over me. I see it now. I haven't done so—and now I'm old. It's too late. It has gone past me—I've lost it. You have time. You are young. Live!"

Listening to Sturges, James could see and hear Howells—and he listened as if the message were for him. He felt old. His best years were gone. He was aware of his unlived life rising within—and yet it seemed "too late." The little anecdote touched the heart of James's sadness. He could do no more, in his own black abyss, than set down Howells's words in his notebook. Five years later they would speak to him again: and then he would pay attention not to the words "too late" but to the words "Live all you can." A long purgatory still lay ahead—and he would have to experience it before he would be ready to write *The Ambassadors*.

BOOK THREE

The Turn of the Screw
1896=1898

A QUIET HERMITAGE

HENRY JAMES RETURNED TO LONDON AT THE BEGINNING OF NOVEM-ber 1895, having had two full months of the autumn at Torquay. The workmen were still in his flat and he would have lingered in Devonshire but for the increasing illness of Jonathan Sturges. Rather than risk having a seriously sick man on his hands he got him to London. The doctors put Sturges straight into a hospital—"where," James wrote to Miss Reubell, "he is (very successfully and comfortably) having his illness now." Sturges remained in his Wimpole Street nursing home all winter, using it "as a kind of safe and comfortable lodging." He had had in reality what the doctors diagnosed as a "nervous prostration."

"I loved my Torquay to the end," James told Miss Reubell. He also now found London lively and "lots of people about." A day or two after his return he helped to entertain Georg Brandes, the Danish critic, who was on a visit to England, dining with him and Andrew Lang and afterwards taking him to the Savile Club and plying the abstemious celebrity with lemon squashes. He found

him of "a very bright and large intercourse" and he told Gosse
that Brandes "did me good—a great good; it is such a joy to
encounter a fine free foreign mind. But it's a peril—it spoils one
fearfully for some of one's other contacts."

The workmen finally left De Vere Gardens and James rejoiced
in the fresh paint and the brightness and cleanliness of his new
electric lamps. He wrote two tales and resumed work on his serial
for the *Atlantic*. Before he knew it, Christmas was approaching, a
time he liked in London; the city was brightly lit and cheerful. To
Mrs. Wister he wrote that he cared more than ever for his work.
With the "necessary isolation the years bring with them (quantities of *acquaintances*—oh yes!)" his writing was "almost the only
thing I do care for." James spoke also in this letter of the death
earlier that year of Leslie Stephen's wife (the mother of Virginia
Stephen who would later be Virginia Woolf). "I had a great
affection for her, and she was—where she was—such a perfectly
precious force for good that one doesn't know what to make of the
economy of things that could do nothing with her—as far as our
measure of the matter goes—but suppress her. She was beautifully
beautiful, and her beauty and her nature were all active *applied*
things, making a great difference for the better for everybody.
Merely not to see her any more is to have a pleasure the less in
life." This was a foreshadowing of Virginia Woolf's picture of
Mrs. Ramsay in *To the Lighthouse* many years later.

Before the Yule season, James visited George Meredith, who
was about to bring out *The Amazing Marriage*; and he wrote to
Daudet about du Maurier's *Trilby* which in its play form seemed
destined to run for at least two or three years. "See what it is to
take the measure of the foot—as we say—of the gross Anglo-Saxon
public," he remarked to Daudet. "The rare Meredith is not that
kind of shoemaker—nor," added Henry, "the poor James."

I

On December 18, 1895, the London newspapers brought the novelist a horrible war scare. There had been for some years a boundary

dispute between Venezuela and British Guiana. Such disputes were frequent in the Latin-American countries, and to a public unaware of the American sense of hemispheric sanctity, these seemed remote and without gravity. Suddenly President Cleveland reasserted the seventy-year-old Monroe Doctrine. He denounced British "aggression" against Venezuela and asserted that the United States had a serious interest in the determination of the disputed boundary. "The American outbreak has darkened all my sky," Henry James wrote to Norris.

He had for so long taken for granted the continuing friendship of the English-speaking peoples—which his own career symbolized —that it came to him as a violent shock to discover how deep trans-Atlantic animosities could run. He knew only too well that the English could be condescending and haughty to their American cousins; but it was new to him to see how nasty some of his fellow-countrymen could be to the English. Feelings between the two nations had been on the whole friendly since their differences during the Civil War. James had witnessed good diplomatic relations during Lowell's term as minister to the Court of St. James's, and an amicable tone of converse between London and Washington in subsequent years. Now Cleveland's belligerence, and a huge outcry against England in the American press, shook the foundations of his security, rooted as it was in an ideal of trans-Atlantic culture. Cleveland, he remarked, had made the United States sound "like one of the big European powers, particularly the Germany of Bismarck."

His letters during the early weeks of 1896 show how deep was his gloom, how profound his anxiety. If there were a war he would have to make a choice, for his allegiance was double. The American tone however seemed wrong and his sympathies lay in London, in Europe, in the cosmopolite world. "One must hope that sanity and civilization, in both countries, will prevail," he wrote to his brother. "But the lurid light the American newspapers seem to project on the quantity of resident Anglophobia in the U.S.—the absolute war-hunger as against this country—is a thing to darken one's meditations. Whence, why does it, today, explode in such immense volume—in such apparent preponderance, and whither does it tend? It stupefies me—seems to me horribly inferior and vulgar—and I shall never go with it." In an outburst of feeling he added: "I had rather my bones were ground into British powder!"

What James experienced in part was the fatalism of the newspaper headlines, the daily presentation of violent alternatives—as if all decisions had to be made on the instant. The British however put on their coolest diplomatic manner; and as days passed, and belligerent words were succeeded by cautionary moves, James could write to the painter, John Everett Millais, "the madness will evaporate." To his old friend Howells he confessed that spring, however, that the war scare had brought home to him the length of his absence from America. He had been away twelve years, and the American "delirium" reached him "as if it came from China or another planet." To his despair, at the end of this terrible year of personal upheaval, was now added a sense of distance from his own country. "Those were weeks of black darkness for me," James told Howells.

11

In mid-winter of 1895-96, James was invited by the *Century* magazine to write a commemorative article on Dumas *fils* who had died recently. He did so promptly; it was a chance to talk "theatre," and Dumas had been a dramatist remembered from his early years; he had heard his name when he was a small boy. He had not been allowed to see *La Dame aux Camélias* because it hadn't been for his time of life. He spoke of this in his article, recalling how his young girl cousins, who had seen the play, had wept "floods" over Madame Doche's performance. "It was the first time I had heard of pocket handkerchiefs as a provision for the play." Later he had not only seen all the leading Camilles, but had found Dumas's *Le Demi-Monde* an inspiration for his own "Siege of London."

In his article he discussed the Anglo-Saxon tendency to be moral and the French tendency to *moralize*. Dumas had been a "professional moralist," a student of the passions. One of his great contentions had been "that seduced girls should under all circumstances be married—by somebody or other, failing the seducer. This is a contention," James wrote, "that, as we feel, barely concerns us, shut up as we are in the antecedent conviction that they should under no circumstances be seduced." When James dispatched his manuscript, he received word from the ponderous Robert Underwood Johnson of the *Century* that it wouldn't do. The *Century* was a "family magazine." Relations between men and women, not least, the seduction of young girls, could not be discussed in its pages. James promptly noted that this would make "a lovely little ironic tale." He wrote it during the following year—"John Delavoy"—and the editor in it tells a young critic emphatically he cannot write about the relations of the sexes. "If you want to know what our public won't stand, there you have it." The *Century* had wanted the article because Dumas was famous. He was famous because he had written certain things—"which they won't for the world have intelligibly mentioned." James may have taken ironic satisfaction in selling the article on Dumas to the New York *Herald* and the Boston *Herald*; it appeared in both under large headlines, as if indeed James had written a shocker— "[Dumas] Reputation for Immorality due to Alien Judgment" and "Life to him Appeared Wholly a Fierce Battle Between Man and Woman." In England the essay was published in the *New Review*.

III

James agreed that winter to do a serial for an unusual medium— for him: the *Illustrated London News*. His friend Mrs. W. K. Clifford had hinted to the editor, Clement Shorter, that he might be willing to strike a "popular" note (it was a little like the author in "The Next Time" who attempts potboilers) and James was very positive about this. "I should be very glad to write you a story energetically designed to meet your requirements of a 'love-story,' " he wrote, and he bargained for a higher price than was offered. They settled for £300. "I shall endeavour to be thrilling," Henry said.

With the final chapters of "The Old Things" still to be written for the *Atlantic*, James decided to quit London early and try to get his books done in some quiet corner of England. He had nursed a dream of going that spring to Italy, but Torquay had demonstrated to him that England had eminently practical places of refuge. They might not be Florence or Venice, but they also were not as distracting. If he could find a house near London, he could be in and out of the city as necessary. Moreover, in De Vere Gardens, there had always been the question of his servants, the Smith couple who took to drink during his absences. He began to lay plans in February 1896. "I've two novels to write before I can dream of anything else," he explained to Norris, who asked whether he would return to Torquay. "I must take a house, this time—a small and cheap one—and I must (deride me not), be somewhere where I can, without disaster, bicycle. Also I must be a little nearer to town than last year."

The house was found for him by his architect friend, Edward Warren, and James moved in punctually at the end of April. "I recapture a cottage on a cliffside," James would remember, "to which at the earliest approach of the summer-time . . . I had betaken myself to finish a book in quiet and to begin another in fear. The cottage was, in its kind, perfection; mainly by reason of a small paved terrace which, curving forward from the cliff-edge like the prow of a ship, overhung a view as level, as pure, as full of rich change as the expanse of a sea; a small red-roofed town, of great antiquity, perched on its sea-rock, clustered within the picture off to the right; while above one's head rustled a dense summer shade, that of a trained and arching ash, rising from the middle of the terrace, brushing the parapet with a heavy fringe and covering the place like a vast umbrella." It was a small house called "Point Hill," located at Playden in Sussex and the novelist got a three-months' occupancy, from May to August 1896. The town at which James looked was one of England's ancient Cinque Ports—Rye in Sussex, unique in Britain in the way in which its red-brick houses, many of them extremely old, huddled about the town's church, set on the highest point of the rock: a church part Norman, with a square tower. For all the world, in the fading light, amid a thick purple haze, it looked from Playden like a miniature Mont St. Michel or one of James's beloved Italian hill towns rising above the Umbrian valleys.

When he explored Rye he found it to be filled with Old World charm. In 1896 it had not yet been invaded by tourists. It had an ancient tower, the Ypres Tower built in the thirteenth century as a watchtower; on the London side the town had a Land Gate also a remnant of the Middle Ages. The waters had long since withdrawn from the base of the rock and the marshes had been drained, so that Romney Marsh, once covered by the sea, now had hundreds of sheep peacefully grazing on it. The High Street of the town was filled with old shops with small-paned windows, reminiscent of old novels; at night when they were lit by candle or smelly oil-lamp it seemed as if he were back in the eighteenth century. Cobbled Mermaid Street, with its Elizabethan houses, went back much farther. During his rambles James was particularly struck by a stout red-brick Georgian house, at a curve in the steep street leading to the church; next to it was a curious little building that looked like a chapel or a banqueting hall. He was told that the house had for decades been in the hands of the Lambs, one of Rye's prominent families.

"It is delightfully quiet and quaint and simple and salubrious, and the bliss of the rural solitude and peace and beauty are a balm to my spirit," Henry wrote to William after a month at Point Hill. "This little corner of the land endears itself to me." To his old friend, Francis Boott, he spoke of Rye and his hillside home as "a very sweet, slumberous corner of the land, wholly unfashionable and very picturesque." His servants took good care of him; the weather was exceptionally fine, and every evening in the thickening twilight he would dine at eight on his terrace, as if he were living in some Florentine villa. He had brought his other companions with him—his faithful fat dog, Tosca, and his canary in its cage, a recent gift from a London friend. When he was not walking the hilly streets, he took the circling sea roads on his bicycle, going to nearby Winchelsea, where Ellen Terry had her cottage, and to a host of little towns with soft quaint names—Brookland, Old Romney, Ivychurch, Dymchurch, Lydd. As the summer deepened, as the shepherds and their dogs passed him in the grassy meadow once marshland, Henry James was reminded of his younger years when he had galloped on horseback past Italian shepherds and their flocks and felt the stir of ancient things in the Roman Campagna.

IV

Long before the first of August, when he was supposed to surrender Point Hill to its returning owners, James decided he did not want to leave. A systematic hunt yielded him a haven for the rest of the summer and early autumn. It was less picturesque but roomier and actually more suited to his needs. This was the town's Old Vicarage, as it was formerly called, situated in Rye itself, to which James moved bird and dog and servants, and his masses of proofs and manuscript. The "musty, bourgeois parsonage" gave him no view, and brought him down to the very cobbles of Rye; but he was able to work well within it. He liked its "very ancient and purple brick-walled garden, where the pears grow yellow in the September sun and the peace of the Lord—or at least of the parson—seems to abide." He amusedly gave himself out as leading the "prosy" life of a *curé de campagne*. "Think of me in a vicarage," he wrote to the church-doctrined Mrs. Humphry Ward; and he clung to it until it was time to give it up at the beginning of October.

"I am nearing the end of a very quiet summer," he wrote to

Grace Norton, "which began May 1st in this rather shabby and unfashionable corner, where 'people' are not and where I've passed the most unpopulated—*de*populated—four or five months that I have *ever* passed. I like the country, which is really rustic, and for the most part remarkably pretty—I like, now, almost *any* country; and I like even a little unsophisticated town, like this, perched picturesquely on its pedestal of rock and overlooking the wide sheep-studded greenness of Romney Marsh." A little red-roofed and clustered Old World town, James told Miss Norton, was "in a manner a small and homely *family*." The image was apt. For the Henry James who ever since *Guy Domville* had felt "homeless," whose mind wandered to the renting or even acquiring of an anchorage (and who indeed was to write three works in succession involving houses), the parochial domesticity of this one of the guardian ports of old England offered a kind of solitude and friendliness which he could not find in London. James said he recognized how intensely Rye must have been a "family" "in the old days of its loneliness, when the French repeatedly harried and took it." It had been the site of constant battle. In later decades it had been a great center of smuggling. All this was but "a quaintness the more, when on one side, away from the steep little street, where the sound of wheels is almost never, one's windows in the rear have a garden and a great country view." He added: "I return to London sometime next month—rather reluctantly—so pleasant to me has provinciality (with books and a bicycle!) become." Before leaving he mentioned, in chatting with the local ironmonger, that he was interested in finding a year-round house in Rye. The ironmonger would, in due course, remember this.

HOUSES AND OLD THINGS

I

"THE SPOILS OF POYNTON"—A STORY OF AN OLD HOUSE AND "OLD things"—marked a turning point in the fiction of Henry James, although the novelist, struggling with his novel on his terrace overlooking Rye, seems hardly to have been aware of this. Rereading the *Spoils* today one is struck by the dramatic quality of its slight but strong theme—the struggle between a mother and son for possession of a houseful of antiques; the scenic deployment of its four principal characters; the shrewd study of personal relations. The novel deals with a woman who values property above people, whose "fine arrogance" and "sense of style" involve the manipulation of persons weaker than herself. But the novel is also —within its technical virtuosity—an amused commentary on the collecting spirit, "that most modern of our current passions, the fierce appetite for the upholsterer's and joiner's and brazier's work, the chairs and tables, the cabinets and presses, the material odds and ends, of the more labouring ages." These are the grouped objects, "all conscious of their eminence and price," which the dedicated owner of Poynton, on the death of her husband, seeks to prevent her son from inheriting—unless he can marry a wife capable of caring for them as she has done.

The "old things" of this novel are moved about a great deal; and we are made to see that certain houses are right for them and others wrong. There is Poynton itself, "written in great syllables of colour and form," held in the embrace of England's composed landscape. There is the dower house of Ricks, a "shallow box," symbol of Mrs. Gereth's dispossession. Here the treasures are rearranged in a dubious compromise. Finally there is Waterbath, "trumpery ornament and scrapbook art," which the embattled Mrs. Gereth regards as enemy territory. She has made a successful work of art of Poynton. She has not succeeded in making her son Owen into anything but a pleasant weak young man. And the story involves her attempts to rectify her failure and his artlessness, to supply him with a woman capable of making up for his deficiencies, that is someone as discriminating and as skilled in maneuver as herself.

II

The original idea for the *Spoils* had been jotted down in James's notebook more than two years earlier, after one of his London dinners, when the woman next to him had spoken of "a small and ugly matter" in which a widowed Scottish lady was suing her son over the rare furniture he had inherited and which she refused to yield. The anecdote became long; and James didn't want its cluttered details. He closed his ears, he said, to the rest: he had his situation in the first few words. In the notebooks we can see that he began by wanting to be sorry for Mrs. Gereth, the displaced and deposed mother, sent away from her grand house and her antiques by the English custom of relegating widows to a dower-house. This very American view of the perpetual "queenship" of the mother faded considerably as James got into his story. What emerged was Mrs. Gereth's destructive rage and her determined effort to marry her son off to the helpless Fleda Vetch, whose name does not suggest the fineness James sought to give her character. She is a young artistic girl, and James regarded her as the moral force of the novel. Mrs. Gereth is clever, but not intelligent; Fleda is intelligent, but not clever. And Mrs. Gereth places her in the impossible position of having to pursue her lighthearted son, who is himself pursued by the ruthless philistine Mona Brigstock. James thus constructs a chain of personal pressures. Mrs. Gereth exerts pressure on Fleda. Fleda in more subtle ways exerts moral pressure on Owen, while Mona presses him from her side. The young man's weakness is greater than his amiability and he has three women on his back. Mona will marry Owen only if he obtains Poynton. Fleda wants to marry Owen, but holds back out of moral scruples, indecision, and an inability to assert herself, perhaps also because she believes her love for him is worthy of more direct recognition. She will marry Owen only if she is sure he can disengage himself from Mona with honor. One develops sympathy for the artless Owen, who is valued largely in terms of a houseful of antiques. Only Fleda shows love for him; but he is passive. And she on her side is more passive still: she values honor and protocol and priority, as much as love. The intensity of her passion is expressed when she says, "I don't know what girls may do, but if he doesn't know that there isn't an inch of me that isn't his—" Thus Fleda to Owen's mother. This same intensity however does not lead to action. Moreover she feels too much "advertised and offered." We have been told that she was armed for "the battle of life" by a season of study with an impressionist painter. Her impressionism, her vacillation, make for self-defeat; holding all the trump cards in her hands she throws them away. These are the emotional and "interpersonal" dilemmas of James's little drama.

Critics have been puzzled by the character of Fleda Vetch and her ill-motivated renunciation of Owen. Her reasons are noble; yet they have no relation to the realities James incorporated into his story. His scenario shows James at odds both with his characters and his plot. He seems to have fixed his mind on the ultimate destruction of Poynton; in the end no one is to have anything—as he had been left with nothing when his own artistic work went up in smoke at the St. James's. The novelist begins, in effect, with the idea for one kind of novel, that of the dispossessed mother, and ends with another. He removes Mrs. Gereth from the center of the stage and puts Fleda in her place. To read James's late preface and his description of his heroine is to recognize that he "thought" one character but another emerged. The Fleda of his preface, the "superior" girl with the "demonic" mind and "free spirit," is not in the book. In the book she is as confused and filled with tergiversation as James had been in the theatre. His traditional ending would have been the triumph of the philistines and the defeat of the noble-minded. But he substituted melodrama instead; perhaps because he had himself been forced to the center of the stage, in a bit of melodrama not of his own making.

His imagery went further back however than the recent disaster at the St. James's. In describing Mrs. Gereth's departure from Poynton and the loss of her antiques, *her* work of art, James wrote "the amputation, as she called it, had been performed. Her leg had come off—she had now begun to stump along with the lovely wooden substitute; she would stump for life, and what her young friend was to come and admire was the beauty of her movement and the noise she made about the house." Thus James had recourse in this work to one of the most personal images out of his childhood. It suggests how vivid for all his lifetime was the memory of his father's amputation and "the noise . . . about the house" of his wooden leg. The father had lost his leg in a stable fire and Henry subsequently had suffered a back injury while helping to fight a stable fire at Newport. Amputation and fire: these symbols out of the past now forced themselves into the story he was telling: Poynton and its "spoils" had to be destroyed as *Guy Domville* was destroyed; and Henry James felt himself amputated—as his father had been. James's five-year struggle to sacrifice art to the Moloch-materialism of the stage was retold in *The Spoils of Poynton* in the form of an irrational issue of a rational conflict, and in terms of irrational behavior. In life everything had been irrational. And the violence of the *Guy Domville* audience had revived the violences of his childhood. Later stories would show just how much had been reawakened. It was as if the injuries of long ago had occurred all over again, within his adult consciousness, and he had to purge himself of them. He was doing this in the only way he knew—he relived them in his art.

III

If *The Spoils of Poynton* represented James's first attempt to use his scenic method and his play-writing techniques, *The Other*

House—the serial which he wrote immediately afterwards for Clement Shorter—was a direct adaptation into the novel form of a play scenario. The play had been sketched for Edward Compton early in 1894. The actor had shown little interest in it, and James had put it aside. The punctuality with which he now dispatched his instalments from Point Hill, and later from the Old Vicarage, suggests that the original scenario must have been in effect a first draft of the play. The work is almost entirely dialogue, save for settings and occasional brief narrative passages. James was to regard the lessons he learned from turning scenario material into fiction as some kind of landmark in his work, for he exclaims in an entry in his notebooks, as late as 1910, "Oh blest *Other House*, which gives me thus at every step a precedent, a support, a divine little light to walk by."

There are two houses in this novel: Eastmead and Bounds. They are separated by a garden and a near-by stream connects them; they are also connected by being the homes of the partners in the banking firm of Beever and Bream. Mrs. Beever, who inherited her husband's share in the bank, lives at Eastmead and to her Bounds is "the other house." Eastmead is "a great, clean, square solitude," and everything we discover about it reinforces our impression of its calm, its order, its uncluttered state. Mrs. Beever's own life is equally ordered—"like a room prepared for a dance; the furniture was all against the walls." A strong, masculine woman, her only concession to maternity is her desire to marry off her son, when he comes down from Oxford, to a girl of her choice. Her choice is a "slim, fair girl," whom James in his notes had designated as his "Good Heroine."

The "Bad Heroine" is installed in "the other house." Unlike Eastmead, Bounds is the reverse of calm. It is in some ways the grander house, handsomely and expensively renovated by the younger partner in the bank, Anthony Bream. In the prelude to this odd story, Bream's wife has just given birth to a daughter. Certain she will not survive childbirth, and having a morbid fear

of stepmothers—her own had been a martinet—the wife exacts ˷
promise from Tony Bream that if she dies, he will not remarry s˷
long as her child lives. At the end of the first "act," she doe˷
indeed die, and the Ibsenite drama can now play itself out be˷
tween the two houses, the house of quiet and the house of passion
between the Good Heroine Jean Martle and the Bad Heroin˷
Rose Armiger, the latter as desperate and frustrated, as intense and
as determined as Hedda Gabler.

Rose had been an old companion of Mrs. Bream's. A difficul˷
and exasperated woman, Rose had loved Tony without hope s˷
long as her old friend lived; and she is now prevented fro˷
marrying him so long as the child Effie lives. Tony on his side i˷
much more interested in the Good Heroine, Jean Martle, than i˷
his wife's friend. Thus the little girl protects him, in a sense
against Rose and indeed against remarriage—as his wife had in˷
tended. The Good Heroine is a sort of child-woman, with a fin˷
complexion and beautiful hair: she is indeed Henry James's ideal
ized female, a simpler Isabel or Mary Garland. Tony is attracte˷
to her in the way in which James was attracted to women, to Mis˷
Woolson, for instance—"there was no one he had ever like˷
whom he could quite like so comfortably." Tony asks himsel˷
what his appreciation of this girl might lead to, and he provide˷
the answer—"it would lead to exactly nothing—that had bee˷
settled all round in advance. This was a happy, lively provision
that kept everything down, made sociability a cool, public out-of
door affair, without a secret or a mystery—confined it, as on˷
might say, to the breezy, sunny forecourt of the temple of friend˷
ship." Everything would be kept "down," as at Eastmead; and th˷
words *cool, public, out-of-doors* are eloquent. No sex, no passion
no secrets, no mysteries, a comfortable Platonic relation.

As for the other girl, she is frightening. She belongs to the
intensity and passion expressed by Tony's own dead wife when sh˷
exacted the sacred promise. Tony looks into Rose Armiger's eyes
They seem at first deep and exquisite. Then he sees something

else, a kind of "measureless white ray of light steadily revolving," and he notes that she could sometimes turn this light away. Nevertheless it was "always somewhere; and now it covered him with a great cold lustre that made everything for the moment look hard and ugly." It *is* hard and ugly; for the frustrated passionate Rose drowns little Effie (the child is four when the crime is committed) and tries to fix the guilt on the Good Heroine. The hero is left undefended.

This is the melodrama James devised for the readers of the *Illustrated London News*. It is the only novel he ever wrote (although he did not consider it part of his fictional canon, always recalling its "inferior" origin in the theatre) in which violence occurs. James had toyed with having the Bad Heroine administer poison to the child; but he chose death by drowning instead, and we are reminded how little more than a year before he had spoken of being himself "subaqueous," in a dim water-world. At the end Tony Bream must ponder "to what tune he had been liked"— which was what James had had to ponder after Fenimore's violent end in Venice.

The Other House is one of James's most unpleasant novels: a piece of subtle mechanical play-tinkering with powerful stuff of the emotions which he does not seem to understand or to command: an outburst of primitive rage that seems irrational and uncontrolled however much it is dramatically "motivated"; and with a crime which defies the tradition of murder stories by going unpunished. It is an Ibsen play without Ibsen's morality—or his insight; we can find in it certain resemblances to *Rosmersholm*, which Miss Robins produced during the year *The Other House* was first planned. Perhaps James felt that his Bad Heroine's future would in itself be sufficient punishment. But the reader puts down the work feeling that for once James has been clever rather than intelligent; that some powerfully controlled areas of feeling within him have burst their bounds (it is significant that the house in which the melodrama is enacted is called Bounds). Reading the cultivated dialogue, and watching the men struggle to shield Rose from punishment, we sense that for once in his career as artist James has seriously faltered. Some instinct told him that he had; for he published the novel, as we have seen, amid the pictured sensationalism of a journal he disliked.

Thus the two novels which James wrote at the outset of this new period of creativity contain within them the violence that had come into his own life. The sudden burning of Poynton was the metaphor for the sudden destruction of his play; the passion of Rose Armiger and its destruction of the little girl meant the murder of innocence—as if some remote little being within James himself had been killed by the audience during that crucial night a year and a half earlier, and he had been left open to the world's indifference. *The Spoils of Poynton* becomes the portal through which we pass into the most curious series of novels James devised in his entire career as a writer: a terrible world of blighted houses and of blighted childhoods—of little girls—and a strange world of female adolescence. The works he now wrote suggest that in the midst of the sun and sea and summer of Rye, the long rides on his bicycle, the change from urban life to quiet English ruralism, James continued to live in a struggling nightmare world, a return to the sensitive hurts of his early life. He was finding outer peace. The quest for inner peace continued.

PARADOX OF SUCCESS

I

ON JULY 30, 1896, HENRY JAMES BROKE HIS STAY AT POINT HILL—
he was on the verge of moving into the Old Vicarage—to attend
the funeral of Mrs. Mahlon Sands, who had died quite suddenly in
London at the early age of forty-one. Her maid had been helping
her to dress in her great house in Portland Place; she was about to
attend a dinner party. The maid left the room for two minutes and
returned to find her mistress dead on the floor. Three days earlier
Mrs. Sands had written to Henry James, at the climax of the
London season: "Are you not coming up at all? I am sick of the
whole thing." He came up for the service in St. George's, Hanover
Square, on an exquisite summer's day; and amid the flowers and
elegant mourners—Harcourts, Rothschilds, Rowtons, Algernon
West who had wanted to marry her—James could hear the irrelevant worldly bustle of Bond Street close at hand. Mrs. Sands had
conquered London fifteen years earlier, almost as if she were one
of his heroines. She had been a friend of the Prince of Wales, she
had known Gladstone, all the late Victorians, moving with ease
through the great houses. James had been fond of her, driven,
nervous, tense creature though she was, enmeshed and trapped in
Society. There was "nothing small or mean" about her and she
had had "a beauty that had once been of the greatest." Sargent
had painted her and James had written her instructions how to
pose:

You can't collaborate or cooperate, except by sitting still and
looking beautiful . . . it's *his* affair, yours is only to be as difficult
for him as possible; and the more difficult you are the more the
artist will be condemned to worry over you, repainting, revolution-
izing, till he, in a rage of ambition and admiration, arrives at the

thing that satisfies him and that enshrines and perpetuates you. There are as good eyes on his palette as ever were caught and yours, on Sargent's canvas, will still be the mystification of posterity, just as they often are that of yours most didactically HENRY JAMES.

Before beauty, the novelist could be both humble and voluble. To the dead woman's daughter, Ethel Sands, who was to be a painter and a distinct personality in Chelsea and Bloomsbury, James wrote a few days after the funeral: "She had no vocation for any *common* happiness, or common answers, small answers, to great questions, and she *had* a great aptitude to struggle and suffer. I say these things to you—but you know them better than I. Better than I too you know her sweetness, her grace, her gifts—you had lived in her beautiful presence. Nothing small had any part in her—and she is an exquisite ineffaceable memory." It was Mrs. Sands who had sent him the bright golden canary that had warbled away the days in Sussex that summer.

11

James experienced a different kind of sorrow that autumn, when he returned to London. His old and cherished friend, George du Maurier, died early in October. James had loved his cartoons in *Punch* long before he had met him; he had studied them as a boy stretched out on the rug before the fire in Fourteenth Street. And then in his first years in London du Maurier had become his friend. He had illustrated *Washington Square* or, as James put it, had consented to make drawings "for a short novel that I had constructed in crude defiance of the illustrator." The two had taken to each other from the first. James had liked the mixture of French seriousness and English drollery in du Maurier; du Maurier liked James's American observation and his French wit. On Sundays, James used to climb the hill to du Maurier's house in Hampstead; they had taken walks on the Heath and in that suburb, amid "red walls and jealous gates, the old benches in the right places and even the young couples in the wrong." Here they sat for hours talking about Flaubert and Paris and English life, and the thousand and one things that drew them together. James had always admired the comedy and craft of this supreme cartoonist—du Maurier's ability to capture people's postures while they wait for dinner, while they are thinking what to say, while they are pretending to listen to music, while they are making speeches they don't mean. Du Maurier could reproduce to the life the gentleman who stares at his boots, the lady who gazes with sudden rapture at the ceiling. And then no one had drawn lovelier women and children. Du Maurier seemed to see all the English as tall and handsome. The world for him had a wonderful simplicity: things were either ugly or they were beautiful.

Du Maurier was blind in one eye, but when they walked his other eye had an extraordinary optical reach. "I always thought I valued the use of my eyes and that I noticed and observed," James wrote, "but the manner in which, when out with him, I mainly exercised my faculty was by remarking how constantly and how easily his own surpassed it." There were winters when the du Mauriers would come down from Hampstead and live in a rented house in Bayswater, and James and the artist would go on long rambles "with dusk enough for the lighted shop-fronts to lend a romantic charm to Westbourne Grove." The novelist remembered du Maurier's alertness: he saw mystery, reality, drollery, irony, in everything.

And then du Maurier had a "sociable habit of abounding in the sense of his own history and his own feelings, his memories, sympathies, contacts, observations, adventures." There were summers when James had gone to the Yorkshire coast, to Whitby, to visit him and to be near Lowell who also stayed there. They used to walk by cold cliffs and beside a cold sea, or on the warm moors, or in Whitby's brown fishing quarter clustered and huddled at the river-mouth. Du Maurier used to like the bleak breakwater, a long wide sea wall with a twinkling lighthouse at the end; he expressed delight in the fishy-smelling town, the bronzed and battered faces of the fishermen and the long procession of their boats. Wherever they were, James and du Maurier took these long walks, and then dined together.

The artist was a marvellous spinner of tales. One night he told James a fantastic story of a pair of lovers changed into albatrosses. They were shot and wounded; one resumed human shape and waited and watched in vain for the other. The germ of *Peter Ibbetson* seemed to be in this tale and du Maurier's idea of "dreaming true." And then there was the famous evening, which James recorded in his notebooks on March 25, 1889: "Last evening before dinner I took a walk with G. du Maurier in the mild March twilight (there was a blessed sense of spring in the air), through the empty streets near Porchester Terrace, and he told me over an idea of his which he thought very good—and I do too—for a short story—he had already mentioned to me—a year or two ago, in a walk at Hampstead, but it had passed from my mind." James then recorded the story. It dealt with a girl with a wonderful voice but no genius for music, who is mesmerized and made to sing by a little foreign Jew "who has mesmeric power, infinite feeling, and no organ." Thus the story of *Trilby* acquired existence first as a note in James's scribbler. James decided he could not write it, though du Maurier urged him to do so; "the want of musical knowledge would hinder *me* somewhat in handling it." He in turn then urged du Maurier to tell it himself. Du Maurier tried but found himself dealing with a different theme. What emerged was his novel *Peter Ibbetson*, about a hero whose dreams become his only reality. James continued to urge him to write the tale about the mesmerized singer. Six years after their evening walk near Porchester Terrace, *Trilby* was published—with the results the world knows.

III

As James stood in the fine old Hampstead churchyard, amid the elite of England, beside the grave of the man he had seen most

often during his London life, and whom he had dearly loved,
Trilby was selling in the tens of thousands and crowds were
flocking to see the play version on both sides of the sea. For James
there was a striking—and mocking—psychological drama in the
final events of his friend's life. Du Maurier had for years lived his
private Hampstead life, with his wife and children and dog, his
drawing board and his notations of London comedy and London
society. Then he had written *Trilby* as a piece of natural and
intimate story-telling. James had expected that it would be liked; he
had not thought it would take the public by storm. The amateur,
writing his tale as it were on the edge of his drawing board, had
achieved what James with all his consummate art of story-telling
could never do. The novelist was not jealous of his old friend, but
he was amazed by the phenomenon, the paradox of "success." Life
was recreating so many of his stories of authorship. In the end
Trilby seemed to have murdered her creator. The old witty intimate du Maurier disappeared; in his place there remained a melancholy successful man. He did not want to be a public figure and
fame insisted on making him one late in middle age. "I dearly
loved George du Maurier," James wrote to Paul Bourget. "I had
with him a long and tender friendship. He had had, late in life, on
the edge of his sixties, the success of a celebrity and of personal
fortune, to which he attached no importance, and which seems
not to have given him much pleasure. He has died in the midst of
this of melancholy and indifference." It had been as if Little
Billee, the handsome and lovable youth of *Trilby*, had suddenly
grown old. What did it mean, this showering of adulation on a
man who loved privacy and quiet? The long article James dedicated to his friend—one of his touching evocative pieces of writing
—takes up this question but finds no answer to it. Why was du
Maurier so "overtaken and overwhelmed"? Why had the public
pounced on his gentle writings with such eagerness, such greed?
He "passed away, I think, with a sigh that was a practical relin-
quishment of the vain effort to probe the mystery of its [*Trilby*'s]
success. The charm was one thing, and the success quite another,

and the number of links missing between the two was greater than his tired spirit could cast about for." Du Maurier had let loose the elements, and "they did violence to his nerves."

The whole phenomenon grew and grew till it became, at any rate for this particular victim, a fountain of gloom and a portent of woe; it darkened all his sky with a hugeness of vulgarity. It became a mere immensity of sound, the senseless hum of a million of newspapers and the irresponsible chatter of ten millions of gossips. The pleasant sense of having done well was deprived of all sweetness, all privacy, all sanctity. . . . He found himself sunk in a landslide of obsessions, of inane, incongruous letters, of interviewers, intruders, invaders. . . . He appears to me to have turned for refuge to the only quarter where peace is deep. . . .

Du Maurier had wanted to simplify, but "the clock of his new period kept striking a different hour from the clock of his old spirit." One more door had closed on James's old "London life."

A FIERCE LEGIBILITY

I

BETWEEN 1895 AND 1898 THE TWENTIETH CENTURY BEGAN TO knock loudly at Henry James's door. He had installed electric light in De Vere Gardens in 1895; in 1897 he purchased a typewriter and engaged a part-time typist; in 1898 he went to one of the earliest movies, the "cinematograph—or whatever they call it," to see pictures of the Fitzsimmons–Corbett prizefight. "We quite revelled," James told his old horseback-riding companion of the Roman period, Mrs. Wister. The novelist now rode a bicycle; and presently he would take to motoring. But it was the purchase of the typewriter that would bring the greatest change into his life.

When the use of the typewriter had become general in the 1880's he had begun to send his manuscripts to a public stenographer. In earlier years he had simply dispatched his pages, written in his rapid flowing hand, directly to editor and publisher; if he was writing a serial the proofs of the instalments served as his clean copy. Early in 1896, he had become aware of increasing pain in his right wrist; he described it as rheumatic and it was probably the familiar writer's cramp, understandable enough in a man who for years had worked six to eight hours a day at his writing table. His brother William, who had acquired stenographic help at Harvard, described the delights of dictating. Henry agreed he might come to this—for his correspondence. It did not at first occur to him that it might also serve for his fiction.

During the autumn of 1896, when he was working on *What Maisie Knew*, his wrist condition became chronic. In February 1897 he accordingly engaged a stenographer, William MacAlpine, a silent Scot from Aberdeen and Edinburgh, who worked regularly as shorthand reporter for medical societies, but had his mornings free to take James's dictation. The novelist began by letting him take his letters in shorthand; and James's typewritten letters from the first announced themselves in elaborate apologies for "this cold-blooded process," this "fierce legibility"—"the only epistolary tongue of my declining years." By the end of the first month, he was dictating directly to the typewriter; it saved time and enabled him to do much more. "I can address you only through an embroidered veil of sound," he dictated to his Parisian friend Morton Fullerton of the *Times*. "The sound is that of the admirable and expensive machine that I have just purchased for the purpose of bridging our silences." He added: "The hand that works it, however, is not the lame *patte* which, after inflicting on you for years its aberrations, I have now definitely relegated to the shelf, or at least to the hospital."

James discovered early that the repose improved his wrist so that he could do a certain amount of letter-writing in the old way; part of his correspondence was thus relegated to the evenings, and remained private, for he did not like to share it with his undemonstrative Scot. A certain number of letters continued to be typewritten; but the machine in the end was reserved for his art. He became so accustomed to its sound that he was unable to dictate one day when his own typewriter broke down and an alien machine temporarily replaced it. Very early, Morton Fullerton raised the question of what the typewriter would do to James's style. "I can be trusted, artless youth," James answered, "not to be simplified by any shortcut or falsified by any facility," and he ended this letter with "am I not meanwhile only more discernibly yours, HENRY JAMES?" To Mrs. Curtis of Venice, who put a similar question, he said that dictation did not hamper him in the least, "in letters quite the reverse, and in commerce with the Muse so little that I foresee the day when it will be pure luxury."

There was no question that he was more discernible, and some of his friends claimed they could put their finger on the exact chapter in *Maisie* where manual effort ceased and dictation began. Henry James writing, and Henry James dictating, were two different artists. His sentences were to become, in time, elaborate—one might indeed say baroque—filled with qualifications and parentheses; he seemed often in a letter to begin a sentence without knowing what its end would be, and he allowed it to meander river-like into surprising turns and loops. Out of several years of consistent dictating the "later manner" of Henry James emerged.

Some part of it would have been there without benefit of the Remington. Certain indirections and qualifications had always been a part of his character. But the spoken voice was to be heard henceforth in James's prose in a way that it had never been heard before, not only in the rhythm and ultimate perfection of his verbal music, but in his use of colloquialisms and in a more extravagant play of fancy, a greater indulgence in elaborate and figured metaphors, and in great proliferating similes. James was Proustian before Proust; and doubtless having a companion always in his work room brought into his creation elements of the "interpersonal." It would be a long time before James would obliterate from his vision the presence of the typist. The actor in him could not resist showing off; extra exhibitory flourishes occurred in the prose—and particularly in some of the dictated letters.

The typewriter was still, in those days, a large and not easily transported object. It never occurred to James—and doubtless he would have been very clumsy at it—to learn to typewrite, as writers would learn to do in the new century. Acquisition of his machine meant not only that he lost his mobility, but that he was dependent upon help to get his daily work done. For more than thirty years he had been able to set up his writing room wherever he went. It was not easy to travel with his machine; and it would have meant employing the typist full-time. Moreover he would have had to lodge and feed him as he journeyed. He explained this in detail to a friend in June 1897: "The voice of Venice, all this time, has called very loud. But it has been drowned a good deal in the click of the typewriter to which I dictate and which, some months ago, crept into my existence through the crevice of a lame hand and now occupies in it a place too big to be left vacant for long periods of hotel and railway life."

11

He passed one of his "quietest, sanest, simplest" winters in London. He went regularly to visit Jonathan Sturges, in his nursing home; it was almost as if he were back in the time when he regularly visited his ailing sister. He declined invitations, worked at his dictation, occasionally went to the theatre. For a few evenings he helped Miss Robins put into English Echegaray's *Mariana* from a literal Spanish translation, for one of her productions; he applauded the actress in *Little Eyolf* and Ibsen's mastery of form in *John Gabriel Borkman*—particularly the way in which, in that play, Ibsen encompassed a great span of tragedy among three or four persons within the space and time of a winter's evening. While writing *Maisie*, he also wrote a monthly letter for *Harper's Weekly*; he was well paid, but in most of the letters he sounds as bored as his readers must have been. When *Harper's* dropped him after ten such letters he was as always indignant. It was his old *Tribune* experience all over again. He had been dismissed "as you scarce would an incompetent housemaid. And yet I tried to be so Base!" As in the theatre and in other attempts at such correspondence, he had begun with contempt for the task; and a part of his haughty anger was anger with himself for stooping to literary drudgery. The best of these *Harper's* letters were reprinted years later in *Notes on Novelists*.

With the spring London gave itself over to preparations for the Diamond Jubilee of Queen Victoria's accession. James was impatient with the scaffold-carpentry, the defacing of the capital, the bidding for seats; this was a drab commercializing of national sentiment. He looked for another house in the country, but found none to his liking: one which he inspected, near Brighton, was "far too Germanic, too Teutonic." So he remained in town, promising himself he would leave just before the "victorian Saturnalia." In a long and vivid letter to *Harper's* he described the preparations as "a great incommodity"—"the gross defacement of London, the uproarious traffic in seats, the miles of unsightly scaffolding between the West End and the City, the screaming advertisements, the sordid struggle." It hurt James's sense of beauty and of stability to have London disfigured, as if there were "some great national penance or mourning." The whole thing was "hugely overdone." This was, he said, "the great clumsy, ugly fate of everything today that's done at all. The machinery of insistence and reverberation—the newspaper deluge and uproar—deflowers and destroys and maddens."

He told William he "saw not the tip of the tail of any part of the show." The young George Vanderbilt offered him a place on his large balcony overlooking Pall Mall. James declined, and a few days before the great day, he abandoned London for Bournemouth. His typist was free and he took him along to the seaside, leaving the "Babylonian barricades" to the hordes. With his private secretary—"for all the world like a cabinet minister"—he engaged rooms at the château-like Royal Bath Hotel, and in a Bournemouth utterly deserted spent the show-day by a hot blue sea. Twelve years had elapsed since his last stay here. The place was prosaic but salubrious; and it was filled with two ghostly presences. His sister Alice had stayed here for weeks after her arrival in England in 1885; and Robert Louis Stevenson had lived at Skerryvore near-by. James had seen almost all he did see of his friend there before his flight to the South Seas—forever.

Save for a couple of absences, James spent most of July 1897 in Bournemouth, enjoying the peace and emptiness of the place. He bicycled; and he purchased a bicycle for MacAlpine, whom he taught, thus providing company for his long rides. The Bourgets visited him there, as had become their custom, but stayed only four days, having scheduled other English visits. The rest of the month was spent in daily dictation and seaside relaxation. MacAlpine was an excellent typist, but a dull companion. James did have to return to London at the end of July, summoned unexpectedly to jury duty; he had learned aliens were not exempt from civic obligation after a ten-years' residence in England. The case, apparently a banal divorce hearing, lasted only two days at the Court of

Queen's Bench, and all we know of the experience is recorded in
Henry's remark to William, "Doing British Juryman threw lights
—and glooms"—which would suggest that the novelist was not
bored. He had discussed a divorce in the opening instalment of
What Maisie Knew—but by the time he went to the court he was
at work on the final pages of the novel.

III

Maisie is a short novel. It was serialized in *The Chap-Book*, a
semi-monthly published in Chicago, between January and August
of 1897 and in England in the *New Review*, where it ran from
February to September. It is a work of intellectual wit and filled
with James's awareness of how a child's world is a piecemeal
world, containing quantities of literal observation but lacking clues
to wider knowledge. Many serious things are said in the presence
of Maisie, and many bawdy things; but she, like a kitten, keeps her
eye on the piece of string, or the direction in which a hand is
moving. She ingeniously parrots characteristic phrases from her
adult world; they seem the right thing to say, but she doesn't know
all that she is saying. Victim of a divorce, handed over in a custody
suit to periodic visits with each of her parents, she becomes the
carrier of the hatred and rage of each to the other. Presently she is
moving in the world of their adulteries and those of her surrogate
parents. The Wilde case had opened the way to greater frankness;
he could now deal with sex more directly in his work. The book is a
bright and brilliant comedy; Maisie moves through an amoral
world, her innocence seemingly intact, and we never know how
much it has been damaged. When the handsome Sir Claude, the
"masher" of the novel, evades her and the governess Mrs. Wix
once too often, she chooses to live with the governess and her
"moral sense," rather than with her unstable multiple parents. The
decision accords with a child's instinct for safety. No digest of the
story can suggest the skill with which James moves his characters

about and keeps the reader constantly within the eye-vision of the little girl; nor can it convey the humor of this novel, the second of his remarkable experiments of this time. The work has the quality of a ballet, of men and women coming together and separating and the little girl dancing alone on the stage among them. It is written scenically, like the *Spoils*, and shows in the way it holds its form and tightness that James was not as yet yielding to the prolixity of dictation.

Like the works of this period it illustrates to an extraordinary degree the way in which the adult mind and professional skill can create a work in the face of an inner bewilderment. Maisie's bewilderment is James's—it is the bewilderment he had felt since the collapse of his world in *Guy Domville*: but it is recreated into a comic vision of benign childish curiosity. Nevertheless, if one looks away from the smooth surface and the intellectual power of the story, one perceives a world of horror: a down-at-heel shoddy middle-class world that treats its children cruelly, and lives in a state of perpetual sexual confusion. In the depths of this novel—which on the surface is very much like a French bedroom farce translated into an English environment—we can discern James's own confusion before the collapsing late-Victorian moral façade. The worldly bachelor of Kensington and Mayfair, in this work, still possessed a fund of innocence and wonder and bewilderment disguised for the moment in the garments of ironic comedy. Maisie's "small demonic foresight," as James was to describe it, harbored his own; and the word "demonic" was apt, for what James was telling in the comic guise was a story of "the death of childhood"—the phrase is in the preface he wrote to the book a decade later. "Small children," he wrote, "have many more percep-tions than they have terms to translate them; their vision is at any moment much richer, their apprehension even constantly stronger, than their prompt, their at all producible, vocabulary." There was "the rich little spectacle of objects embalmed in her wonder" and "she wonders to the end, to the death—the death of her child-hood." It is Maisie's sense of wonder that makes the sordid elements of her life appear phantasmagoric, like a child's fairy tale, something out of the *Arabian Nights*, or the images projected by a magic lantern. But the reader sees both the wonder and the nightmare. James's next work would bring this nightmare—his own—to the surface.

A FAINT CONVERGENCE

ESTABLISHED IN BOURNEMOUTH, OUT OF REACH OF THE CROWDS AND the Jubilee, Henry James had done a curious thing. The Jubilee was celebrated on the 22nd of June. On the morning of the 23rd he took train to Waterloo Station, traversed a London clogged with people—"a woeful squeeze through the town"—to Paddington Station. Here he boarded a train for Oxford. His friend Paul Bourget was incongruously scheduled, on this day—"after the great fair"—to deliver a lecture in the Taylor Institute on Gustave Flaubert. James found the occasion irresistible.

It is clear from his account of it later, that the journey was made by him out of an acute sense of his status as novelist. Oxford had thus far largely ignored artists in fiction. It had bestowed honorary degrees on kings and generals, statesmen and prelates, and a few poets—Wordsworth and Tennyson, and the trans-Atlantic Longfellow, but it had never taken notice of Scott or Dickens, Thackeray or Trollope. James may not have been aware of it at the time, but when he had feted Turgenev's honorary Doctor of Civil Law in 1879, he was actually celebrating the first occasion on which Oxford had paid such a compliment to a novelist. The present occasion involved no such elaborate honor. It was simply a lecture in the institute devoted to modern languages. But James was intrigued by the idea that old Oxford, which did not concern itself with modern literature, should have invited a novelist as controversial as Bourget to speak on a novelist who had not yet acquired the glamour and critical significance accorded to him in later decades. This was a "faint convergence," as he called it, a convergence of staid Oxford with what was almost a kind of nineteenth-century avant-garde. He doubtless made the troublesome journey out of loyalty also to Bourget and to his memories of his own friendship and his admiration for Flaubert. He went above all, however, as the exponent of the "modern" novel, at a time when the novel—a century and a half old—was still regarded as an upstart in English literature. Little more than ten years had elapsed since Walter Besant's plea that novelists should be taken seriously as men of their craft. James had agreed with Besant's insistence on the importance of fiction, but had argued that novel-writing was not a "trade" to be learned at will: and his reply of 1884—his essay on "The Art of Fiction"—had not as yet acquired the status of a manifesto that it has today. That Oxford, the academic stronghold of conservatism and tradition, should want to hear his friend Bourget, whose novels were hardly of the kind that good Victorians should read, lecture on the author of *Madame Bovary*, a novel deemed immoral by many critics, teased James's sense of paradox and irony. James could muster for such occasions an enormous energy: and he still had the gift of easy travel.

The weather for his little trip was splendid; an uncommonly hot English day. He had difficulty getting a cab in London, so filled was it with people—"millions of eyes, opening to dust and glare from the scenery of dreams, seemed slowly to stare and to try to recollect." When James arrived in Oxford in mid-afternoon the town was pulling itself together as if after a binge; but by 5 P.M. the bare scholastic Taylorian was filled, and Paul Bourget spoke felicitously and with intimate knowledge of his subject. "Just the fact of the occasion itself," struck James as significant. "That the day should have come for M. Bourget to lecture at Oxford, and should have come by the same stroke for Gustave Flaubert to be lectured about, filled the mind to a degree, and left it in an agitation of violence." If as a novelist James rejoiced in the occasion, he also had misgivings.

The whole affair was a little miracle of our breathless pace, and no corner from which another member of the craft could watch it was so quiet as to attenuate the small magnificence of the hour. No novelist, in a word, worth his salt could fail of a consciousness, under the impression, of his becoming rather more of a novelist than before. Was it not, on the whole, just the essence of the matter that had for the moment there its official recognition? were not the blest mystery and art ushered forward in a more expectant and consecrating hush than had ever yet been known to wait upon them?

He found in the occasion a singular solemnity; it was, he wrote, "a date" in literary history—a modest one, to be sure.

He knew that Flaubert probably would have regarded the affair with bewilderment, had he lived to know it. In the seventeen years since his death, *Madame Bovary* had slowly gained adherents outside of France; nevertheless Oxford was at the time "strangely alien air" into which his glory strayed. James sat in the crowded hall, at the drowsy end of the summer's afternoon, mindful of old gray quads and old green gardens—and of traditions totally different from those of France; and yet there was a "seed of contact" at the moment which at the same time raised brooding questions. Here was "the seat and habit of the classics, the famous frequenta-

tion and discipline." Henry James knew what this could do for
literature: but what could it do for the "modern"—and for the
novel? The danger, as he formulated it—with a great deal of
cautious wording—in his recollection of the occasion, was that
there was an "anomalous gap"—"the light kindled by the immense academic privilege is apt suddenly to turn to thick smoke in
the air of contemporary letters."

The danger, in a word, was that there might be in all this a
singular want of perspective. "There are movements of the classic
torch round modern subjects—strange drips and drops and wondrous waverings—that have the effect of putting it straight out." A
place like Oxford was designed for "an education of the taste"; it
might be a risk to introduce into it a strange new unevaluated
work; this might produce "unexpected raptures, bewildering revelations of a failure of the sense of perspective." James was afraid
"Euripides might give an arm to Sarah Grand and Ibsen to
Virgil." (Later in revising this passage he substituted Octave
Feuillet for Ibsen.) "It is the breath of a madness in which one
gropes for a method." Henry James wasn't sure that the particular
occasion, this discreet dose of Flaubert via Bourget, would in itself
have much effect. Yet his forward-looking mind was seeing the
wave of the future: the hint of para-scholarship, the "age of
criticism," the frenetic espousal of the avant-garde, the bridging
"of this queerest of all chasms," now so tenuously undertaken,
between the established old and the relative new. Then James
remembered that in this same lecture hall Renan and Taine had
spoken in other years; but they were not novelists and there would
have to be many more such episodes before the meaning of
"contemporaneity" in the seat of the ancient could be fully explored. The American novelist left Oxford for his seaside resort
pleased at the new recognition bestowed upon the form he practiced. But it was a mixed pleasure: and he recorded it in one of his
Harper's letters.

A QUESTION OF SPEECH

I

ON JULY 3, 1897 AT BOURNEMOUTH, WHILE READING THE LETTERS OF the Suffolk genius, Edward FitzGerald, whose rendering of *Omar Khayyam* had brought an emanation of—a breath of—hedonism into Victorian England, James had come on the name of Saxmundham, which had for him a certain "strangeness and handsomeness." That same afternoon, during a long beach-walk, he encountered a rugged boatman from Suffolk—from Saxmundham—whose brother, FitzGerald's boatman, figured in the letters James had just read. And on returning from the walk, he found a letter—from Saxmundham, from an American cousin, sister of the long-dead Minny Temple, who was staying in the FitzGerald country, at Dunwich on the Suffolk coast, with her three daughters. She urged James to join her. The coincidence of a thrice-encountered mouth-filling topographical name and his feeling that he should get to know his American cousins better combined to make James promptly agree. Moreover, he was at loose ends. He had not known what to do with the rest of his summer. Thinking perhaps of *Omar Khayyam*, he wrote to his cousin Ellen Hunter (she had been Ellen James Temple in his Newport days) that she had described "a little Paradise." He beseeched her "to keep a divan for me there." He would come for most of August; and he hoped a room could be found also for his typist.

Elly Temple had married one of the New York Emmets. One of her sisters had married his brother. There was a proliferation thus of Temple Emmets to whom James would apply a generic term, "the Emmetry." The novelist had seen the widowed Elly (now remarried to an Englishman) the previous winter, at Harrow, but had not yet met her two older daughters who were studying in Paris. The three Emmet daughters were described by one of James's nephews as being "of devastating charm and attractiveness." The oldest was Rosina, then twenty-four, who had sent her uncle Henry some of her writings and had been warned by him against introducing too much low-life and slang into fiction. "There is, after all, another psychology than that of the brutes and another vocabulary than that of the slangermongers." Her sister, Ellen Gertrude, called "Bay," twenty-two, had been studying art in Paris and was to become a portrait painter of distinction. The youngest, just turned twenty, was Edith Leslie. The three were lively, buoyant, curious. They had had little education; it had been interrupted by their displacement from America to Europe. "They just knew everything by instinct," the same nephew used to say; but their instincts were on the whole good. Henry James in writing to Rosina the previous February had said he hoped to see her and her artist sister later in the year, "by which time you and Bay will have become still more interesting than you are already" —as a result of exposure to the art world of Paris.

Ellen and her three daughters, supplemented by another Emmet cousin named Jane, seem to have awaited the coming of the novelist to the rural retreat as for the descent of a royal personage. The bedroom and sitting room he wanted were found in one of the local houses, although Ellen could not guarantee the softness of the Omaresque "divan" he craved. The landlady promised, and James hoped, they would get "all achievable elasticity" into it. Cousin Ellen had a more serious problem; there was neither butcher, baker nor grocer in Dunwich, a decayed little seaport in an area where there had been centuries of erosion by the sea and where the roads were bad. Everything was off the beaten path. However she organized the food services "Bonapartistically," James was later to say. She had warned him that he would be roughing it. Delayed by his jury duty at the end of July, he sent

MacAlpine ahead. We get some feeling of the excitement the awe-inspiring writer-cousin created in a letter written by the visiting Jane: "Henry James is expected to arrive *sans faute* tonight. I don't believe there is such a person. I think it is always exciting to see a person you have heard of all your life, especially if you have been so delighted and amused as I have always been by his books. H. James's horrible young meek Scotch typewriter came down a day or two ago."

From Jane Emmet (later Mrs. Wilfrid Von Glehn) in Dunwich, Saxmundham, Suffolk, to her sister Lydia Emmet, August 6, 1897:

Well, at last Henry James arrived, and he is the nicest thing, but what a mental epicure. He is awfully sweet and affectionate and nonterrifying, and tragic-eyed. He hangs poised for the right word while the wheels of life go round. . . . This afternoon Rosina, H. J. and I went for a walk and got caught in the rain and had to wade through ponds of muddy water to Henry James's unfeigned horror. I don't think he has been through a mud puddle for years. He rides a bicycle which is his only attempt at sport. Poor thing, he must miss so much, being so horrified by accent. He can't get past it. He must miss so much real refinement and cleverness and niceness. We do nothing but thank our stars that we are not Henry James. He is so pathetic and cramped and has such a bad combination with almost everything except the English tongue in its most perfected form. I am afraid our voices and sentences hurt his ear-drums. He and his typewriter spend their mornings together and the simple villagers of Dunwich may hear subleties being dictated from ten to one.

From Henry James in Dunwich, Saxmundham, Suffolk, September 1, 1897, to William James in Cambridge, Massachusetts:

The resources of Dunwich are not infinite, and I should, without the Cousins, have made a briefer dip of it. It was of course for them I came and for them I am staying on a little. The girls accept with the extreme sweetness and tact that, I think, they show in all relations to the situation their mother has made for them, a rather extended stretch of a place offering a good deal less luxuriance of charm than many another they might, with more chance to look about, have found for their English summer. Meanwhile this little corner, where all is in the minor, the minimum key, is not without sweetness and character. I have done, with great pleasure and profit, a good deal of the bicycle; for which this region offers every inducement that can be offered without roads. We are miles from a good one—which is partly indeed why we are quaint and curious. . . . But I stray, even now, from the Cousins—as to whom you will be glad to hear more of whatever there may be to say. This last is summed up in a nutshell: they would be thoroughly "sympathetic" if they only had a language to be it in! Their speech, absolutely unaffected as yet, so far as I can see, by a year of Europe—thanks to the antecedent cycle of Cathay—remains really their only fault. But it is a grave one. I attack it, however, boldly, and as much as I can. It will be hopeless, I fear, ever—or at least for a long time—to interfuse Bay and Leslie with a few consonants, or to make any of them sound the letter "i" in any of the connections in which it occurs and especially in the word "him" and "it" where they replace it inveterately by "o", "u" and even "a"! However, they *want* to improve, and are full of life and humour and sentiment and intelligence.

II

Small wonder that among the enduring memories the Cousins were to have of the distinguished man were those of his efforts to adjust the American language as they pronounced it. In later years Rosina was to relate how on one of their walks together Henry James, with much affection and yet a kind of merciless regularity, kept her attention fixed on the sound of her own voice. Hoping to engage him in conversation she had commented on how charming she found the jewel in his tie-pin.

"Jew-*el*, not *jool*," her Distinguished Cousin rejoined, ignoring the compliment.

"I'm afraid American girls don't speak their vowels distinctly," Rosina ventured.

"Vow-*el*, not *vowl*, Rosina."

Tears came. "Oh Cousin Henry, you are so cruel."

"Cru-*el*, not *crool*, Rosina."

And the youngest cousin Leslie remembered that when she said, "I must go upstairs and fix my hair," Cousin Henry looked at her fixedly, and then said solemnly:

"To fix your hair, my dear Leslie, to *fix* it to what—and *with* what?"

In later years, the language of the American young, and the ways in which, they spoke it, was to become an obsession with Henry James. Language was sacred; speech was sacred. Invited to speak at the Commencement at Bryn Mawr, during his 1904-05 visit to the United States, Henry James found occasion for his fullest statement to his young and captive audience. He titled it "The Question of Our Speech" and with good humor appealed seriously for a "tone-standard." He reminded his hearers that "the human side of vocal sound" was being corrupted by slovenly speech and kept "as little distinct as possible from the grunting, the squealing, the barking or the roaring of animals." He deplored, this time, the failure in the "emission of the consonant," so that speech became "a mere helpless slobber of disconnected vowel noises—the weakest and cheapest attempt at human expression that we shall easily encounter, I imagine, in any community pretending to the general instructed state. Observe, too, that the vowel sounds in themselves, at this rate, quite fail of any purity." His illustration was the way in which "Yes" became "Yeh-eh," and when the need for a final consonant showed it became the still more questionable "Yeh-ep." He had many more examples, all testifying to his own listening and conscious ear, and to his belief that language—one's own—was to be learned and cultivated and cherished and not allowed to degenerate. He criticized the failure to teach the language properly to the immigrants, the careless writing in newspapers, and the refusal of school, pulpit and parents to pay attention to the verbal forms of communication. "Flames, however, even the most sacred, do not go on burning of themselves," Henry James said in his discourse. "They require to be kept up." And doubtless that summer at Dunwich Henry James felt one of the responsibilities of his cousinship to be the handing on of the torch of language, of tone, of discrimination, of civilization—to the *jeunes filles en fleur* of the Emmetry.

III

That he enjoyed himself enormously at Dunwich, in spite of the absence of luxuries and the bad roads, is clear from the lengthy article he wrote for *Harper's Weekly*, one of his last fugitive travel pieces—he had written so many in other years. There was enough to fascinate in Suffolk—the wide pebbly beaches, the towns that had disappeared in the great wash of the sea during the centuries, the boatmen and coast-guard men with whom he talked on every occasion, garnering their tales as FitzGerald had done. He remembered that he was in the country of David Copperfield; and that in nearby Aldeburgh was the birthplace of the poet Crabbe. He delighted in names such as Great Yarmouth, Blundeston and of course Saxmundham, and in the appeal of "desolate exquisite Dunwich." He surveyed with his professional eye the ruins of the great church and its tall tower, and the crumbled ivy wall of the Priory, where FitzGerald had admired the pale Dunwich rose that grew on its walls; the low heathery bareness of the countryside, the rare purple and gold that ran to the edge of the sea. There was enough left by the predatory sea to feed the fancy; "what is left is just the stony beach and the big gales, and the cluster of fishermen's huts and the small, wide, short street of decent, homely, shoppy houses." And there were "the private emotions of the historic sense," the recognition of "a mere pinch of manners and customs in the midst of wind and waves!"

There were afternoons when he would go on long bicycle runs to a main artery six miles inland, and he remembered stopping at such sleepy towns as Westleton to refresh himself at an old red inn with lemonade and a "dash"—only of beer, but the refreshment was "immense." Since the cuisine at Dunwich was rudimentary, he had big afternoon teas en route at various pubs and inns, consuming large numbers of buns and quantities of jam. Best of all he liked his talks with the seafaring folk. "I had often dreamed that the ideal refuge for a man of letters was a cottage so placed on the coast as to be circled, as it were, by the protecting arm of the Admiralty." As if it were a private thought he added, "may the last darkness close before I cease to care for sea-folk."

To his friend Gosse he wrote that it was "all delicious—if there were only a cuisine." Things were "the most primitive as to bed and board that I have yet had to do with in the islands." He wore with obvious pleasure his old baggy trousers and his rough-textured Norfolk jackets, jaunty bow-ties and golf cap. Snapshots taken by the cousins show that by this time he had trimmed his beard to the spadelike shape it has in the well-known Rothenstein lithograph. There is one picture of James standing with a large grin beside a lifeguard on the stony beach; and another of him leaning on a cane as if he were Neptune himself.

After a fortnight, he went off for a dozen days to Devonshire to visit Norris. A little of Dunwich went a long way. He returned, however, late in August and remained into the first days of September.

As he left he wrote a long letter to his brother and in it he spoke of his sense of being a nomad. "I should like to put in a couple of more months in the country—but am tired of oscillating between bad lodgings and expensive hotels. The latter, moreover, are all in prosaic places. The moral of it all is the cot beside the rill, which would keep one happily out of town till November 1st. Even Point Hill, had I taken it again this year (as I daresay I shall next), would have helped me but little, as it is not available for August and September." He had had a "casual" summer; later he called it "my rather incoherent summer . . . of a rather patched-together, hand-to-mouth, unhoused and accidental sort." He had moved about more than he wanted. This would continue to be his lot, he said, "until I can put my hand on the lowly refuge of my own, for which, from year to year, I thirst." And he added, "On the day I do get it—for the day must come—I shall feel my fortune is made. It can only be made so; for to wander, even in the very slight degree in which I now do it, is more and more intolerable to me."

The day of which he spoke was only a fortnight away.

LAMB HOUSE

DURING THE WINTER OF 1895–96, HENRY JAMES HAD SEEN IN THE Cowley Street home of Edward Warren, the architect, a pleasant little watercolor sketch. It showed the solid brick front of a house in Rye, with Roman-arched bow windows rising above the street, a peaked roof, an old-fashioned lantern set in the wall and ivy climbing up one side. Warren told him it was the detached "garden room" of a house known as Lamb House he had lately sketched. The following summer, when James lived at Point Hill and later in the Old Vicarage, he saw the house often and became fond of it. During this period, it will be recalled, he had casually mentioned to the local ironmonger, a man named Milson, that he was house-hunting.

Now, a few days after his return from Dunwich, he went on a long day's bicycle ride with Warren. They had a talk about houses. Lamb House was mentioned. Two days later came a brief note from the ironmonger; he remembered James's remark. He wished him to know that Lamb House had fallen vacant. It was available on a long lease. "Telepathy does indeed mark the case for its own," James wrote to Warren. Confronted with the possibility, and a decision affecting his entire way of life, James felt the news to be "a little like a blow in the stomach."

Dream houses were delightful; the reality had in it anxious elements. James rushed off to Rye and Warren promised to give the house a close inspection.

I

Lamb House stands at the top of the steep and cobbled West Street which climbs the hilltop of Rye out of the High Street. It is located at the turn, where West Street curves toward St. Mary's Church. The house looks out on the ancient church, while the detached garden room, which Warren had sketched and whose casemented bow windows stood high above the cobbles, looked down the hilly street up which James had come. The garden room was called the "banqueting room"; doubtless the Lamb family (its members had been mayors of Rye for over a century) had used it for civic purposes. Rye itself had long ago received a visit from the great Elizabeth and Lamb House had provided shelter for the first George, whose tempest-tossed ship homeward bound from Hanover put in at one of the Cinque Ports. Thus the house had a "King's Room" in which later George II and his son, the Duke of Cumberland, also slept during visits to the town. The house was of

red brick that had turned russet; the garden room at a right angle
to it, built somewhat later, was of brick that had faded to a tawny
color.

James probably entered Lamb House for the first time by its
high canopied Georgian doorway; the knocker had to be turned
sharply to the right to unlatch the door. Inside, the precautions of
more violent times were visible: bolts, latches, chains: the door
could be fastened in nine different ways. A well-proportioned and
handsome balustraded staircase of oak faced the entrance. To the
right was a small panelled room, a kind of waiting room, that
might serve as a small *cabinet de travail*. On the left, was an
oak-panelled parlor, or so James was assured, for the panelling had
been covered by modern wallpaper. A door opened from the parlor
into a comfortable stretch of garden—a little less than an acre.
Next to this room was a squarish dining room, with another
French door giving on the garden, very much as James would
describe it in "The Turn of the Screw." Opposite, under the stair,
the novelist passed into a high and spacious kitchen. The upstairs
was laid out similarly: the King's Room, panelled from floor to
ceiling, but also papered, with a benched window, looked toward
the church; across the hallway on the right was a small square
panelled room looking toward Winchelsea and on the Lamb
House garden. There were two more bedrooms, also a dressing
room, with a handsome pedimented cupboard, leading to the
bathroom. On the floor above were four attic rooms that could be
the servants' quarters.

James passed through the ground-floor parlor into the garden; to
the left was a short flight of curved stone steps, with a graceful
iron hand-rail leading into the garden room. This was spacious and
would make an ideal study and workroom; its bow window commanded the downward sloping street and a fine expanse of the
changeable Sussex sky. The house was not, as family houses go,
large; all the rooms except the garden room were small; but with

four bedrooms on the second floor and four in the attic Lamb
House was more than sufficient for a sedentary writing bachelor.
One of the upstairs bedrooms—it would be known as the Green
Room—would serve as a second study.

The garden was charming. There was a big mulberry tree throwing generous shade; there was a kitchen garden at the upper end
and a row of greenhouses. There were peaches—a memory of
Albany—and an old bignonia which had climbed the southwest
corner nearly to the roof. There was also an annex to the property,
a studio with a pillared entrance in adjacent Watchbell Lane,
which James would be able to use or to let. Behind Lamb House
proper was a cobbled court and a delivery entrance to the street.

The house was in good condition, and Warren's verdict was
favorable, even enthusiastic. The paper could be peeled from the
fine old panels; some improvements in the sanitary arrangements
were needed; the place required redecorating. The renovation
could be done during the coming winter, so that the house would
be ready for the spring. Alfred Parsons, the landscape painter who
had done the sets for *Domville*, inspected the garden for James
and pronounced in an equally favorable manner. The back windows of houses facing the church threatened the privacy of the
garden, but it could be screened from view by planting Lombardy
poplars at that end. High trellises on the walk would do the rest.

Before the end of September 1897 James had signed a twenty-
one-year lease. He got the house for £70 a year, about $350. The
large parchment, setting forth the usual commitments of lessor
and lessee, bound James to upkeep and improvements and, among
other things, to a life of horticulture, or at least to the employment
of an efficient gardener. The novelist undertook to keep the Lamb
House garden, the hothouse and greenhouses "well and properly
stocked, cropped and manured." He promised to "improve, prune
and preserve all the flowers, shrubs and fruit trees, plant vines and
other trees." He covenanted to replace such plants or trees as

decayed or died by others "as good or of the better sort." He agreed to repaint the woodwork with three coats of "good oil color" at the end of the seventh and fourteenth years of his lease; and at the end of these years he had the option to surrender the lease if he wished.

As soon as he had signed the document James left for a visit to Ford Castle in Northumberland, a week-end stay of the kind he now rarely made. There, asked to put his name in the visitors' book at the village school, he proudly, and with a flourish, signed it "Henry James, Lamb House, Rye, Sussex." It was as if he were already in residence. To A. C. Benson he wrote that his house was "really good enough to be a kind of little becoming, high door'd, brass knockered *façade* to one's life." This indeed was what Lamb House became.

I I

In the midst of his joy at his acquisition Henry James had a sense of great complications. There was the problem of what to do with De Vere Gardens during his long absences; there was the need to find a gardener and to deploy his servants, the bibulous Smith couple.

Looking ahead to the time when he might spend a greater part of his year in the country and would therefore get rid of his flat, he put himself down at the Reform Club for one of the bedrooms looking out on Carlton Gardens. These were let by the year, and it would be some time before a chamber would be vacant. In the future he would be assured of a *pied-à-terre* in the city.

Then there was the question of furnishings: he could hardly despoil De Vere Gardens if he wanted to sublet it, though he would want to move some of his books. Lamb House fairly obviously would need "old things," preferably eighteenth-century, certainly not of the costly Poynton kind; nor could he afford the sort of rarities Mrs. Jack captured on her European forays. Some good mahogany and brass, some Chippendale and Sheraton, a little faded tapestry, he gaily said in one letter, "a handful of feeble relics," would do. And he began his search immediately, for he wrote Warren from Northumberland: "I have bought two maps, five prints and a chest of drawers." He was to have long leisurely winter rambles that year in London curiosity shops, as in the days, a decade earlier, when he had furnished De Vere Gardens. His lady friends rallied to his aid and Mrs. Warren promptly announced she would take care of his curtains.

To accomplish all this however he would need extra funds. In other years James had skillfully mobilized his resources to earn enough for his trips to the Continent. Now, with the same business alertness, he looked about for opportunities. He committed himself to a monthly "American Letter" for a new journal, *Literature*, published by *The Times* (it would be a precursor of the *Literary Supplement*). This would yield him £40 a month. Then the family of William Wetmore Story renewed a plea made earlier that James write a life of the sculptor. James had been delaying his answer, suggesting that he would examine the family papers on his next trip to Rome. But now, when the Waldo Storys sent him a sampling of the material available, James decided to inquire what moneys he could obtain in advance of undertaking a piece of writing he was reluctant to do. He wrote to William Blackwood in Edinburgh, who had published Story's amateur verses and his various plays and essays. He explained that his time was "too valuable, much, for me to write Mr. Story's life, even on the restricted scale on which alone I should be willing to proceed, as a mere friendly and unremunerated task." He found it embarrassing to discuss "business" with the Storys. Moreover he could not do the book at once. "It would be possible for me to do the book only for a definite *fee* on its completion—which should exhaust my interest in it." He recognized that there must not be undue delay; but the deadline would have to be for him to determine. Blackwood was sufficiently interested. He paid James £250 or $1250 in advance and agreed to pay a further £100 after 7,000 copies were sold and a like sum for every 2,000 copies sold thereafter.

Within a month of signing the lease to Lamb House, James had thus provided himself with a financial "cushion." Now he had a further bit of luck. Howells suddenly turned up in Europe. They had not seen each other in many years. James offered to meet his old editor and literary adviser in Paris if necessary, but Howells passed through London before sailing and they had a long quiet *déjeuner* in De Vere Gardens on a morning of thick fog, and talked for six hours. Howells had come (as James was to tell him later) at a "psychological" moment. James had been too long away from America; he no longer knew how to place his work there, nor what prices to ask. The reunion of the two old friends was a mixture of reminiscence and practical literary purpose. James later wrote of the "miraculous" effect of "your admirable counsel and comfort." He had come to feel, in the marketplace, he said, "like an old maid against the wall and on her lonely bench." Now he knew that he wasn't one "for the blessed trade, quite yet." And he added, "you *were* Don Quixote."

Howells acted promptly on his return to America, with the result that *Harper's Weekly* expressed an interest in a serial and James asked a steep price for it, $3,000. He promised them the tale that had begun to shape itself as a novel, *The Awkward Age*. Even before this, James had contracted to do a short serial for *Collier's* to be delivered by the new year. This he would have to write at once, since it would carry an illustrative headpiece by his old friend La Farge, and another illustrator would do a series of scenes from the story. James's efforts to give himself financial leeway for his installation in Lamb House were more than successful: his earnings for the next year, he said, would be much larger "than for any year of my existence."

He could now with greater ease and sureness talk of his house to his own family; but it wasn't until Howells had come and gone, and more than two months had elapsed, that he described Lamb House and the good fortune that had come to him in a long letter to Mrs. William James. He told how he had two years before made "sheep's eyes" at the place "the more so that it is called Lamb House"; he was writing at the beginning of December 1897 and he could report that things were still flourishing out of doors near the southern exposure of the russet garden wall. The letter is cheerful and filled with the sense of possession. It also contained a significant piece of literary intelligence. "I *have*, at last, finished my little book—that is *a* little book." This was the story for *Collier's*. It was called "The Turn of the Screw."

THE LITTLE BOYS

HENRY JAMES'S DECISION TO TAKE LAMB HOUSE ON A LONG LEASE sounded eminently sensible—and practical—as he described it to his sister-in-law. He was forsaking London. He was providing for his old age. He had chosen the kind of house that suited the taste and sensitivities of an artist. It was a reversal of all that he had done in the past. He had been from the first a footloose American in Europe; his expatriation had been in part a revolt against embeddedness. The lodging house, the foreign *pension*, the hotel had been his way of life for the greater part of a quarter of a century—or at least until he had committed himself to De Vere

Gardens in 1886. But even possession of a London flat, while it
had rooted him more securely, had not altered his practice of
spending many months on the Continent—in Paris, Venice, Florence. Moreover he had always travelled "light." His most important possession on his trips had been his writing portfolio; and he
could work anywhere. All this, to be sure, had had to be revised in
recent months. The typewriter had begun to limit his freedom. He
could no longer write his novels with the ease with which he had
written *The American*—begun in Paris, continued in Normandy,
then in the south of France, then again in Paris in a small Left
Bank hotel, then at St. Germain-en-Laye, and finally in a large
Paris apartment that had in it portrait-medallions of the Empire.
Last touches had been put to the manuscript in London. Those
carefree days were gone. And then he was also accustomed to the
sounds of cities and towns as he worked, the feeling that he moved
in a dense human medium, always available to him whether urban
or seaside. He depended on his clubs in London, and friendly
houses both at home and abroad, a mode of existence that combined great industry with the civilized amenities and comforts of
"society." Even his later dream of finding a "great good place"—
once his immediate anxieties were assuaged—envisaged an escape
from worldly pressures into a brotherhood, all discretion and quiet,
the house of an Order, celibate and fraternal at the same time.

His deeper feelings seem to have been that in Lamb House he
would be an anchorite, a lonely dweller, a "prisoner" beyond the
suburbs. His immediate artistic response to his contemplated
change was a tale of nightmare terror. He had set down the idea
for "The Turn of the Screw" in his notebooks more than two years
earlier, at the horrible moment when he had described himself as
drowning after the *débacle* of *Guy Domville*. It had been the old
Archbishop's hint for a tale of horror: that of haunted children.
James had been writing tales about children victimized by an adult
world—murdered Effie, tormented Maisie—and he had written

stories in which houses occupied the center of the scene—Poynton, Covering End, Eastmead, Bounds. Preparing now to settle in Rye, in Sussex, he called his fictional house Bly, and placed it in Essex; and to this house he dispatched a young governess, who would narrate strange eerie events, involving a boy and girl, that would give an extra "turn" to the screw—by which, in old torture chambers, pain was made more excruciating. To be confronted by the possibility of Lamb House had felt "a little like a blow in the stomach." What followed seemed to be a period on the rack. The remark indeed turns up early in the tale. When Mrs. Grose is told by the governess that she had seen the ghost of Miss Jessel, she takes it "as she might have taken a blow in the stomach." There are similar strange remarks in James's letters at the moment he signed the lease. "All my inclination is to take it—I feel in fact *doomed* to do so." This was a curious way of describing fate or destiny, when the fate had made his wish come true. It sounded rather as if some extraneous coercion were occurring, as if some ominous oracle had intervened. The word *coerce* is used also in a letter to the Emmetry; he felt "coerced by some supernatural power that relieves me of all the botheration of a decision or an alternative. I feel quite absolutely foredoomed to take a lease."

James is clearly invoking an idea of magic. It had been uncanny. He had looked at the house, liked it—and suddenly he had been told he could have it. This was like rubbing a lamp in some old tale of the *Arabian Nights*. It was also a way of absolving himself of all responsibility. The fates had decided; and he was "doomed." From this kind of magical fantasy to a tale of the supernatural might seem a logical step in a writer of imagination; but that the tale should be one of the greatest horror stories of its kind—as the public and posterity would judge it—suggests that James was in some kind of abject terror himself, over a decision he believed not to have been his own. Something far deeper in his being had been touched than the mere thought that he was leaving bright London and "the world" for a rural life of solitude. "The Turn of the Screw" is a tale of a governess frightened by her own imaginings. And we must look at it closely to see what were the hidden imaginings of its author.

I

"The imagination," Henry James was to say to Bernard Shaw, "leads a life of its own." Between September and December 1897, James rapidly dictated the strange history of an untried young woman, fresh from a Hampshire vicarage, who is sent by her employer to a remote house to care for his nephew and niece, aged ten and eight. The employer is a handsome man who lives in Harley Street, and the governess's girlish "crush" on him prevents her from recognizing how callous he is toward the orphaned children. In effect, he washes his hands of them; he makes her the head, in spite of her inexperience, of the small household at Bly and instructs her not to trouble him, not even to write him letters. The governess, flushed and anxious with her new-found authority, arrives at Bly in a state both of euphoria and anxiety. She finds her little charges precocious and charming. She is seconded in her responsibilities by Mrs. Grose, the housekeeper, a good-natured, efficient woman, who acts as a kind of semi-articulate chorus in the story.

The governess's tale begins in June, during the long English twilight when the rooks circle above the crenellated towers of Bly and the evening's hush is on the land; it ends in bleak November, when the trees in the churchyard are bare and Bly has been blighted. In these few months the governess—the narrator—with eyes "unsealed" encounters the apparitions of Miss Jessel, the governess who preceded her, and Peter Quint, the master's valet, both of whom had died some time before. The governess puts on a bold show of courage, always thinking that her heroism will win the approval of her handsome employer who is constantly in her

thoughts. But her courage is a mask for a deep hysteria, which is
unveiled for us in two crucial scenes: that in which she confronts
the little girl on the far side of the pond, and the final one in
which she confronts the boy. Exalted and arrayed against the
works of the devil, she believes the ghosts have come for the
children; a true daughter of the manse, she is determined to
exorcise the evil that she feels and sees around her.

Bly, however, is filled not so much with the evil of the ghosts as
with the terror of the governess, her wild suppositions and soothing self-consoling explanations. There are the escapades of the
children, which seem harmless, but which she describes as sinister,
and there is the shock of the "recognition" scene, when the
governess tells Mrs. Grose of the man on the tower and leads her,
by elaborate cross-examination, to pronounce the name of Peter
Quint and to utter the words (Joseph Conrad would echo them in
another tale of evil, *Heart of Darkness*, the following year) "Mr
Quint is dead." The controversial "recognition" scene is filled with
ambiguities, and it tends to draw the reader's attention away from
the essential data, which is not the identification of the ghosts, but
the history of the governess and her way of relating to the children
and to the housekeeper. As the summer advances, and the children
grow restless under the constantly protective eyes of the governess,
she sees in their liveliness confirmation of her suspicions. She
expects them, in her own immature understanding of how children behave, to confide everything to her. And when little Miles,
in the country churchyard, reminds the governess that he is a boy
and doesn't want to be cooped up constantly with females, she
regards this as an act of defiance against herself. There is a parallel
scene with Flora in which the governess accuses the little girl of
communicating with the apparition of Miss Jessel. Defied by
Flora, who has all the aplomb of Maisie, the governess has a
moment of amnesia, and finds herself stretched out and sobbing
on the damp ground. We are in a kind of Brontë world in which

calm and hysteria mingle—and we are in the Brontë period, for James carefully places the tale (as we can determine with the aid of simple arithmetic) in the decade of the 1840's. It happens to be also the decade of James's own early childhood.

As the tale unfolds, it gives us a picture of the constantly haunted state of the governess; her "turn of the screw" of pain resides in her belief that evil has come into the lives of the innocent. There is, however, a further "turn" for the reader; consciously or unconsciously we begin to sense that it is the governess herself who haunts the children. For by all the testimony of the story, she alone sees the ghosts: neither the children nor Mrs. Grose ever see them—their eyes, as she puts it, are "sealed." Peter Quint and Miss Jessel are private phantoms. James was very clear about this, both in the story and in his remarks in the preface he wrote ten years later. The ghosts are not ghosts at all, "as we now know the ghost, but goblins, elves, imps, demons, as loosely constructed as those of the old trials for witchcraft." When we remember the testimony of the bewitched children of Salem, who said with the discernment of childhood what their approving elders wanted to hear, we have a fundamental clue to "The Turn of the Screw." In the charged account of the governess, with her phantoms, her "certitude," her suppositions which she turns into "fact," her "facts" which are mere suppositions, we recognize the materials of the witch-burners and executioners of old. Her narrative, with its consummate interweaving of paranoid fancy with circumstantial reality, is indeed capable of making readers pronounce the innocents guilty—as the testimony of the Salem children long ago turned innocent men and women into sorcerers and magicians.

Here lies the deepest horror of James's story: the nightmare element in "The Turn of the Screw" resides in our becoming aware of the ways in which Flora, Miles and Mrs. Grose seek constantly to accommodate themselves to the obsessions of the governess. The children are shown to us as direct and guileless, even as the governess is indirect and filled with guile. She is always putting words into Mrs. Grose's mouth; she asks the children questions they cannot understand or answer. Small wonder that little Flora, whose beautiful eight-year-old innocence has been carefully described for us, responds to the governess's hysteria at the pond with all the force of her childhood—"I don't know what you mean. I see nobody. I see nothing. I never *have*. I think you're cruel. I don't like you!" The governess gets as firm a dressing-down as if she and the child had changed roles. To Mrs. Grose, the little girl turns and says, "Take me away, take me away—oh, take me away from *her*." Her instincts are right. In the last scene, which is like that of an Elizabethan tragedy, Miles never sees Quint. The boy is described as if he were a dumb trapped little animal seeking a way of escape from the smothering presence not of the ghost but of the intense and exigent governess. "No more, no more, no more," she shrieks thinking she has banished the phantom. When Miles, after guessing wrongly, dredges up the name she wants him to pronounce, that of Peter Quint, he is able in his frightened state to add the words "you devil!" A careless reader might think that he is addressing the apparition. However throughout this scene Miles has his back to the window where the governess sees Quint hovering ominously. It is indeed the governess who has become the devil; and the subtlest twist of the story is that the demon she seeks to exorcise is the demon within herself. She rids herself of her private ghost; and in the process little Miles's heart is "dispossessed," and she is left "alone with the quiet day," with the dead boy in her arms—as in the medieval tales of possession. Her evil spirit has been driven out; but innocence has died.

11

James had never written at a greater pitch of intensity. In his series of brief scenes he had woven a hell-fire tale and given it a horrible tension, made it vague, ambiguous, filled with overtones of mystical and supernatural terror. What arrests our attention when we re-examine the story is James's choice of a young boy as protagonist at a season of his life when all his stories dealt with little girls at various stages of their growth. Little Miles is the sole masculine figure in the series of Effies, Maisies, Aggies, Nandas, including the young unnamed governess herself and the unnamed girl "in the cage." Miles's fate resembles that of earlier little boys—the murdered Dolcino of "The Author of Beltraffio," killed by a Medea-mother who like the governess would save him from external evil; or Morgan Moreen, whose young heart gives way at the very moment when his hope of freedom seems frustrated; or the young adult, Owen Wingrave, who in the old haunted mansion of Paramore proves his bravery by facing the family incubus—and dying. In James's world little boys died. It was safer to be a little girl. They usually endured.

In this light, the confrontation scene between the governess and Miles in the country churchyard, in which they deal not with supernatural events but with Miles's normal wish to go back to school, illuminates a large area of Jamesian experience. The scene is striking in its sharpness and "objectivity." They walk to church on a crisp cold autumn morning; and the governess describes Miles in terms of his masculinity—"turned out for Sunday by his uncle's tailor, who had had a free hand and a notion of pretty waistcoats." She notes the boy's "grand little air," his "whole title to independence" and "the rights of his sex and situation." At the same time she is admitting to herself that she has been overpossessive—"I had all but pinned the boy to my shawl . . . I was like a gaoler with an eye to possible surprises and escapes." Thinking this, she remarks that if the boy struck for freedom she would find herself with nothing to say.

There was, as a matter of fact, a great deal she could say. Miles has been expelled from school with no explanation from the headmaster. Instead of asking the boy about this she has silently waited for his confession. This makes the conversation in the churchyard—in the little city of the dead under the leafless trees of autumn—a mixture of the governess's deception and the boy's candor. What Miles asks is "When in the world, please, am I going back to school?" His complaint is that he spends all his time with a lady—the governess; or his sister Flora whom he considers a baby. "I want my own sort," says little Miles. "I want to see more life." Also, "I'm a fellow, don't you see?"

Two things emerge from this: Miles's strong will to masculinity, and his sense of entrapment, confined in a house wholly in the company of females. In the days when Peter Quint was alive he had had a male companion; but now he demands the company of his peers. Later, when the governess at long last asks him about his expulsion, his answer is direct enough: "I said things." He had said them to boys he liked; and the boys had said them to others, and what he had said had finally reached the ears of the masters. James supplies no clue as to what he said, and by his policy of letting the reader's imagination fill such blanks we can choose between blasphemy and obscenity. The story keeps the misdemeanor in the realm of speech, not sex. Miles probably used words he had heard from Peter Quint. It little matters. The essential point the story makes is to show Miles's wish to be a boy among boys—and the fact that his expression of such a wish is deemed evil by the governess.

III

We are reminded as we think of the trapped and dead little boys and young adults in James's fictional world—the boy Miles, the adolescent Morgan, the young Owen—of events in James's own life, during the long-ago period when his rivalry with his strong and active older brother William led to eternal conflict within the James family. William was masculine and active, and punished often for his excess of activity; and Henry his junior, as spectator and outsider, pushed away by his elder brother, discovered that it was dangerous to be like his brother; he was safest when he identified himself with his younger sister, and stayed at home with his mother and the vigorous Aunt Kate. "*I* play with boys who curse and swear," William James had said to him once, when Henry was about as old as little Miles. It was William's way of telling Henry that he wasn't fit for the company of older boys. The novelist, remembering this in the autobiographies of his old age, looked sadly upon his boyish self and agreed that he "simply wasn't qualified"; William could "say things" *he* apparently had not yet learned. He smarted at being "mere junior," and the picture we have of him at a later stage at Newport (in the memories of T. S. Perry) is that of a lonely adolescent, sitting on a window-seat reading while "the rest of us were chattering." This "certain air of remoteness" was the first thing that struck Perry when they met. Another young man, a friend of William's, had a further memory. Steele MacKaye long after (when he was famous as a stage designer and actor) described how the older boys had called Henry "sissy" at the time when he was already beginning to write. And we get still another picture of the extent to which Henry retained a sense of his divorce from masculine activity when he recalled his life in New York, during his thirty-second year. He had felt shut out—because he was a writer—from the great male business world of "downtown." Like his father before him, Henry was "uptown" and "at the very moderate altitude of Twenty Fifth Street" he felt himself "day by day alone . . . with the music teachers and French pastry-cooks, the ladies and children—immensely present and immensely numerous these, but testifying with a collective voice to the extraordinary absence (save as pieced together through a thousand gaps and indirectnesses) of serious male interest." Like Miles he was not with his own "sort." He was in a feminine world.

We have then evidence at different stages of Henry James's life —from childhood to maturity—of the masculine-feminine problem exemplified repeatedly in his fiction. There was, in the novelist, a compelling drive to masculinity which Miles expressed; but it had been driven underground. To be male was to risk (in the remote fantasy of childhood) such things as amputation like his father's; females seemed the most serious threat to his sense of himself, as a boy, and later—by the disguises of the imagination, by thinking himself a little girl and by being quiet and observant —he could escape "amputations" and punishments. The stratagem succeeded. His mother had called him "Angel." He could be above all an observant exploratory young female. The disguise of femininity was necessary mainly when he was confined to "Family" and had to contend with his elder brother; in that relationship he always saw William as strong and active and himself as inhibited and passive. This is true in the many tales in which the old rivalry is re-imagined, and in which William is present, but usually reduced to a shoddy adventurer, an impostor, or a weakling. In the stories in which older brothers are banished, the second son can be his masculine self, but this can have fatal consequences. Owen's older brother we remember was locked away in an asylum and the full responsibility of the Wingrave name fell on the second son. In "The Pupil" the older brother is an effete young man; it is little Morgan who is the focus of family attention—and neglect. There remained in James (as we can see in "The Turn of the Screw") a young assertive male who wanted a life of action and of courage, who wanted to curse and swear with his fellows and possess the heroism of the Napoleonic Marbots or the seasoned Wolseleys. But long-ago inhibitions, reinforced by later experiences, had taught him how dangerous this could be.*

---

* I omit in this discussion Henry James's relation to his younger brothers, Garth Wilkinson and Robertson, who were two and three years younger. Henry and William were well out of the nursery during the infancy of Garth and Robertson. On the other hand, the slight age difference between the two

The personal history enables us to understand the lack of conviction that lay behind *Guy Domville*; James's self-assertion in the theatre had been half-hearted out of his fear of committing his art totally to "the world." He had tried; and, because he had been half-hearted, he had lessened his chance of success. Failure then confirmed him in his constituted mode of being. The very subject of the play expressed this: the young priest had been called upon to be a man, go into the world, have progeny. James, in effect, had concluded that Guy was incapable of this. The world was too bad, too dangerous. He would be safer in the monastery.

In this light it is possible to surmise what the "blow in the stomach" was, when Lamb House fell easily, almost magically, into James's hands and fulfilled a profound wish. The house symbolized the world of his childhood, the place where he had been least free, where he had had to resort to disguise and subterfuge in order to possess himself and his identity. In the house of Family he had had to defend himself to escape William, and also to avoid the restrictions he saw placed upon William's excess of activity. To change from London to Rye, to take a house, represented (for one part of Henry James) an act of assertion not unlike Owen's act, in sleeping in the old haunted family room at Paramore. In "The Turn of the Screw" James was saying, on the remote levels of his buried life, that Lamb House was a severe threat to his inner peace. It was haunted. It contained all the ghosts of his boyhood—pushing, demanding governesses, Aunt Kate, his mother in her moods of severity. He could not be "a fellow, don't you see?" in such an environment. In the house of Family, Henry had always thought of himself as a claimant, as his early tales had shown. To establish his claim, to take possession, carried with it the certitude of punishment—the demanding

. . . .

older brothers—fifteen months—made them contemporaries during all their formative years. See *The Untried Years*, the chapters "Mere Junior," "The Younger Brothers," and "Jacob and Esau"; and, in *The Conquest of London*, the chapters "William" and "Angel and Brother."

ghosts would exact their price, and little Miles's, or Owen's, or
Morgan's sacrifice had shown what—somewhere beyond rational
existence—he believed that price would be.

These, we may see, were the feelings that arose out of the past
within the adult Henry James, in a kind of conscious nightmare
called "The Turn of the Screw"—within an atmosphere of the
uncanny and the supernatural. We can understand why he felt
"doomed" in the inexorable way in which oracles doom men to
prescribed experience. The children and the governess are the
voices of James's past, early terrors re-expressed through his imagi
nation and through art—the eternal power of fantasy and thought
that can turn the calm quiet of day into a place of evil and horror.

IV

"The Turn of the Screw" was published in *Collier's*, from January
to April 1898. Later that year it appeared in the volume to which
James gave the title *The Two Magics*, its companion piece being
"Covering End," the story version of the Ellen Terry play: two
tales of houses, and the title embodied the element of "magic"
relating to them—black magic and white, the baleful and the
benign. Not since "Daisy Miller" had James written a tale that
caught the public fancy as did "The Turn of the Screw." As
inquiries from mystified and fascinated readers poured in, James
was careful not to give away his secret. Like most artists, he did
not like to "explain" his art, and he was determined not to spoil
the mystification he had created. He was to tease both readers and
critics in his later preface by saying the story was "a trap for the
unwary," and he quite regularly reminded questioners that he
regarded the tale as a piece of hack work. Doubtless it was, in the
sense that he wrote it in a hurry and for money; but James himself
knew that what sometimes begins as hack work can end as a
masterpiece.

When one psychologist, interested in the unconscious, queried

James about his intentions he replied that he blushed "to see real substance" read into his "wanton little tale," and added, "Ah, the exposure indeed, the helpless plasticity of childhood that isn't dear or sacred to *somebody*." To his brother's friend, F. W. H. Myers, the psychical researcher, James described the tale as a "very mechanical matter," but he did add that he had wanted to create the impression of "the communication to the children of the most infernal imaginable evil and danger—the condition on their part, of being as *exposed* as we can humanly conceive children to be"—exposed, we judge, to the too-vivid imagination of one of their elders. To H. G. Wells, who asked him a story-teller's question—why he had not described the governess in greater detail —he gave a fellow-craftsman's answer. He had sought "singleness of effect" and so had confined himself to letting the governess strike her own "little note of neatness, firmness and courage." He was to elaborate on this in his later preface, writing, "we have surely as much of her own nature as we can swallow in watching it reflect her anxieties and inductions."

There exists evidence that James said in private exactly what he said in public about "The Turn of the Screw," and the elaborate divagations of some of the critics of this much-discussed tale have never sufficiently taken this evidence into account. The private comment was made in his doctor's consulting room; and it is known only because the doctor recorded the conversation in a learned study, *Angina Pectoris*, without discerning the uniqueness of "The Turn of the Screw," and how easily it can be recognized. It figures as "Case 97" in a series of cases described by Sir James Mackenzie, a great Edwardian heart specialist, who dealt with emotional factors in heart ailments.

I was once consulted by a distinguished novelist. Just before he came to see me I had read one of his short stories, in which an account was given of an extraordinary occurrence that happened to two children. Several scenes were recounted in which these children seemed to hold converse with invisible people, after which they were greatly upset. After one occasion one of them turned and fled, screaming with terror, and died in the arms of the narrator of the story.

"You did not explain the nature of the mysterious interviews," Mackenzie said to his distinguished novelist. The latter then explained to Mackenzie the principles on which a mystery is created. "So long as the events are veiled the imagination will run riot and depict all sorts of horrors, but as soon as the veil is lifted, all mystery disappears and with it the sense of terror."

This idea is expressed in James's theory of the ghostly tale. He liked "the strange and the sinister embroidered on the very type of the normal and the easy." In a word, terror exists for us anywhere, and at any time that we imagine it. That is why James preferred daylight ghosts. And the secret of his story, as he finally revealed it in his late preface, was that he allowed his readers to imagine for themselves horrors never named. For an author to specify, to produce the corpse or rattle the chains, was to limit the potential of nightmare. "Explained" ghosts and attested and certified psychical phenomena did not interest him. He sought to "make the reader's general vision of evil intense enough . . . make him *think* the evil, make him think it for himself." By doing this the author was released from weakening "specifications."

James wrote "The Turn of the Screw" accordingly on a theory of unexplained extra human terror, that terror within himself that could not tell him why he had felt a sinking of the heart, at the simple daylight act of providing himself with an anchorage for the rest of his days.

HENRY JAMES AT DUNWICH
From a snapshot taken by Miss Leslie Emmet, 1897

LAMB HOUSE FROM THE GARDEN
The garden room is to the right

THE GREEN ROOM, LAMB HOUSE
From a photograph

PART OF THE HALL AND "TELEPHONE ROOM," LAMB HOUSE
From an unpublished photograph by Alvin Langdon Coburn

BOOK FOUR

The Great Good Place

1898–1899

TWO DIARIES

EXCERPTS FROM A DIARY KEPT BY HENRY JAMES, AGED NINE-teen, son of William James and nephew of the novelist, during a summer's journey abroad:

Lamb House, Rye, Friday July 14, 1898—I came down here a week ago last Wednesday and was met at the station by Uncle H. who brought me up the hill to the house, showed me over part of it, holding me by the arm and keeping up a perpetual vocal search for words even when he wasn't saying anything. He left me in my oak panelled room to dress, with the injunction that I must "come down" bursting with news. In the evening he walked me about the town, to the old tower with its little terrace, to the "land-gate," down round the back passed [past] the bit of shipping. It is all extremely pretty, pleasant, charming, or picturesque, but owing to my self-consciousness and slowness of expression I was much bothered by the duty of seeming properly appreciative.

I doubt myself how much H. cares for me. He takes no interest at all in my plans projects or ambitions and at any rate does not wish to show any curiosity about my tastes or peculiarities. And as his only way of condemning seems to be by faint praise, I don't feel much reassured by his commendations. But on the other hand he is always most kind and seems most anxious that I be properly amused, and I am beginning to think that he is naturally, socially rather duller and less genial than I thought. When a man named Orred came here to lunch a couple of days ago he was just as conversationally short-winded and nervous as with me. He knows it all so that I can't tell him anything (about my impressions of England etc.)

I am sitting out here now under the shade of a mulberry tree, with the reddish wicker chair in front of me, and the pleasant sunny lawn, the flowers, the white washed hot-house, the ivy-covered side of Lamb House, (with one half the sitting room door open), and the sunlit brick wall of the gardenhouse across it on my left. There is a pleasant humming of flies above in the mulberry tree, and occasional sparrows chirp in the neighboring garden.

[Harrow] July 26, 1898—Got a note from Uncle H. a couple of days ago saying he missed me. He told me he cherished me when I left. These things encouraging . . .

Aboard the cattleboat Armenian, one day out of Boston Harbour, September 27th 1898—

This diary has not been kept with the greatest regularity after all, but I shall jot down a word or two of what followed during the summer. From Edinburgh we came back to Harrow again and for a day or two I waited to hear from Uncle H. that Rosina was to arrive. . . . The week and a half that followed were the best of those that I spent at Rye. Poor Rosina was pitifully personal and limited in her point of view and also over-prone to talk self and her own friends. . . . This, especially when addressed to strangers, appalled Uncle Henry. Yet he never made a sign and treated even her most Rosinaish outpourings and questionings with perfect respect. It was, however, but what was to have been expected of him. It [had] the effect of waking him conversationally, and when Edmund Gosse, a very perceptive, but genial and at times almost playful personage, came down he [H.J.] came out of himself completely, was at times quite frolicsome and even descended to a pun.

One evening they got to talking about Meredith and about his origin. Gosse knew a lady who had been a friend of Meredith's when he was a very young man. . . . He had married first at the age of eighteen. Later his wife ran away from him and Meredith subsequently disappeared. Where he had been was not known, but Gosse said that he supposed he had been in Germany during the two years. Uncle Henry said he thought he had never been in Germany, that he had once been a war correspondent in Austria (if I remember rightly) and that "of that experience he had made the very utmost." . . . Uncle Henry said that he lived out of the world in a rather shabby little house with a beautiful garden. He had wonderful wine of which he drank very little. . . .

11

From the diary of Mrs. J. T. Fields of 148 Charles Street, Boston:

Monday, September 13, 1898—We [Mrs. Fields and Sarah Orne Jewett] left London about 11 o'clock for Rye, to pass the day with Mr. Henry James. He was waiting for us at the station with a carriage, and in five minutes we found ourselves at the top of a silent little winding street, at a green door with a brass knocker, wearing the air of impenetrable respectability which is so well known in England. Another instant and an old servant, Smith, opened the door and helped us from the carriage. It was a pretty interior—large enough for elegance, and simple enough to suit the severe taste of a scholar and private gentleman. Mr. James was intent on the largest hospitality. We were asked upstairs over a staircase with a pretty balustrade and plain green drugget on the steps; everything was of the severest plainness, but in the best taste, "not at all austere," as he himself wrote us. We soon went down again after leaving our hats, to find a young gentleman, Mr. MacAlpine, who is Mr. James's secretary, with him, awaiting us. This young man is just the person to help Mr. James. He has a bump of reverence and appreciates his position and opportunity.

We sat in the parlor opening on a pretty garden for some time, until Mr. James said he could not conceive why luncheon was not ready and he must go and inquire, which he did in a very responsible manner, and soon after Smith appeared to announce the feast. Again a pretty room and table. We enjoyed our talk together sincerely at luncheon and afterward strolled into the garden. The dominating note was dear Mr. James's pleasure in having a home of his own to which he might ask us. From the garden, of course, we could see the pretty old house still more satisfactorily. An old brick wall concealed by vines and laurels surrounds the whole irregular domain; a door from the garden leads into a paved courtyard which seemed to give Mr. James peculiar satisfaction; returning to the garden, and on the other side, at an angle with the house, is a building which he laughingly called the temple of the Muse. This is his own place *par excellence*. A good writing-table and one for his secretary, a typewriter, books, and a sketch by du Maurier, with a few other pictures (rather mementoes than works of art), excellent windows with clear light, such is the temple! Evidently an admirable spot for his work.

A RUSSET ARCADIA

HENRY JAMES SLEPT FOR THE FIRST TIME IN LAMB HOUSE TOWARD the end of June 1898, probably on the 28th. The furniture acquired during the winter months was moved in on June 9; his servants followed—the liquor-loving Smiths, who showed some uneasiness and took to the bottle in anticipation of exile from

London. James's uneasiness, at the time of the signing of the lease, had long been banished. "The Turn of the Screw" had taken care of the ghosts. Presently carpets were laid and curtains were hung. James supervised every detail. He engaged a local gardener, George Gammon; he remained in flurried consultation with his architect; he acted with a sense of well-being and happy accomplishment. He brought with him his amanuensis, MacAlpine, complaining however that his work was uneven. He described it as a mixture of "capacity and failure," which he found surprising in a Scot: Scots, he explained to his nephew, usually made the most of their capacities, even if these were limited. "He is excellent for my work," he explained, "but with the fault that there's too much— *much* too much—of him for it." However he kept him that summer and into the autumn for the writing of *The Awkward Age*. Later MacAlpine worked only occasionally for the novelist and boarded out in Rye, so that James did not have to cope with his presence in Lamb House during non-working hours, that is in the afternoons and evenings.

In the midst of the installation, and because there was chaos both at De Vere Gardens and at Lamb House, James paid country visits, and just before he finally quitted town he went to Brighton and thence to Rottingdean to the funeral of his old friend, Sir Edward Burne-Jones. He stood in the gray-towered churchyard, which was smothered in spring flowers, and watched the committal of the ashes, in sight of a glistening sea. He had known the painter since his earliest days in London and he wrote another elegiac tribute, this time to Charles Eliot Norton, who had originally introduced him to Burne-Jones. "There was no false note in him. He knew his direction and held it hard—wrought with passion and went as straight as he could."

I

Rye proved a constant delight, a "russet Arcadia." James liked the brown tints in the town and the glimpse of the Channel; the quiet at night seemed almost audible, and he could hear with great comfort in every room the friendly tick of the clock in his hallway. His new life had begun with the visit of his nephew and namesake, the eldest son of William, who came to England to spend a few weeks. "I have but just scrambled in here by the skin of my teeth," he wrote to the young Harry James who was arriving on a cattle boat at Liverpool, "and am all ready—nay yearningly impatient for you. (I have slept here two nights—tonight the third, and shall feel an old inhabitant.) Your room awaits you—right royally—and the garden grins in anticipation." His first visitor to his new domain was, appropriately enough, "family" and the "right royally" indicates he was installing his nephew in the "King's Room" which became the guest chamber of Lamb House.

At the time of his visit to his uncle, James's nephew, Harry, was a solemn, rather conceited youth, as his diary notes show, articulate, thoughtful, but a little too much absorbed in himself to take note of all that was going on around him. Henry James found himself drawn to him and pronounced him extraordinarily nice, "only too silent and inward for absolutely easy intercourse." If Harry wasn't sure, during his stay, whether his uncle liked him he soon had abundant evidence in warm, affectionate letters filled with travel advice and urging an early return to Lamb House, where the uncle expected a visit from the charming if "incurably crude" Rosina—she of the missing vowels.

So began a famous tenancy that would from this time on link Henry James to this corner of Sussex. The novelist's first two months in Lamb House were a cavalcade of visitors. In letter after letter James reported "the bump of luggage has been too frequent on my stair." This also meant anxious conferences with his cook. It was one thing to entertain at luncheon or dinner in De Vere Gardens; it was another to have friends and relatives descend at the little Rye station to spend twenty-four hours or more. James invariably met the train escorted by his servant who brought a little hand-cart or wheelbarrow for the luggage. If the guests were elderly, he sometimes had a carriage; more often he would saunter with them up the cobbled hill, pointing out the delights of his rural existence. In fast succession that first summer came his old friends, the future Justice Holmes, Mrs. Fields and Miss Jewett, the Bourgets, the Curtises, the Edward Warrens, the Gosses, Howard Sturgis—"a good many irrepressible sojourners"—and Henry James complained that he did not achieve at first "all the concentration I settled myself in this supposedly sequestered spot in search of."

However he himself issued the invitations; he wanted company. In spite of his joy in the place he felt abruptly cut off from London. He could not shed so easily the habits of twenty years: he felt "out of things." He needed to know what was going on in Mayfair. He was reduced now to communication with London friends by letter and telegram; indeed the telegram began to play a large role in his life. The medium itself provided a delightful challenge. "Are you utterly absent or can you dine with me Friday at seven to go afterwards with three others to the theatre," was a typical message dispatched that summer when he planned a foray into town. This sense of isolation from his clubs and the murmurs of London society contributed probably to his tale—the first written in Lamb House—of a young girl confined to her cage in a branch post office at the back of a Mayfair grocery store, seeking to deduce from the telegrams she handles the goings-on of society. As with the story "The Great Good Place," which he wrote just before he moved, James created "In the Cage" out of immediate emotion. And no matter how much he might complain, as guests descended from the Ashford local and the luggage bumped on his eighteenth-century stairs, he actually felt himself protected by visitors against the solitude of country life with which he would now have to come to terms.

Bit by bit, however, the sense of the place asserted itself. The morning click of the typewriter in the garden room became known to Rye—and the distant sound of a grave and measured voice weaving sentences. By midsummer Henry James had been offered (and declined) the vice-presidency of the local cricket club. Later he would join the Golf Club, not to play golf, but to partake of tea in the clubhouse. He had indeed found a great good place; and late that year he could proclaim to Francis Boott, his Florentine friend, now living in Cambridge, Massachusetts, "Lamb House . . . is my Bellosguardo." He had never dreamed, in the old Italian days, when he envied Boott and his daughter Lizzie their tranquil existence in the Villa Castellani, that he too would have something resembling a villa, in—of all places—a rural and decayed out-of-the-way corner of England.

I I

He had planned his move from London with the greatest care. Workmen had peeled off the paper and disclosed the handsome panelling in certain rooms of Lamb House; fresh paint had been applied; tile fireplaces had been repaired. "Getting into" Lamb House, the novelist wrote to his brother, "is the biggest job of the sort I have ever tackled and the end is not yet." He had bought, aided by Lady Wolseley, discreet pieces of Georgian mahogany, "a handful of feeble relics," he said—and some of his books were moved from De Vere Gardens. He hoped as we know ultimately to let the London flat for part of each year.

His possessions were not as "humble" as he suggested; they showed discrimination and taste. If he had not assembled a Poynton, he had nevertheless taken care of creature comfort—and with modest elegance. The "Green Room" would lodge many of his books; and presently certain pictures were hung—a Burne-Jones, an inscribed photograph from Daudet, a small portrait of Flaubert, some illustrations from an edition of "Daisy Miller," a Whistler etching. Elsewhere he would place family portraits and, prominently, a picture of Constance Fenimore Woolson. The garden room was also furnished for work and James installed here many of the inscribed volumes received from author-friends, as well as works of reference. There were books in the entrance hall, in massive bookcases. James's library was not that of a systematic book-buyer; he did much of his reading at his clubs. His Lamb House shelves contained volumes from his early years, sets of major English and French writers, a good deal of history and many memoirs—he read eagerly anything that related to manners, customs, rituals in older societies—a goodly amount of Napoleonic material and certain books, pencil-marked and scrawled over in his large hand, which he had reviewed in the days of his literary journalism. It would be some time however before his library would be weeded out and fully transferred from De Vere Gardens, where he had at this moment more books than Lamb House could accommodate.

At first James's staff consisted of MacAlpine, the husband and wife from De Vere Gardens and his newly acquired part-time gardener. Later there would be a housemaid; and early in his life at Rye he took in an "apprentice," a diminutive local lad named Burgess Noakes. Burgess was a mere fourteen and still lived at home when he became James's house-boy. His master treated him as he would a son; he corrected his English, taught him manners, made him conform to personal ritual. Ultimately he was his valet. Burgess learned, after 1900, to shave the novelist and to minister to his personal wants; he looked after his clothes, did his errands. He remained small, wiry, athletic, with a love for football and boxing. "My gnome Burgess," James used to say of this sturdy bantamweight—he ultimately won the Sussex championship—and there was always pride and loyalty in this relationship. Noakes survived, like James's fictional butler Brooksmith, a cultivated emanation of his master, a relic of the civilized Edwardian life of Lamb House.

III

The visit of Mrs. Fields to Henry James, bringing with her the delicate and gifted Miss Jewett, was an echo from an early time, a

revival of memories of youth. Mrs. Fields had been a beautiful
Bostonian in James's apprentice years; her husband had published
him in the *Atlantic*, and she had welcomed him as a precocious
young man of letters to her salon in Charles Street. James remembered her as a singularly graceful young wife, with a beautiful head
and hair and smile and voice and as a singularly winning hostess,
who had enabled him to meet Mrs. Stowe, and to hear Julia Ward
Howe recite the "Battle Hymn" with her finale of a great clap of
hands as she rose to deliver the last line, "Be swift my soul to
answer him, be jubilant my feet." To receive a note from Mrs.
Fields, from London, after all these years, was to receive a flood of
old and welcome Charles Street memories; and James invited her
and her companion to Lamb House to spend the night. The ladies
preferred to come to luncheon and return by a late afternoon
train.

Mrs. Fields on her side had other memories of Henry. What she
had experienced long ago was the freshness of the youthful tales
her husband brought home, in James's large sprawling handwrit-
ing. On one such occasion, recorded in her journal, the couple on
a beautiful summer's day went to a nook in the pasture "where we
could hear the sea and catch a distant gleam of its blue face," and
lying in the cool grass, she read Henry James Jr.'s tale called
"Compagnons de Voyage" (later published in the *Atlantic* with
the English title "Travelling Companions"). "I do not know," she
had written, "why success in work should affect us so powerfully,
but I could have wept as I finished reading, not from the sweet
low pathos of the tale, which was not tearful, but from the
knowledge of the writer's success."

They met now, in middle age, with this long reach backward to
the time of the Civil War. Boston—Charles Street—had come to
ancient Rye. As James put it a few days later, writing to Mrs.
Humphry Ward, "Mrs. Fields took me back to my far-away youth
and *hers*—when she was so pretty and I was so aspiring." She
wore, for her visit, a black lace mantilla, allowing it to descend

from the head, as George Eliot had done when James had known the novelist; it gave Mrs. Fields, with the traces of her earlier beauty, "a general fine benignity." In Sarah Orne Jewett, whose tales he had admired, and whom he now met for the first time, James found "a sort of elegance of humility or fine flame of modesty." Her work was minor; it combined the sober and the tender note. On the evidence of Mrs. Fields's diary of that day at Rye, Henry James cross-examined Miss Jewett closely, and in its pages we seem to hear the talk in the parlor of Lamb House after the lunch.

"It is foolish to ask, I know," said James to Miss Jewett, "but were you in just such a place as you describe in the *Pointed Firs?*"

"No," replied Miss Jewett, "not precisely; the book was chiefly written before I visited the locality itself."

"And such an island?" James persisted.

"Not exactly," she said again.

"Ah! I thought so," the novelist said. And then, perhaps sensing the aggressiveness of his questions, he told Miss Jewett that her famous sketches were done with "elegance and exactness," they were "absolutely true—not a word overdone." The pertinent queries must have been sufficiently kind; Mrs. Fields at any rate wrote that Miss Jewett and Henry James were "very much at home together after this."

James had ordered a carriage, and he took his two visitors to Winchelsea where he showed them the ancient village and Ellen Terry's cottage. The memorable day—memorable both for the visitors and Henry James—ended with their going to Hastings, where they drank tea and consumed a quantity of buns. After that they took their respective trains, the ladies back to London, the novelist back to Rye.

IV

Aside from his hospitality much of the novelist's time was given over to exploring the region; there were long leisurely spins on his bicycle and a slow and deliberate "living into" the new-found Arcadia. He would go to Winchelsea, the decayed sister port, and study the view of Rye in the distance—the crowned hill, of which he now had such complete possession. Was there a touch of Mont St. Michel in the aspect of the Sussex town—the little churched hilltop, rising from the lonely marshes, the open gates, the walls, the towers? James made such a comparison, but his thoughts ran rather on the Robert Louis Stevenson aspect of the place—the contraband running from the Continent and the yards where once the King's ships had been built out of solid Sussex oak, until iron began to be used. The shipyard had declined, as had the town itself, from its ancient commerce. But there were always three or four fishing boats on the ways and some ship in the shrunken harbor. James liked to go to pubs and talk to the sailors; to wander on his bicycle to every nook and cranny. He reread Thackeray's unfinished *Denis Duval*, which was set in this region, and day-dreamed of Thackeray, ensconced in his garden room, writing this novel. In an article on Rye and Winchelsea, written a couple of years later, when James had thoroughly made himself a part of the place, he indulged in this Thackerayan fancy. He spoke of

the open, sunny terrace of a dear little old garden—a garden brown-walled, red-walled, rose-covered on its other sides, divided by the width of a quiet street of grass-grown cobbles from the house of its master, and possessed of a little old glass-fronted, panelled pavilion which I hold to be the special spot in the world where Thackeray might most fitly have figured out his story. There is not much room in the pavilion, but there is room for the hard-pressed table and the tilted chair—there is room for a novelist and his friends. The panels have a queer paint and a venerable slant; the small chimney-place is at your back; the south window is perfect, the privacy bright and open.

He was reminded he said of some "far-away foolish fiction, absorbed in extreme youth," which made this place "an echo of an old premonition." "I seem to myself to have lain on the grass somewhere, as a boy, poring over an English novel of the period, presumably quite bad,—for they were pretty bad then too,—and losing myself in the idea of just such another scene as this." Fiction had a way—in the existence of Henry James—of becoming life. But the fiction, he observed, "couldn't have been so good as this." James could see other little gardens, other odds and ends of crooked brown wall and supported terrace, and the view from the Rye cliff, with the river below, the tide that came and went, the mile or more of the old salt flats and the sea at the near horizon where during these golden summer days he caught in the depth of blue a scattered gleam of sails.

A SUMMER EMBASSY

HENRY JAMES'S INSTALLATION IN LAMB HOUSE WAS ACCOMPANIED by the far-away alarums of the Spanish-American War. The *Maine* blew up in Havana harbor in February 1898; and the press headlines, the dispatches from the United States, and finally the outbreak of hostilities in April, were a heavy burden to the novelist for whom any conflict evoked memories of the Civil War. He carried with him always those old feelings "buried under all the accumulated other emotions and years." To his brother he wrote, "I see nothing but the madness, the passions, the hideous clumsiness of rage." He blamed the newspapers "for the horrible way in which they envenomise all dangers and reverberate all lies." It was true that the Hearst newspapers had been responsible for much of the war hysteria in America.

James's letters however showed less involvement now than in

the Venezuela dispute two years earlier. On that occasion his double allegiance had been in conflict. The new hostilities, largely naval, touched his ingrained pacifism; and from the outset he reflected fears that America's seaward cities might come under Spanish shells. Spain had been for a long time, Henry remarked, "a picturesque and harmless member of the European family," and England could be counted upon to stay out of the fight. James said he was averting his eyes from the press—"one must save one's life if one can." He was "mainly glad Harvard College isn't—nor Irving street—the thing nearest Boston Bay."

On the day after the United States issued its call for volunteers, James wrote to his old friend, Frances Morse, in Boston that he felt "in a vile unrest . . . wretchedly nervous and overdarkened." Once again he was distant from his country; "and besides, it's too late—and one must swallow one's discriminations." Less of a public figure than his brother or Howells, he watched the war without declaring himself; but then he always avoided talking to reporters. He received at this moment however a letter from Howells pronouncing the war "the most stupid and causeless that was ever imagined by a kindly and sensible nation." Howells added, referring to the drama of Dreyfus in France, "If there could be anything worse than the Zola trial, it would be our behavior to Spain."

I

It turned out that James was to be extremely well briefed on this war that, in a matter of weeks, turned the United States into a world power—in the sense that its frontiers were suddenly thrust beyond the seas. The defeat of the Spanish navy at Manila, the blockade and destruction of the Spanish ships, the surrender of the Philippines, the ultimate cession of Puerto Rico, the freeing of Cuba, the annexation of Hawaii—all this James learned not only through the newspapers but from his friends at the American Embassy in London—the Ambassador himself, John Hay, and the

First Secretary Henry White. He had known both for many years.

In the autumn of 1897, the Ambassador had invited James to join him and Henry Adams in a trip up the Nile. James, whose journeyings had always been confined to the European continent, was sorely tempted. But Lamb House beckoned; and he was guarding his finances. "I can't go—I *can't*." James wrote to Hay; it was, he said, "perversely *impossible*." As it was, Hay was soon recalled to London from Egypt because of the impending war. And shortly after James installed himself in Lamb House he learned that the Hays, Henry Adams, Senator Don Cameron and his wife Elizabeth—the woman to whom Adams had been most closely attached in recent years—had taken the large Elizabethan manor house of Surrenden Dering, in Kent. It was but a dozen miles from Ashford, the change-point for Rye. Thus a group of Americans—for the house was filled with Adams nieces and Hay children and transient relatives and friends—were within easy distance of Lamb House. Surrenden Dering, set in its large park, amusedly described by Adams as "about the size of Versailles," was the "summer Embassy." James could find, at any time, authoritative reports and the diplomatic background for the American history being written overseas. "I have had," he wrote, "Henry Adams spending the summer not very far off—in the wonderful old country house of Surrenden Dering, which he has been occupying in the delightful way made possible by the possession of Shekels, in conjunction with the Don Camerons." James could not visit frequently; his own house was filled; but he did go for a short stay on a couple of occasions.

He found the summer establishment interesting in many ways, for, as Adams's biographer remarks, "behind the feudal scale of hospitality" there went on the work of diplomacy "as the secretaries hurried back and forth to London." Perhaps even more than in the echoes of Washington within the greenery of Kent, James was interested in the human relations in this large house on the vast estate. He had been fascinated for some time by the way in which Adams had become a part of Elizabeth Cameron's large entourage. "Everyone is doing—to my vision—all over the place—such extraordinary things that one's faculty of wonder and envy begins at last rather to cease to vibrate," he wrote to a friend in Boston. There were signs that his faculty of wonder (like Maisie's) and his novelist's curiosity were vibrating as strongly as those of his narrator in *The Sacred Fount*, whom he would place two years later on as peopled an estate as Surrenden Dering. Concerning Adams and Mrs. Cameron James remarked that he "envied him as much as was permitted by my feeling that the affair was only what I should *once* have found maddeningly romantic." He had met Mrs. Cameron on other occasions; she was, he found, "hard"—considering her "prettiness, grace and cleverness." The word "clever" in James's lexicon was not always a compliment. Mrs. Cameron was indeed a skilful managerial woman—a Mrs. Touchett or a Mrs. Gereth. Adams's niece, Abigail, has testified that at the manor house that summer Mrs. Cameron "was not only the hostess for this big and complicated caravanserai, but she ran it as well, and I doubt if many details escaped her eagle eye." She was "the most socially competent person that I have ever met," the niece, writing in her old age, remembered—a woman who could "tackle any situation and appear to enjoy it." In his notebooks James wrote that he was "somehow haunted with the *American* family, represented to me by Mrs. Cameron," but set this aside as demanding "a large, comprehensive picture." He did not elaborate. The allusion would seem to have been to Mrs. Cameron's ability to be a senator's wife, keep tight control of his busy home and his social life in Washington, and at the same time be available as a social resource and comfort to the widowed Adams. James was to say, in a letter to Henrietta Reubell, two or three years later, in the vein of *The Sacred Fount*, that Mrs. Cameron had "sucked the lifeblood of poor Henry Adams and made him more 'snappish' than nature intended." He added that "it's one of the longest and oddest American *liaisons* I've ever

known. Women have been hanged for less—and yet men have
been too, I judge, rewarded with more."

11

It was at Surrenden Dering that John Hay that August received
the cable from President McKinley summoning him to Washington to be Secretary of State. James had known the diplomat and
writer—Hay had long ago won a popular reputation with his *Pike
County Ballads*—for many years. It was John Hay's good offices
which had obtained for Henry the Paris correspondence of the
Tribune in 1875. And they had come to know each other well
during a certain period in the 1880's when Hay and Clarence
King, the geologist, were in Paris at the Grand Hôtel. Henry
found them there—the boon companions of Henry Adams—and
had fallen into breakfasting with them and roaming the boule-
vards. Clarence King was a well-known "charmer," a conversation-
alist of great spontaneity, and he quite eclipsed in interest the
meticulous and politic Hay. Hay had in him something of the
distance of a politician and statesman; and Henry had his kind of
"distance" as well. Thus their relations were framed within a
double distance; they were on the whole pleasant and warm, yet
remained always formal. "He cares nothing for me," Hay remarked of Henry James. "I have always known it, and it came out
again, plainly, in Paris. But I care a great deal for him." Hay
continued throughout his lifetime to testify to this. Henry on his
side remained a loyal and distantly admiring friend, although he
developed considerable tenderness for the statesman at the moment of Miss Woolson's death, Hay having happened to be in
Rome at the time and performing all the offices of friendship for
James at her funeral. Otherwise, a kind of top-hatted ceremonious-
ness prevailed between them. How highly Henry thought of Hay
may be attested however by the fact that he journeyed to South-
ampton to greet him on his arrival as American Ambassador to
England. Hay's writing activities were, from James's high profes-

sional point of view, simply gentlemanly ventures into literature. He read Hay's novel *The Bread-Winners* and identified the author in spite of its anonymity. It had, Henry told his sister, much "crude force" and imitated the best in American fiction—the best being, he wryly remarked to her, "Howells and me." He also read Hay and Nicolay's life of Lincoln, "a wonderful gallery of pictures of the vast democratic American life," and called it an "epic" biography. For Hay, the pillar of Republicanism, the one-time secretary of Lincoln, the ambassador and Secretary of State, James had all the respect of an individual outside of politics who admires probity and distinction in public life. "I shall never, never, my dear Hay," he wrote to him once, "forget that you are the person in the world who has said to me the three or four things about my lucubrations that have most uplifted me—and them."

He came to Surrenden one September day to salute his honored friend before his departure for Washington. He was to remember "with the vision not denied me, thank God, of the drama of life" —the way in which Hay "paused before the plunge, on the great high Surrenden terrace"; and he wondered often if Hay had remembered that moment—the soft September day, the baronial quiet of the place, the general air of enchantment—as well as the "lovely women and distinguished men just respectfully hanging on to your coat-tails."

III

Hay, King and Adams were a kind of private Washington trium-virate, and their friendship, watched from a distance by James, would be memorialized by Adams himself in later years. Hay was the party-office holder and man of political action that the ironical and worldly-wise Adams could not allow himself to be. Clarence King, a man of the out-of-doors who could accept the irrational and primitive forces within himself, represented that part of Adams which was most nearly submerged in his New England rigidity. These two men—Hay and King—had become more than

Adams's close companions. In the Conradian sense, it might be said they had been his "secret sharers." They helped complete a life that Adams felt to be incomplete; for Hay and King, each in his own way, acted out what Adams sometimes scarcely allowed himself to feel. The son of Quincy, the habitué of Washington, who felt himself swaddled in his puritan heritage—and damned by it—could experience vicariously King's love for "archaic races" (this was Adams's way of putting it), that is his sympathy with the Negro and the Indian, and his corresponding dislike of their enemies.

Hay was simply "the good Hay," in James's letters; but Clarence King he had watched with the eyes of a story-teller and a lover of character. He found him "charming, but a queer, incomplete, unsatisfactory creature." One day King would be "buying old silk tapestries or the petticoats of Madame de Pompadour to cover New York chairs," or "selling silver mines to the Banque de Paris or philandering with Ferdinand de Rothschild, who appears to be unable to live without him." Then suddenly he would ignore Rothschild and dine "with publicans, barmaids and other sinners." James saw these paradoxes from his Olympus. "The most delightful man in the world, Clarence King!" he said, yet he was also "slippery and elusive, and as unmanageable as he is delightful."

King on his side read James with a closeness that the novelist would have appreciated and wrote to Hay:

How clever Harry James's London is, but how Jacobean. Whenever he describes the periphery, as anywhere over one cab-fare from his dear Piccadilly, there is a nervous, almost nostalgic, cutting and running for the better quarters of the town. Even when talking of Blackwell or Hampstead, you feel that he looks a little askance, that he wants to go home; and you positively know that before going into these gruesome and out-of-the-way parts of the town, he gathers up a few unmistakeably good invitations and buttons them in his inner pocket, so that there should be no mistaking the social position of his corpse if violence befell him.

King had apparently been reading *The Princess Casamassima*, and perhaps remembering some of his visits with James to the then more "unsavory" sections of London, though his remark about Hampstead was obviously a joke. He expressed admiration however for James's ability to create "such airy webs" and drape them over the objective facts of life," so that the dew shall sparkle on them and the amusing little insects glitter and tangle in them, like the fabrics of the spiders. It is a charming gift. I wish I had a little of it. I'd give worlds to be able to spin one inch."

"He was in his way a fascinator," Henry said of King at the time of the latter's nervous breakdown, some years before his death. "It's miserable to think one may never again see him as he delightfully was. In truth I never thought there was no madness at all in his sanity—and feel indeed as if there may be some sanity in his madness."

IV

Surrenden Dering was a minor incident in the crowded life of Henry James that summer, although it evoked old memories and kept him in touch with America and Americans. Not least, he felt, for a moment, the current pulse of Washington. The war had been "a deep embarrassment of thought—of imagination. I have hated, I have almost loathed it." For some friends there was no qualification. "I detest the war," he said. When it was over, and America's frontiers were extended to the southeast, and westward, far into the Pacific, James shrank from the thought of "remote colonies run by bosses." At the same time—perhaps as a consequence of the rationalizations of diplomacy heard at Surrenden Dering—James began to take a more benign view of the matter. The extension of American power was perhaps a New World version of Britain's *imperium*; the British he felt had been good colonizers, and the cause of civilization had, on the whole, been advanced. This was the way in which he spoke, at any rate, to his British friends, combining a gracious attitude toward his host-country with the wish to put his own nation in the best light possible. He wanted, however, he said, "to curl up more closely in this little old-world corner, where I can successfully beg such questions. They become a spectacle merely." His probing intelligence nevertheless tugged at the questions continually, and much as he hated the newspapers he read them closely, with critical curiosity.

He put the matter in another way to his nephew Harry, some months later when he had had time to absorb the shocks of the war and the ramifications of the peace. "To live in England," he explained, "is, inevitably, to feel the 'Imperial' question, in a different way and take it at a different angle from what one might, with the same mind even, do in America. Expansion," he said, "has so made the English what they are—for good or for ill, but on the whole for good—that one doesn't quite feel one's way to say for one's country 'No—I'll have *none* of it!' It has educated the English. Will it only demoralise *us?*"

Then he had another thought. "I suppose the answer to that is that we can get at home a bigger education than they—in short as big a one as we require." After offering these suggestive thoughts, he told his nephew he thanked God he had "no *opinions*—not even on the Dreyfus case." He was he said more and more aware of things "as a more or less mad panorama, phantasmagoria and dime museum." The truth was he did have opinions—not least on the Dreyfus case.

BROTHER JONATHAN

IN LONDON THAT SPRING, BEFORE HE HAD MOVED TO LAMB HOUSE, Henry James had reached a moment of intense weariness. The war was a burden to him; every morning there was the same little mountain of newspapers, the casual bundles of proof, journals, books from publishers, from friends, from booksellers, the tide of the world's words sweeping into De Vere Gardens and overwhelming him. What could any creature want of so much print? He was to ask the question, and to speak disconsolately of "the irrelevant, destructive, brutalizing" side of life, in a fantasy called "The Great Good Place." The tale was a pre-vision of Lamb House. "The Turn of the Screw" had recorded old lingering fears of childhood when the occupancy of Lamb House was in prospect; but once these fears had been expressed, once the terror had been siphoned off, James could dream peacefully and pleasantly, and the "place" he imagined was more than a private retreat. In his story (which was to wait two years for publication—was to appear indeed on the eve of another, a new, century) the good and great place is a curious mixture of monastery, hotel, club, country house, an ideal cushioned silent refuge, "some great abode, of an Order, some mild Monte Cassino, some Grand Chartreuse" accessible to the Protestant as a "retreat" yet not a retreat of the religious sort: a place of material simplification.

The interest of the story, on its biographical side, is not only in its obvious wish for some surcease from the worldly pressure Henry James was experiencing, but his wish for an exclusive man's world, a monastic Order, a sheltering brotherhood. The tale has in it distinct homo-erotic overtones. The young admiring acolyte who comes to the great writer, George Dane, sits beside him, puts a hand on his knee, and gives him at once a "feeling of delicious ease." At the mysterious "place" the "dream-sweetness" experienced by the harried writer resides in the absence of all demands upon him and in the discreet quiet—a place of "slow receding footsteps" where "slow sweet bells" are heard in the distance and the Brothers compose "a landscape of quiet figures." Above all there is the blessing of anonymity. George Dane can exist "without the complication of an identity." He is freed from being a *persona* in the world; the inner life can wake up again. He can repossess his soul.

This was a very old fantasy of Henry James's. In *Roderick Hudson* of 1875 he had depicted a similar place, near Fiesole, where Rowland Mallet finds peace within a cool cloister, and lays his hand on the arm of a Brother to whom he speaks of the temptations of the devil. James had always been fascinated by the moment in Hawthorne's *Marble Faun* when Hilda, the little American dove-girl in Rome, filled with the horror of the crime she has accidentally witnessed, goes to confession—though a Protestant—to ease herself of her burden. In a monastery the world's burdens drop away; this had indeed been the theme of the ill-fated *Guy Domville,* and we may capture some touch of James's "associational magic" in noting that the names George Dane and Guy Domville have the same initials. The craving for a great good place and the touch of a Brother's hand had existed for years. There is however one other element in this dream-fantasy. It resides in George Dane's identifying himself with the young man who has come to his flat and who, while Dane sleeps, gets rid of the newspapers and proofs, and answers the letters and telegrams. The great good place is also the place of youth. James's fantasy expresses the wish to be young again, to be the younger brother that he had once been. He had long ago embodied this fancy in his little tale of Browning, about "The Private Life," in which the poet of the drawing room carries his worldly burdens while his liberated other self, in the quiet of the study, writes his immortal verse.

The language of the passage in *Roderick Hudson* describing

Rowland's visit to the monastery, written almost twenty-five years before, is close to that of "The Great Good Place." The feelings are exactly the same. In James's secular religion of beauty "the great good place" is also "the great want met"—and the want is not so much "the putting off of one's self" as in a religious retreat; it is "the getting it back—if one has a self worth sixpence."

I

He was getting it back at Lamb House. The autumn that year was dry and warm and Rye seemed even more beautiful—more *nuancé*, as he said—than in the summer. He awoke on clear days "no longer with the London blackness and foulness, the curtain of fog and smoke that one has each morning muscularly to lift and fasten back; but with the pleasant sunny garden outlook, the grass all haunted with starlings and chaffinches." The war, now that it was over, seemed merely to have flashed by; whatever dreadful marks it had left were beyond his reach; he felt, more than ever, that he could stay close to his little plot of land, cultivate his little garden, and he watched his gardener plant bulbs and seedlings—hyacinths, tulips, crocuses—for the winter's shelter, with the promise they held for the spring. He relished the mellow fruit of autumn from his south wall. The novelist decided to linger in Rye until Christmas. De Vere Gardens—London—could wait. Presently great gales blew and his garden shook off "in each gust, some article of clothing." To Francis Boott he wrote, "I like this place —I like my little old house and little old garden. . . . It blows, today,—it blew all last night—great guns; and I hear them magnificently boom in my old chimneys. But my little house stands firm and gives me most refreshing assurance of the thickness of its walls and the depth of its foundations. After so many years of London flats and other fearsome fragilities, I feel quite housed in a feudal fortress."

The summer's end had brought an end to the rush of visitors; the bump of the luggage had ceased. He had finished writing "In the Cage" shortly after settling in Rye and now, undisturbed, he worked steadily at the *Harper's* serial, *The Awkward Age*. Jonathan Sturges came to stay with him for a few days in the middle of October and remained for two months. He was not as the other visitors; he made no inroads on James's working hours—in his crippled state he was accustomed to quiet; and he was excellent company at other hours of the day. "Brother Jonathan," James had called him when he had met him eight years before; this was an evocation not so much of the old Roundhead or Puritan name (Sturges was not from New England but from New York); the illusion was rather to the early image—particularly the stage image—of the stock American, the predecessor of the traditional "uncle Sam." "Little Brother Jonathan has his share of the national genius," James had written to Edmund Gosse, and this quality, plus his bright eyes, his mordant wit, his fund of gossip, made him always a delightful companion. Since his visit to James at Torquay, three years before, Sturges had been through a long illness. He was well now, that is as well as he would ever be. He evoked in James, as always, the tender feelings the novelist had shown to his invalid sister when she lived in London; like Alice James, Jonathan Sturges had a sharp tongue, which was why James also called him "the little demon." "Do you remember young Jonathan Sturges?" he asked Henrietta Reubell. "He is full of talk and intelligence, and of the absence of prejudice, and is saturated with London, and with all sorts of contrasted elements of it, to which he has given himself up. Handicapped, crippled, invalidical, he has yet made his way there in a wondrous fashion, and knows nine thousand people, of most of whom *I've* never heard. So he's amusing, and to him (as I'm very fond of him), I make sacrifices. But they *are* sacrifices."

They were, insofar as James gave up total solitude, though he liked that less than he was ready to admit. He got in exchange this "mine of conversation and a little blaze of intelligence." Having forsaken London, he had a small incarnation of London beside

him. There was something more, however, than the amusing asper
ities and touching physical helplessness of the younger man
(Sturges was thirty-four). He was literary, he was sentient; he
observed; he was a civilized presence. Among the papers of James'
journalist friend in Paris, Morton Fullerton, there is preserved a
fragment of a letter written by Sturges on Lamb House stationery.
It suggests a little the qualities in the younger man which made
him sympathetic to James. Sturges wrote to Fullerton,

I wish I could give you a picture of this little, red, pointed, almost
medieval town with its sea-wall and its Norman relic of Ypres
Castle which they call here 'Wipers'—perched on a hill in the
midst of the grey-green, sand coloured waste of Romney Marsh, an
Anglo-Saxon Mont St. Michel, long deserted by the sea yet with
the colour and scent of the sea in its quiet brown streets, a brown
of the tone of fishermen's sails and nets. The blue-jerseyed retired
fishermen themselves are to be found at any hour, on the deserted
bastion of Ypres Castle happily armed against the French invasion
a hundred years ago. They address one another with a classical
"what Ho!" which seems almost too beautiful to be true, and
through brass telescopes they study the sails upon the distant
Channel. In southwesterly gales one hears the roar and sees the
long white raselier * of the surf. The sheep huddle together upon
the marsh and the fishing boats huddle with bare poles in The
Robber in Rye "Harbor," a hamlet like a Dutch picture against
the wild grey sky—three miles away.

The old house itself is early Georgian, an impression of red brick
and white marble, oak-panelled rooms and brass knockers. There
is a "garden-house" in the garden and a quantity of beautiful old
pink wall. And H.J. . . .

At this point the fragment ends and we are deprived of Sturges's
picture of Henry James in his rural setting. There is abundant

. . . .
* Apparently a word coined by Sturges to suggest the "shave-and-lather" effect
of the surf. There is no such word in the French dictionaries.

eference to Sturges, however, in James's correspondence, for he
dmired the crippled young man's stoicism—"he is only a little
ody-blighted intelligence—a little frustrate universal curiosity—
nd a little pathetic Jack-the-Giant Killer's soul." In "The Great
Good Place" James had dreamed of being cared for in a company
f Brothers. At Lamb House he cared for Brother Jonathan; and
t was as if he were being cared for himself. For he had reached
hat time of life when he was turning to younger men to capture
ome image in them of his own youth.

II

f we are deprived of Jonathan Sturges's glimpse of Henry James
t middle age in his rural retreat, we have another picture, set
lown a year later by an assiduous diarist, a schoolmasterly man
who lived with his pen in his hand in a constant state of self-com-
nunion. This was Arthur Christopher Benson, the second son of
he Archbishop of Canterbury. Benson lived on to memorialize
ames on various occasions; and this has suggested a closer friend-
hip than actually existed. The younger man sent his early verses
o James, and the novelist replied in large pleasing phrases that
evertheless showed he found them wanting: they lacked form,
hey were false poems, however much they seemed to render
eeling. Benson was born in a school, his father was a schoolmaster
nd later an archbishop, and his own career was divided between
Eton and Cambridge. He was a writer of familiar essays; they
ame out in such quantity and sold so well that someone said of
im (and of his brothers) that the Bensons wrote as easily as they
breathed—adding however that it was uncomfortable to have
hem breathing down one's neck all the time. A. C. Benson was a
nelancholy man and, like certain Victorians, a great mountaineer:
ne was much given to his books and his thoughts. In later years he
had long fits of depression. James responded to his melancholy; he
had a certain affection for him, but one gets the feeling of a cool
nd courteous distance between them; the novelist is mild, and

friendly yet aloof. There was something dry and commonplace in Benson to which James could not respond; and yet he seems also to have had a feeling of pity for him and his circumscribed academic-churchly world.

A. C. Benson came to spend a night at Lamb House at the beginning of 1900, after receiving a warm invitation—"I want immensely to hear the history of your triumphant Book and to assure you of my participation in your labour, your rest and your success. The way you heirs of all the ages knock off these things! But I want the inside view—I want indeed, from you, many things." The visit occurred on January 17, and Benson felt impelled to "dip my pen in rainbow hues—or rather let me be exact, finished, delicate, to describe the charm of this place." There followed in his diary a brief picture of Rye and of Lamb House, and then the picture of its master. James had met him at the station, as was his custom, but "looking somewhat cold, tired and old." He was as always affectionate in his greeting; he patted the younger man on the shoulder, and was "really welcoming, with abundance of *petits soins*." They dined simply at 7:30 with many apologies from the host about the fare. "He was full of talk, though he looked weary, often passing his hand over his eyes; but he refined and defined, was intricate, magniloquent, rhetorical, humorous, not so much like a talker, but like a writer repeating his technical processes aloud—like a savant working out a problem." They gossiped; and James talked also "with hatred of business and the monetary side of art. He evidently thinks that art is nearly dead among English writers—no criticism, no instinct for what is good."

Benson's diary records some of James's talk. They got on to the subject of Mrs. Oliphant:

I had not read a *line* that the poor woman had written for *years*—not for years; and when she died, Henley—do you know him, the rude, boisterous, windy, headstrong Henley?—Henley, as I say, said to me "Have you read *Kirsteen?*" I replied that as a matter of fact, no—h'm—I had not read it. Henley said, "That you should have any pretensions to interest in literature and should dare to say that you have not read *Kirsteen!*" I took my bludgeoning patiently and humbly, my dear Arthur—went back and read it, and was at once confirmed, after twenty pages, in my belief— I laboured through the book—that the poor soul had a simply *feminine* conception of literature: such slipshod, imperfect, halting, faltering, peeping, down-at-heel work—buffeting along like a ragged creature in a high wind, and just struggling to the goal, and falling in a quivering mass of faintness and fatuity. Yes, no doubt she was a gallant woman—though with no species of wisdom—but an artist, an artist—!

James held up his hands "and stared woefully" at Benson.

The tone of the novelist and the orotund phrasing is in this passage set down by Benson shortly after hearing it. The Johnsonian James was beginning to emerge; the figure who would be called Master by the younger men.

"Henry James works hard," Benson wrote after his visit.

He establishes me in a little high-walled white parlour, very comfortable, but is full of fear that I am unhappy. He comes in, pokes the fire, presses a cigarette on me, puts his hand on my shoulder, looks inquiringly at me, and hurries away. His eyes are *piercing*. To see him, when I came down to breakfast this morning, in a kind of Holbein square cap of velvet and black velvet coat, scattering bread on the frozen lawn to the birds was delightful. . . . We lunched together with his secretary, a young Scot. H.J. ate little, rolled his eyes, waited on us, walked about, talked—finally hurried me off for a stroll before my train. All his instincts are of a kind that makes me feel vulgar—his consideration, his hospitality, care of arrangements, thoughtfulness. . . . He seemed to know everyone to speak to—an elderly clergyman in a pony-carriage, a young man riding. Three nice-looking girls met us, two of fourteen and fifteen, and a little maid of seven or eight, who threw herself upon H.J. with cooing noises of delight and kissed him repeatedly and effusively, the dogs also bounding up to him. He introduced me

with great gravity. . . . We got to the station; he said an affectionate farewell, pressing me to come again; I went away refreshed,
stimulated, sobered, and journeyed under a dark and stormy sky to
the dreary and loathsome town of Hastings.

I I I

The story called "In the Cage" which James published as a
volume-size tale in the autumn of 1898 is of a piece as we have
seen with his immediate feeling of being cut off from London.
The profound change in his mode of existence, his sense at times
of being confined and "out of things," seems to have contributed
at this moment to his imagining a young girl, handling the brief
and cryptic telegrams of the outer world, counting the words and
reckoning the fees. She is curious and sufficiently alert to take in
the meanings of the messages; they tell her of certain scandals.
James gives the girl no name. Like the governess in "The Turn of
the Screw" she is identified by her thoughts and her conversations
with a lady of some social pretension who works in the rich houses
as an arranger of flowers. We know the girl only as a troubled
observer, using her inductive and deductive capacities to satisfy an
insatiable curiosity about her environment. The cage-girl and the
governess both feel shut out—or shut in—as James in Rye now felt
shut out from the great world, or as he had pictured Hyacinth
Robinson long before in *The Princess Casamassima*, wondering
what went on behind the impressive closed doors of noble man-
sions in London. The cage-girl's notions of the world are derived
in part from romantic novels; the telegrams handed in through the
high aperture of her cage become a part of the fictional furnishings of her mind. Where the governess remains locked in her own
imaginings and lives with phantoms which she tries to explain to
the readers of her tale, the cage-girl constantly returns to reality—
to her fellow-employees in the grocery shop, to her young man,
Mr. Mudge, and to Mr. Buckton, the manager, in a setting of
hams and cheeses, dried fish and paraffin. She is always aware of

her poverty, her station in life, and the contrast between this and the world's splendours about which she is so touchingly curious and with which she feels she must make her peace. The moment of tension is reached in the story when she rescues from some undefined imbroglio a dashing Captain Everard, by remembering a telegram he has sent. Her dream of romance is quickly ended however and she discovers the world's indifference when "without a look, without a word of thanks, without time for anything or anybody" Everard strides out of the grocery shop, as if young telegraph girls were expected always to bail out embroiled young gentlemen. She comes down to earth from her fantasies with a thump. Reality has quickly reasserted itself. Society may be blind to people of her station—but she sees, and without the distortions that complicated the life of the governess.

By many delicate and subtle touches, "In the Cage" keeps us within the girl's limited range of vision (as well as the vision of her creator) and we are enabled to accompany her in her practice, in a modest and simplified form, of the deductive methods celebrated in Sherlock Holmes. She is a detective of her own confined soul; she must make the best of her world. "In the Cage" shows James thus going about the business of seeing what he can do with his own alienation from Mayfair. That he should assume the disguise of an adolescent girl is of a piece with his creation of his stories of little girls; they had served their purpose in the earlier stages of his progress from his hurt and bewilderment in the theatre through the madnesses and terrors of his soul. Now in the stages of his recovery, he had reached the moment when he needed no longer to take refuge within the bright-eyed world of Maisie; he could substitute the cogitations of a young adult. But like the girl he feels abandoned—almost as if London had left him rather than he London—and like Captain Everard without so much as a "thank you." If he no longer had his London, he at any rate had his little plot of ground in Rye, as the telegraphist, once she leaves her cage, will have her modest home with Mr. Mudge and be the humble wife of a tradesman. James had had, after all, his "position in society," had it for a quarter of a century; indeed he still had it. But society had turned out to be full of pitfalls and deceptions. If "In the Cage" shows us an adolescent yearning for knowledge of this society, *The Awkward Age*, which James now wrote, showed an adolescent caught up in its treacheries. In a certain sense this novel seems to have been James's way of telling himself that he was well out of London and its corrupt society: for *The Awkward Age* was to be his strongest indictment of England's upper-middle class, its arrogant sense of privilege, and its erosion of human values. With the writing of this novel, the most complex of his fictional experiments following *Guy Domville*, James was on the verge of becoming his old self again. He seemed ready to shed the protective disguises of girlhood he had assumed and to take his own shape in his fiction—that of the elderly and fastidious observer of his world, the grave figure described by the melancholy Arthur Benson.

THE AWKWARD AGE

I

"THE TURN OF THE SCREW" HAD HAD ITS INITIAL IMPULSE IN Henry James's anxieties over his impending retirement to the country; "In the Cage" reflected his sense of actual divorce from London—from that "London life" which he had lived with such

vigor and delight for a quarter of a century. *The Awkward Age,* the
long and brilliant novel which he now wrote, between September
and December 1898, was a serious inquiry into the society he had
abandoned. The work suggests that James, in this crisis of his
middle age, was writing not only about the "awkward age" of the
female young, but about the awkwardness of aging. His elderly
character is named as if he were invoking the rejected metropolis
—Mr. Longdon. He gave him his own age, fifty-five, the age at
which he was writing the novel. Mr. Longdon has lived for a very
long time in the country, in Suffolk. His house is square and
red-roofed and be-gardened and russet-walled, like Lamb House in
Sussex; indeed the frontispiece to the novel, in the New York
Edition, offers us a picture of the entrance to Lamb House. It is
captioned "Mr. Longdon's." At the beginning of *The Awkward
Age,* Mr. Longdon—in London—accompanies a younger man,
Gustavus Vanderbank, to his rooms during a night of downpour.
There they discuss at great length the drawing room they have just
quitted. It is like the rising of a curtain on a play. Mr. Longdon
seems to be the novelist's idealized self. James still wore his beard;
his counterpart is clean-shaven. James was stocky and thick. Longdon is slight and delicate. James was bald; Longdon is silver-
haired. But if he thus seems to be the image of what James would
have liked to see in the mirror, he talks brilliantly, as James talked,
of London and its *mœurs;* and he reminds his thirty-four-year-old
companion that he is "an old boy, who remembers the mothers."

Mr. Longdon's descent upon London is like that of an ancient
traveller visiting a remote civilization. He compares himself indeed
to "a stranger at an Eastern court, comically helpless without his
interpreter." He cross-examines Vanderbank closely about the life
of the Brookenhams in their expensive Buckingham Crescent flat.
Their drawing room is extremely articulate but Mr. Longdon has
been "rather frightened." Vanderbank, a heavy fashion-plate, senses that. "We're cold and sarcastic and cynical," he says, "without
the soft human spot." The novel becomes the story of the elderly

man's attempt to discover a "human spot" for the young Nanda (Fernanda) Brookenham, a charming adolescent who mingles knowingly with her elders and hears outrageous things in her mother's entourage.

Decidedly Henry James was writing as if he felt "out of it"—of the London scene. And "what's London life?" Vanderbank asks point blank. He provides the answer: "It's tit for tat!" Everything has its price. "Ah, but what becomes of friendship?" Mr. Longdon inquires "earnestly and pleadingly"—we might say almost ruefully. There is a poignant suggestion of isolation and loneliness in the question. It was as if, after his long inner struggle with the demons of "success" and neglect, of feeling himself "unwanted" and cast aside, James had to start all over again. Having once conquered London, and learned it intimately, he must now re-explore it from a new distance. He sees now a society hard-rimmed and cruel, an aristocracy in *déchéance* savage in its civilization—"through its own want of imagination, of nobleness, of delicacy, of the exquisite." He was aware that "everything is allowed to a closed caste persuaded of its superiority"; but there has been "a great modern collapse of all the forms"; and without form society—life—was void and chaos. And then, had he really learned to know "society"?—the British aristocracy? Had he really grasped from his novelist-cage what went on in the gilded salons? Behind the façade of bright and brittle talk he could now discern intricate human relations, meetings, partings. One couldn't be quite certain who was sleeping with whom. In the old days one didn't ask such questions. Mr. Longdon's curiosity about what Nanda "knows" is but an enlargement of James's inquiry into what Maisie "knew." It is but one more stage in the curiosity of the governess, the cage-girl—or Henry James's own bewilderment and bachelor innocence—that ingrained Adamic bliss bestowed on him by his unworldly father.

James knew well that somewhere, in some extra-human zone of being, there was evil. He had never been as innocent as Emerson in that respect. But he had lived in a kind of luminous sexless and unphysical world—at least until his descent into the theatre. That had been the beginning of change. He had become aware by degrees that women in life as well as in fiction were not immaculate; they were organisms, possessors of temperament and passion who like Miss Robins could serve him cocoa in her rooms amid a smell of powder and perfume and greasepaint, and talk about the men who fell in love with her. He had watched this calculating actress, in the world of fakery and illusion—so intelligent about the stage and about Ibsen, so interesting a sexual object—use poise and appearance to impress and advance herself, in her struggle for existence and fame. James's world of Daisies and Pandoras and Isabels had indeed vanished. In the wings of the theatre, in the dowdy dressing rooms, in the costly defeat he had suffered, a process of re-education had been going on. The young Henry James, for whom life had been codes and manners and observances, had encountered the fleshly in place of the verbal and the ethereal. He had witnessed the pettiness and egotism of struggle for place and for power. He who had learned to trust the truths of his fancy had by a long and painful process been learning certain truths of fact. Mr. Longdon, or the unnamed narrator of *The Sacred Fount*, or the curious New England "ambassador" Lambert Strether, would re-embody a new, still slightly bewildered, novelist who had once chided Maupassant for looking too much at the monkeys in the monkey-cage.

Perhaps Henry James had looked too much at the reflective side of man—and too often looked away from the monkeys? Edmund Wilson long ago remarked—was indeed the first critic to perceive —that in James's novels of "the death of childhood," and in his final large fictions, there was a kind of "subsidence" into himself. Now sex does appear—it becomes a kind of obsession—in a queer, left-handed puritanical way, as of a man who has never allowed himself to think about sexual intercourse save as something to be read about in lemon-colored French novels. "There are plenty of love affairs now and plenty of irregular relationships," wrote Mr. Wilson, "but there are always thick screens between them and us; illicit appetites, maleficent passions, now provide the chief interest, but they are invariably seen from a distance." The "distance" in the works of 1895–1900 is created in part by the limited vision of the little girls or the limited experience of the adolescents. There is another kind of distance in those works—the confusion of feeling in the author himself. He had dramatized, always, the loss of American innocence in its encounter with a corrupt and decadent Europe. Now, by the process of living, feeling, suffering, he seemed on the verge of losing his own safeguarded, almost unbelievable innocence. In his citadel of art he had remained one of the pure of mind.

II

We are à l'ombre des jeunes filles en fleur in Henry James's The Awkward Age, although the novelist is hardly telling us the same story as Proust. The jeunes filles of James's story are English and Italian; they are products of two distinct methods in education. The English girl Nanda has been treated, as we now say, "permissively." She has put up her hair and come down into the drawing room and been exposed to her mother's "fast" set. The Anglo-Italian girl Aggie has been brought up by a determined English duchess, her aunt, in the Continental manner: she has been treated like "a little ivory princess," hand-fed "the small sweet biscuit of unobjectionable knowledge," in anticipation of an early marriage. This is an engaging theme—it seems almost "quaint" in our time—in The Awkward Age. The era of "emphasized virginity" is no more; but what makes James's treatment of the subject highly contemporaneous is his grasp of the dilemmas of adolescence. Published in 1899, The Awkward Age would qualify as an outmoded Victorian novel were it not for James's vision of the essence of his dual subject—and the formidable technique he used to give it a frame.

The "frame" puzzled the early readers of the novel. In the manner of "Gyp," the French countess who wrote dialogue-novels in the 1880's and 1890's, James constructed his novel almost entirely out of drawing-room "talk," and set scenes. His dialogue book possesses thus the immediacy of a stage play. The reader tells himself that he reads the novel as he reads a play; he enjoys none of the usual privileges of fiction: little is told about the characters, save as they tell it themselves. The reader is asked to supply voices, inflections, gestures, the very things actors give to a script. *The Awkward Age* must be read with the inner ear to grasp its tone and idiom. This done, the characters come to life, move about in their scenes, endow the novel with its enveloping emotion. *The Awkward Age* is no more artificial than Oscar Wilde's comedies, and it is considerably more humane. But it would be more accurate to compare it with Molière—the high wit and the self-characterizations remind us of the French dramatist; also the personages and the materials are in his tradition: two young marriageable girls, two duennas, two eligible but difficult young men, and a strange assortment of society characters who circle about the protagonists. The story is dramatized, as James put it, in a series of "presented episodes." Each episode is a piece of the building—and it is we who build as we read. In this way James demonstrated, after his own miserable failure in the theatre, that a fine dramatic comedy could be placed within the novel form.

The risk James ran was that his series of "set" scenes would thwart the movement of the story. He must have felt this, for he gave to his Mr. Longdon a special function. He is the invented observer, initially intended as a puppet-string character, but also a chorus. He asks the right questions; he insists on the right answers; he bridges gaps created for the reader by James's strict dialogue method. He has however much more than a mere "structural" function. He comes alive as one of the "poor, sensitive gentlemen" for whom James had a predilection in his late works. Mr. Longdon and Nanda reveal two kinds of innocence, those of age and of youth; and both are engaged in voyages of discovery. Mr. Longdon rediscovers the London from which he has been long absent; he knew it in its Victorian prime, when Nanda's grandmother was alive, when society was fearfully respectable on the surface and all its corruptions were carefully concealed. Now the corruptions are in the open, embodied in fact in a civilized "system" of wit and urbanity which is the mainstay of Mrs. Brookenham's salon. Nanda's voyage of discovery is more painful. She has had to learn too early to struggle with alien "instincts and forebodings." And James recognizes that however much we may "free" the young, the buds within the budding grove must still be given time to burst into leaf. *The Awkward Age* is the story of Nanda's growing up. James may seem, at first, to approve of the Continental way of rearing young girls; yet he returns at the end to the truths of the Garden of Eden. Knowledge need not be dangerous, he seems to say to us, if men and women learn to face it with eyes unsealed, in full awareness of what is real and what is factitious in the world around them.

III

Once we are able to cope with its obsessive dialogue and its humorous gravity, we discover in *The Awkward Age* a kind of "theory of education" for the female young. James had indeed been offering such theories or opinions in his works since he created Daisy Miller or the *jeune fille* Pansy of *The Portrait of a Lady*. If he protested against the permissiveness in America's upbringing of its young, he also admired their spirit, their candor, their innocence. But what he now seems to be saying more clearly than before, though not without his old ambivalence, is that a corrupt society corrupts its young: that sentience and "awareness," carefully cultivated, constitute a greater safeguard than ignorance. Mrs. Brookenham's salon contains a queer assortment of characters: the complacent, the newly rich, the divorced—idle women, scheming mothers, questionable "affairs." Like Molière, James is the wise and objective moralist, but without falling for a moment into didacticism. Lord Petherton lives off Mitchett, the son of a bootmaker to royalty with a weak social position and vast wealth. Mitchy is one of James's characteristic weaklings. We have met him as Ralph Touchett, we will meet him in other forms in the later novels. Vanderbank, the hesitating, irresolute and handsome "heavy" of the novel, hesitates before Nanda as Winterbourne did before Daisy, two decades before; but he is at home with older women, with Nanda's mother, for instance. Mrs. Brookenham, born of the aristocracy, is married to a nonentity who owes his small government job to his wife's good connections. Their son has an offhand way of "borrowing" five-pound notes, or helping himself to money if it should be left in a desk drawer. Lady Fanny is on the verge of quitting her husband; Mr. Cashmore wants "Mrs. Brook" to "square" him with his wife so he can philander; and Mrs. Brook herself, in the end, is in competition with her daughter for Vanderbank whom Mr. Longdon, in desperation, tries to "buy" for Nanda by offering a handsome marriage settlement. Vanderbank isn't sure—above all whether Nanda, just becoming a young adult, still possesses the virginity of heart to go with that of her body.

Mrs. Brook is the great creation of the novel: disillusioned, ambiguous, arbitrary, she is beset by all the troubles of her world: her vapid, ineffectual husband, her daughter who loves her lover, her light-fingered son; even her cherished salon is foundering in the crisis between mother and daughter. In the midst of her tottering empire Mrs. Brook holds her head high, looks out at us with her "lovely silly eyes" and speaks with an absurd wit that is often deadly serious, and with a wry twist in her logic that steers her through her perilous situations. Mrs. Brook must place her daughter in life; and Nanda's exposure to the corrupt morals of the salon makes her unplaceable: her virginity has been "de-emphasized." She will have difficulty finding a husband. Moreover she loves Vanderbank. In the end Nanda leaves her mother's precious salon; and what remains with us when we try to visualize this civilized, corrupt world is the sadness of the young, the awkwardness of the aging.

We experience above all the touching predicament of Nanda, who between eighteen and twenty-one has been asked to be solemn beyond her years. She has had to acquire the wisdom of Eve in an Edenless Victorian world that seems bent on depriving her of all that she has learned to value—truth of feeling, truth of statement, truth to life. She is indeed pure in heart but her exposure to her mother's world makes her tough in mind. Very much like the less fortunate Maisie, she moves us by the candor of her innocence. And when her bold front dissolves in tears—as it must—we can experience her ultimate pain that life is not always as arrangeable as her room, or its furniture. Life itself indeed *is* the arranger. Like all of James's late heroes and heroines, Nanda has to arrive at self-awarenesses through a vision of the cold determining world with which she must make her peace. In the process of muddling through, she recognizes that her most important discovery has been herself. She will not therefore judge little Aggie harshly, when that Continentalized virgin runs wild the moment she is "safely" married. "Aggie's only trying to find out what sort of person she is," Nanda carefully explains to the attentive Mr. Longdon. "How can she ever have known? It was carefully, elaborately hidden from her—kept so obscure that she could make out nothing. She isn't now like *me*." Nanda *knows*. And she learns that one pays a price for knowledge. If she cannot have the younger man, Vanderbank, she will accept the protection of the elderly Mr. Longdon. We recognize that the relationship will be chaste; she will be a treasured virgin, a priestess at a bachelor's altar. He will minister to her mind and endow her with the eternal richness of the heart rather than the ephemeral torments of passion.

The aging moralist in 1898 thus ended his late novel almost as he had ended his first, *Watch and Ward*, almost thirty years before. In that fiction a female adolescent is reared by her guardian in the hope that he will ultimately be able to marry her. For the middle-aged Henry James such a consummation was not necessary. And it seems in *The Awkward Age* that in removing Nanda from her mother's drawing room, Mr. Longdon can now do what Henry James had done all his life—harbor within his house, the house of the novelist's inner world, the spirit of a young adult female, worldly-wise and curious, possessing a treasure of unassailable virginity and innocence and able to yield to the masculine active world-searching side of James an ever-fresh and exquisite vision of feminine youth and innocence. For this was the androgynous nature of the creator and the drama of his novels: innocence and worldliness, the paradisiacal America and the cruel and corrupt Europe—or in other variations, youthful ignorant America and wise and civilized Europe.

In no earlier novel had James called British society so to account. *The Awkward Age* records his complete disenchantment. He tells himself in effect that he is well out of London, well out of its lies and camouflage. A letter written at this moment to Paul Bourget expressed his deepest feelings about the endowed classes. He had, he says, "an inalienable mistrust of the great ones of the earth and a thorough disbelief in any security with people who have no imagination. They are the objects, not the subjects, of imagination and it is not in their compass to *conceive* of anything whatever. They can only live their hard functional lives."

A compromise with the functional-living was however possible. If the creator has to maintain himself within an unimaginative world he can do so by cherishing certain illusions. In such a world, it is better to use harmless deception so long as one knows what the deception is: so long as one doesn't pretend that the lies are the truth. James was beginning to say that civilization and society, forms and manners which ennoble man and make rich his life, would founder without their illusions, or their artistic lies, their "suspension of disbelief." In a word, society must have faith in its illusions and yet paradoxically remember they are illusions. It must have its mythology, like the Greeks; and live by its myths. This would be the philosophy of his last and greatest works.

—

THE LITTLE GIRLS

"THE AWKWARD AGE" WAS THE LAST NOVEL IN HENRY JAMES'S series dealing with female children, juveniles and adolescents, written between 1895 and 1900. He had, in earlier years, written about young adults—Catherine in *Washington Square*, Daisy Miller, Isabel Archer—American girls with a certain sense of their own worth and a distinct will to freedom. But he had never, save for his early novel *Watch and Ward*, and the single scene of little Hyacinth's visit to his mother in *The Princess Casamassima*, concerned himself with childhood. In the years after his play-writing—the years of his life within the black abyss—he not only lived in a world of childhood wonder and terror, but had written his stories in a remarkable sequence. His precocious little females grow a little older in each story, as if they were a single child whose life experience is being traced from the cradle to coming-of-age. *Watch and Ward* of 1871 had been a limited story of an "education"; and in it he had traced Nora Lambert's growth from twelve to twenty. He had written that novel during months of depression, when his future looked bleak, and his longing for Europe was acute. Was it mere coincidence, this return to child-hood during the years of public failure and renewed depression, or was there some inner need to relive forgotten experience, some compulsion to revisit, step by step, the hidden stages of his own growth and development, within his safety-disguise of a little girl —as if indeed these books were the single book of little Harry James of Washington Square and Fourteenth Street, of Paris, Geneva, Boulogne and Newport?

Taking them in their sequence as he wrote them, we begin in the cradle with Effie, who is murdered at four (*The Other House*, 1896); she is resurrected at five (*What Maisie Knew*, 1897) and we leave her at seven or eight, or perhaps a bit older. Flora is eight ("The Turn of the Screw," 1898) and the one little boy in the series, Miles, is ten: we are in the period of the child from eight to ten. Then we arrive at adolescence: the adolescence of an unnamed girl in a branch post office ("In the Cage," 1898). Little Aggie, in the next novel, is sixteen, and Nanda Brookenham eighteen when the story begins (*The Awkward Age*, 1899). With the writing of this novel, James completes the series. He wrote also a goodly number of tales during this time, but the childhood sequence is embodied in the longer works. After the story of Nora in *Watch and Ward* which was serialized in 1871, the novelist had gone to Italy. Now after recording the education of Nanda (and we pause over the associative recall of the names, Nora and Nanda, although they are separated by almost thirty years) James also went to Italy. The repetition of old experience in new contexts is striking.

I

It is sufficiently clear from James's notes and prefaces that he wrote these novels one by one, not as a series; that he did not deliberately set out to create a sequence. And yet the sequence is there—and the astonishing fact that in his imagination he moved from infancy to childhood, from childhood to adolescence and then to young adulthood. Taken as a whole, the series shows the curiosity of these children, their challenges, their questionings, in terms of the bewilderment, wonder, imagination, phantasmagoria of their years—and their drive to attain omniscience in a world of negligent and terrifying adults. If we remind ourselves of the personal origin of these tales, we can discern within the total record a series of parables, an extensive personal allegory of the growing up of Henry James. Beyond the conscious intellectual exploration of states of childhood, Henry James was intuitively questioning his unconscious experience, reliving the long-ago "education" of his emotions.

The murder of little Effie in *The Other House*, which inaugurates the series, can be read as inflicted at the age at which the little Henry, within the mature artist, felt himself annihilated by the brutality of the audience at *Guy Domville*. It will be recalled that James originally planned to have the child poisoned; but his selective imagination chose the form of death he himself had described at the Archbishop's when he had spoken of having been under water—"subaqueous"—at the time of his *débacle*.

Maisie is a careful presentation of the Henry James of the late autobiography, *A Small Boy and Others:* she possesses his curiosity, she is engaged in a systematic study of her elders, she searches determinedly for her identity amid her absent and estranged parents and governesses. Nanda describes this phase later in *The Awkward Age*—"there was never a time when I didn't know *something* or other and . . . I became more and more aware, as I grew older, of a hundred little chinks of daylight." Maisie is not "real," her precocity partakes of James's boyish precocity. James endowed her with his own resistance to "the assaults of experience" by having "simply to wonder," and so preserve the integrity of her years. He gives her his own "undestroyed freshness." Her "vivacity of intelligence" and her "small vibrations" are those of a story-teller in the making. She might have been "rather coarsened, blurred, sterilised, by ignorance and pain." Art saves her and protects her innocence, as it had saved Henry; art and the ability he acquired to "convert, convert, convert"; raw experience was always convertible into the stuff of poetry. Maisie is able to give us a vision of her shoddy mother which becomes "concrete, immense, awful." For the little girl follows, as her creator tells us, "some stray fragrance of an ideal." In his late preface he describes the "exquisite interest" he found in his study of this little girl, for in reality she is a study of himself; unwittingly he has treated her as a kind of psychological "case history." *A Small Boy* gives us abundant data about Henry's governesses—those he had during his boyhood, that is when he was a little older than Maisie, and into his teens, particularly the memorable Augustine Danse, the most Parisian, "the most brilliant and most genial of irregular characters," who was sent away—"a cloud of revelations succeeding her withdrawal." Shades of the shade of Miss Jessel! She had been "all-knowing and all-imposing," and she had had a "flexible *taille*" and "salient smiling eyes." James's boyhood memories endow her with strong sexual attributes. Her views had had "a range that she not only permitted us to guess but agreeably invited us to follow almost to their furthest limits." Little Maisie among her variegated parents is but another version of the slightly older Henry among variegated governesses.

After Maisie we arrive at the latency period, represented by little Miles, the one boy in the series. We may speculate that Henry James, having sought the disguise of a little girl, remained fundamentally a little boy, strongly masculine, save when this masculinity was confronted by his older brother, or the pushing hands of governesses. The price of Miles's self-assertion was death; after that James reverted in his stories to the disguise of female adolescence. The anecdote he tells in his autobiography of his hiding under the table to listen to a reading of Dickens, his stories of himself as an observant little outsider, seem to parallel the adolescent girl who, from her cage, tries to understand the society around her. Then, in Nanda and little Aggie of *The Awkward*

Age, we may see a projection of two sides of the Henry of late adolescence—one part of him Continentalized and ranging freely in the forbidden fruit of French novels, and the other the serious young literary novice who had to make what he could out of the New England environment to which he was brought, the life of Newport, when he was Nanda's age. We remember how Nanda at the end is surrounded by "sets" of authors.

Some such history of the psychical "growing up" of Henry James is traced in the depths of these stories. There has been a revisiting of earliest childhood following the recoil from the horror of public rejection and the destruction of self-esteem. And as human cells act to heal a wound and create scar tissue, we have in this sequence of stories a logical, chronologically accurate remounting of the steps of early experiences of feeling in the service of a wounded ego. This was more than an intricate rewriting by the imagination of the biography of James's psyche. In resuming the disguise of a female child, the protective disguise of his early years, James performed imaginative self-therapy. The record of these stories can be seen as the unconscious revisiting of perceptions and feelings, to minister to adult hurts. As his old feelings and imaginings had defended his childish self long ago against the brutal world, they now served as aid against the new brutalities. He underwent a kind of "self-analysis," strangely enough in the very years in which Sigmund Freud was undergoing his self-analysis and writing his book on dreams. There is a striking historical parallel—the return of both men to the stuff of childhood; in the case of Freud it was partly voluntary and with full use of his ratiocinative powers. In the case of James it was an involuntary, intuitive, unerringly accurate historical search, conducted subliminally. In neither case was there a complete cure; but in the history of both Freud and James the process restored, after a period of crisis, the subject's functional power—more important his creative power. Each could move forward into new depths of adult experience.

11

Henry James was not wholly unaware of the process of "unconscious cerebration," as he had called it as early as the writing of "The Figure in the Carpet" in 1895. He asked himself certain pertinent questions a dozen years later when he was writing his prefaces. But he did not press for answers, as Freud, working to other ends, might have done. James's first question to himself was why had he shown such a predilection in these stories for little girls? His rational answer was that they were more sensitive recorders of their environment—more sensitive than "rude" little boys. This answer satisfied him for a while. Suddenly a second question came up—and for a moment he looked at it. Then he simply set it aside. "Rude" little boys, perhaps, he had said—but wasn't Morgan Moreen, for instance, every bit as sensitive as his girl characters? And wasn't it curious that if the little girls were more sensitive than his boys, they certainly were tougher? As he put it, "they bear up, oddly enough . . . beyond their brothers." He made this observation; but the answer would have led him too far into the spiritual transvestitism that he had practiced. Besides, it is extremely difficult to read the riddle of the self. The masculine adult side of James could not explore the threats to his young masculinity, save as he had explored them in his inner dreamwork, in his art—in the violence of the governess toward little Miles.

The little girls had thus emerged out of a personal healing process during the years from 1895 to 1900. And this process had in itself, in its stages, served a fascinating function. The period of nightmare had been short-circuited by the writing out of the nightmare; the bewilderment over his buffeting by the theatrical world and its audience had been eased by his study of the bewilderment of female adolescence. Each tale had eased some of his emotional suffering, so that from story to story he had divested himself of certain intensities of pain. He had undergone a continuing moral rebirth and regrowth, as if his body were shedding dead skin. This mobilization of inner resource occurred while the novelist's outward self moved in the world in full command of its intellectual powers. The mature Henry leased houses, visited friends, dined in clubs, wrote and discussed his art, grew in authority and dedication to his craft; struggled moreover against failure and commanded the attention of editors and publishers. Below or beyond the adult self, the hurt self discovered its healing substance. The subject, the essence, of these works was that of the growth and development of the human, the artistic, imagination. What else are these children doing if not trying to match magic-lantern phantasmagoria with reality? By the way of art, and within the form of his technical experiments, Henry James re-encountered his buried life, in the manner in which he had known it—as a struggling little girl, as a beleaguered little boy, as a troubled female adolescent. A striking instance of this kind of self-exploration of the personal myth is to be found in *Orlando* by Virginia Woolf, in which she retraces the history of her emotional education, seeing herself first as a boy in the Elizabethan era, and later becoming a young woman in the eighteenth century and a suffragette and matron in the time of Victoria. There was some such allegory of the self in Henry James's work of the late 1890's. Whether we call this a "crisis of identity" or a "middle-age crisis," the sequence of his stories reveals the benign workings of the imagination moving—in this instance in chronological fashion—from direct confrontation of disaster through the death of the spirit to its re-emergence and growth within the familiar shapes of the past.

James had spoken four years earlier of his quest for "compensations and solutions." The language of his notebooks during these and later years, in his eloquent and mystical prayers to his Muse and his Genius, reflects his strong feeling that his art was the very source of his life. He speaks of his "workings-out" of his stories as "the dear old blessed healing, consoling way." In the act of constructing a plot he writes, "My troubled mind overflows with the whole deep sense of it all—overflows with reflection and perception." By this awareness—perceiving, reflecting—he could discover, he told himself, "all passions, all combinations." "Oh, sacred beneficence of *doing!*" he suddenly exclaims. And again, "Oh, celestial, soothing, sanctifying process!"

Healing, consoling, soothing, sanctifying! Art was for James an anodyne, a balm, a religion, a sacred fount. In the service of art he renewed himself. As Proust was discovering memory and association at the very moment when Freud was asking his patients to "associate" and remember—remember in particular their childhood—so Henry James, also at this moment, intuitively had gone in search of his childhood—consciously for the purpose of creation, unconsciously in answer to the imperatives of his imagination, the demands of his spirit. Some geniuses at such crises turn to the anesthesia of drugs, the artificial dream-worlds of opium or the modern acids of hallucination; others seek the consolations of alcohol, the numbing exhilaration of the bottle. James wanted no anesthetic. His need was to stay awake, to perceive, to reflect; his art, and what he came to call in the end the "religion of doing," steadied him and sustained him.

III

His long-deferred trip to Italy, and with it his promised visit to the Bourgets in France, suddenly became possible early in 1899 with the letting of De Vere Gardens on a six-months' lease. To make arrangements for this he had to go to London after his prolonged residence in Rye, and he had the sensation of his Mr. Longdon, of returning to the city as from another country. He felt himself an outsider; and he fled back to Lamb House. He had not yet acquired his room at the Reform and his one-room lodging at the Grosvenor Club made him feel "so on the streets."

James had to read large bundles of proof of *The Awkward Age* before leaving. January and February were mild, however, save for winter gales; and he was alone in Lamb House for the first time.

Sturges was laid up in London with the flu. MacAlpine had left on completion of the novel with the understanding that he would be available later as necessary and on a boarding-out basis. James settled down beside great fires in his hearths, and he spoke with pleasure of the "indoor winter cosiness." Solitude meant a return to self-communion. "This is a grey, gusty, lonely Sunday at Rye, the tail of a great, of an almost, in fact, *perpetual* winter gale," he wrote in his notebook. "The wind booms in the old chimneys, wails and shrieks about the old walls. I sit, however, in the little warm white study—and many things come back to me. I've been in London for three weeks—came back here on the [January] 20th; and feel the old reviving ache of desire to get back to work. Yes, I yearn for that—the divine unrest again touches me."

The "divine unrest" was in evidence—after his long troubled months; he wanted to write, to travel, to be in strange cities as of old. He even began to think charitably of the theatre. It was only a momentary thought. Alexander asked him to turn the tale of "Covering End" into a one-acter, it seemed so like a play. He was right, of course; it had been the Ellen Terry play. James said he might do "a fresh one-act thing," and in his notebook he mused on the way the very thought of the drama "with the divine little difficult, artistic, ingenious, architectural FORM" could still make the "old pulses throb and old tears rise again. The blended anguish and amusement again touch me with their breath." However he was in no mood for dramatic trifles. Rather than one-act plays he wanted to write "big" novels—"How, through all hesitations and conflicts and worries, *the* thing, the desire to get back only to the *big* (scenic, constructive, 'architectural' effects) seizes me and carries me off my feet." For the first time in many months he prayed to his muse, as of old—"Ah, once more, to let myself go! The very thought of it soothes and sustains, lays a divine hand on my nerves, and lights, so beneficently, my uncertainties and obscurities. *Begin* it—and it will grow. Put in now some strong short novel, and come back from the continent, with it all figured out. I must have a long *tête à tête* with myself, a long ciphering bout, on it, before I really start. *Basta*."

His notebooks record however no *tête-à-têtes* on the subjects of his contemplated novels—rather a series of jottings for tales; an idea for one given him by George Meredith during a visit early in February in Dorking; a return to other ideas noted during the past twelvemonth. He could not think of big novels on the eve of his journey. He read his galleys; suffered a longish bout of influenza; made arrangements to have Jonathan Sturges live in Lamb House while he was away—it would give the servants something to do—packed his bags and late in February sat up till the early hours clearing his desk before his departure. "I go to Italy after more than five years' interlude," he wrote to a friend. At this moment he became aware that his room was filled with a smoky haze; and then he saw smoke squeezing through the planks of his floor, and around the edges of his rugs. He ran down the stairs to the dining room below to see what was burning, but everything was normal. He then roused his servants. Smith hacked, sawed and pried up a couple of planks nearest the fireplace. Thick smoke poured out: a charred beam was smoldering under the hearthstone. It was a matter of minutes to douse it with water, and for safety's sake pack it with soaked sponges. The Smiths returned to bed, and James resumed his letter. He thanked his friend for being an agent in his discovering the fire: it would have been serious had he been asleep in bed. And he signed himself with a "Good-night—it's 2.45 and all's well. I *must* turn in."

All was not well. There was flame now beneath his floor. He shouted anew for the servants. Firemen and police were summoned. Lamb House could not be another Poynton. To reach the burning beam they had to pickax their way through the wall and ceiling of the dining room below, for the underside had ignited and the fire was spreading downward. His parlor was smoked up a bit; but on the whole he felt he got off lightly, for the firemen were "cool as well as prompt"; moreover they used water sparingly. His epistolary passion in the small hours of the morning had saved his house, perhaps his life. After a sleepless night James dispatched a long telegram to his architect which ended "now helpless in face of reconstructions of injured portions and will bless you mightily if you come departure of course put off HENRY JAMES."

JONATHAN STURGES
From a posthumous drawing by Albert Sterner

BOOK FIVE

The Sacred Fount

1899 = 1901

L'AFFAIRE

IN THE NEW YORK "TIMES" OF JANUARY 7, 1895, PROMINENTLY displayed, with a large headline, is the account of the public humiliation of a Jewish officer on the parade ground of the École Militaire in Paris. Found guilty of selling military secrets to Germany, the officer had been marched two days earlier before 5,000 soldiers for the removal of the symbols of rank and honor: his epaulets were torn from his uniform, his sword was broken—while beyond the stiff ranks a mob hissed and jeered. Below this bit of ancient history in the press, the disgrace of Captain Alfred Dreyfus, one may read a small headline. It describes the jeering of Henry James in London on the first night of *Guy Domville*. The two episodes are related only in time, and in emotional content: they speak of humiliation, outrage, hurt—and a howling mob. The military humiliation in France was sinister, tragic, world-shaking; the literary humiliation was minor, limited, private.

Henry James's response to the Dreyfus "affair," in the ensuing years, may have had in it, in part, an unconscious element of recognition. He had from the first been fascinated by the sinister drama on the other side of the Channel. More than four years had elapsed since Dreyfus's incarceration on charges of high treason. Early in 1898, Zola, out of his profound sense of justice and his deep social convictions—but also with a strange and compelling megalomania—had published his letter to the President of the French Republic, known as *J'accuse*. "Truth is on the march and nothing will halt it." In February 1898 he had been put on trial for libel. James had felt as if he were "every a.m. in Paris by the side of the big brave Zola, whom I find really a hero." He thought *J'accuse* "one of the most courageous things ever done and an immense honour to our too-puling corporation! But his [Zola's] compatriots—!" he added, as with a Gallic shrug, in writing to his cosmopolitan friend, Henry Brewster. On the day that Zola was found guilty, James had "worked off" some of his emotions by writing a letter of support and encouragement to his old friend of the Flaubert *cénacle*. The letter does not seem to have survived among Zola's papers and one wonders whether it reached him at so difficult an hour; for the French writer fled to England, to a retreat in Surrey, on the advice of his lawyers and friends. James believed Zola's life to be in danger. "He will appeal, and there will be delays and things will happen—elections and revulsions and convulsions and other things—but it was, I think—I fully believe —his sentence,* on Wednesday, [that] saved his life. If he had got life or acquittal, or attenuation, he would have been *torn limb from limb* by the howling mob in the streets. That's why I wrote to him." Whether the two novelists met during Zola's exile is doubtful. James was too busy settling into his house in Sussex and Zola was isolated in Surrey and unhappy to be out of France at this crucial a moment. "I sit in the garden and read *l'Affaire*

. . . .
* James means the verdict of guilty of "defaming the French army." Zola fled. and sentence was never pronounced.

Dreyfus," James wrote to Mrs. Humphry Ward in September 1898. "What a bottomless and sinister *affaire* and in what a strange mill it is grinding. The poor French." He took the same attitude of sympathy with France in a letter to Bourget who had written him in great detail and with much hatred for the Jews. James told Bourget his letter dealt

almost solely with these unfortunate things in France, about which you speak so sombrely and about which I can't offer you any word in the world, alas, that might be comforting. I don't understand, I am too distant both from the experience of them and the way in which you feel them. Nothing here corresponds to them—neither the good relations which we maintain with the Jews, and, in sum, with one another, nor the supreme importance we attach to civil justice, nor the "short work" which we would make of the military if they attempted to substitute their justice for it. I can well sympathize however—to the point of tears—with your stricken country. Let us hope it will emerge by the door open to it (or the door that will be open to it) of revision [of the case]. I must confess that if France refuses to do this, I will find her less subject for sympathy—a less interesting sufferer. But France will not refuse.

I I

The Dreyfus affair was much in his mind, as he journeyed to Paris on March 8, 1899, and later to the Riviera, at the end of the month, to visit the Paul Bourgets. He knew that his French friends believed in Dreyfus's guilt; and he was aware of Bourget's pronounced anti-Semitism. James was stoutly convinced of Dreyfus's innocence—and he had no hatred for any people. He might satirize national manners or national idiosyncrasies, or use national stereotypes, but there was no touch of bigotry or racism in his make-up. At the moment of his journey all France was split by *l'affaire*; and as a consequence of Zola's action and the clamor of the League for the Rights of Man a court martial was scheduled to review the case.

James had committed himself long before to visiting the Bourgets. To travel south and avoid them would require an open break in a friendship he valued. He had always enjoyed Bourget's conversation, his intelligence, his *art de dire*. He also recognized in the French novelist a certain discipleship, much as he disliked his novels. Now history was throwing up a barrier to their intercourse —history and Bourget's Catholic and conservative view of the world. "The odious affair is rather in the air between me and that [Riviera] retreat," James told Mrs. Gardner. "I don't feel about it as I gather our friends there do." He added, "one must duck one's head and pass quickly."

He ducked his head at first by lingering in Paris. There was a distinct reluctance to proceed. He explained his delay by saying that he was proceeding by slow stages, and he remained at the Meurice, reading page-proofs of his novel and receiving regular dispatches from Edward Warren about the repairs in Lamb House. The fireplace in the dining room would be remodelled; the hazards would be eliminated. James's insurance would cover the costs. "Scientific reconstruction is already under way," he reported to his friends the Curtises in Venice. He was lighthearted and happy to be travelling again. Five years had elapsed since his last journey: and now he brought to old familiar scenes on the Continent the eyes of middle age, eyes that saw things not only in their immediacy but in merging memories—old crossings, old associations, old emotions going back to his boyhood during the Second Empire. The early spring sun in the French capital was comforting; and he found there his young cousins, Rosina and Leslie Emmet. Ever avuncular, he gave the young women the benefit of his Parisianism. "I breakfasted, dined, theatr'd, museumed, walked and talked them," he told William—without counting constant teas and little cakes of which he was a large consumer. He had lunch also one day with the young French novelist, Marcel Prévost; and he paid his usual homage to the salon of Henrietta Reubell, and the apartment of Morton Fullerton. "This extraordinary Paris," he wrote to Edward Warren, "with its new—I mean more and more multiplied—manifestations of luxurious and extravagant extension, grandeur and general chronic *expositionism* . . . it strikes me as a monstrous massive flower of national decadence, the biggest temple ever built to material joys and the lust of the eyes, and drawing to it thereby all the forces of the nation as to a substitute for other—I mean other than Parisian—achievement. It is a strange great phenomenon—with a deal of beauty still in its great expansive symmetries and perspectives—and *such* a beauty of light."

The beauty would prevail over the poisonous items in the newspapers. During this visit he received a large impression of the capital that lingered in his memory; it would emerge in the novel he began to write within the year about an American returning to Paris in middle age.

III

After hanging back for a fortnight, James went to the Riviera in one straight jump; he spent the night at Marseille and reached the Bourget villa, Le Plantier, at Costebelle near Hyères, the next day. He enjoyed the warmth of late March, the flowers, the views, the terraces. Bourget, after endless travels around the world, and a long hotel-life, had finally settled for the winters at least on a twenty-five-acre estate in one of the most beautiful spots on the Riviera. Everything spoke for the French writer's literary prosperity. There was the large house, and the guest pavilion in which James was placed with another visitor, the Vicomte E. Melchior de Vogüé, a minor novelist and one of the early interpreters of the Russian writers in France. The estate was on a terraced mountain slope; the walled park of pine and cedar afforded views both inland and to the sea. "It's classic—Claude—Virgil," James wrote to his brother. Before these splendors, "poor dear little Lamb House veils its face with humility and misery." The "misery" resided not so much in the differences in scale and landscape

between Rye and Costebelle as in James's sense of his own modest
income from his writings compared with that of the *mondain* and
best-selling Bourget. For, almost in the same breath, he avowed
that he was homesick for Lamb House—"never again will I leave
it." That James was not altogether at his ease with the Bourgets is
clear enough from his letters; it is suggested also by his managing
very promptly to set fire to the curtains in the guest house.
Nothing was damaged but the curtains. Still, the carelessness was
not in character, especially after his own brief ordeal of fire in
Lamb House.

James had always liked Bourget, even while recognizing his
shortcomings. He knew his snobberies, his social platitudes, his
aristocratic pretensions. For a Frenchman he was uncommonly
cosmopolitan; he had an interest in moral questions and psychology, and above all he was a gifted talker. James was prepared to
stomach his rigidity, his dogmatism, even sometimes his conservatism and his fixed ideas, in order to enjoy the play of his mind, its
lucidity, its bright logic. He had been embarrassed when Bourget
dedicated an early novel to him long ago, in the year of their first
meeting. Bourget "notes with extraordinary closeness the action of
life on the soul," James had written in an essay of 1888, but he
added, "especially the corrosive and destructive action." There was
something corrosive in Bourget; and his being such a monument
to success only sharpened James's ironic view of him. As James put
it in 1900 to their common friend, Urbain Mengin (who had
parted company with Bourget on the issues of the Dreyfus case),
Bourget was primarily interested in the grand life, the life of
luxury, the "*spectacles de la grande richesse, de l'éternelle élé-
gance*," and this meant that he wished to perpetuate systems "*qui
font fleurier ce genre de beauté.*" He added in English (for his
correspondence with Mengin jumped from one language to the
other), "the manner in which his imagination, his admirable
intelligence and his generous and sensitive soul have been led
captive by a certain abnormal vision of 'high life' remains for me

one of the oddest and most indescribable facts with which literary, with which moral criticism, just now, has to deal. He's a moralist so strangely conditioned!" Bourget on his side recognized James's "love for a complex experience of life," and publicly praised his technical virtuosity. "No one," he said, "has rendered as this master has, the exact nuance of remarks exchanged by New Yorkers or Bostonians in a corner of a drawing room or around a dinner-table." He greatly admired James's tales of the artist-life. His own airless view of the world, however, made him see James as "subtle rather than colourful, delicate rather than powerful, inquiring rather than deeply moved." James would indeed have said as much—and more—of Bourget.

In the guest pavilion at Le Plantier, it amused the American novelist to observe the seriousness and assiduity of Melchior de Vogüé, whom he described as a *gentilhomme* turned journalist-novelist—in other words an amateur. Daily the Vicomte locked himself up to do his stint: a serial of his was running in the *Revue des Deux Mondes*. James found in him "a fine gentlemanly tension," but his mind was "too conscious and too cultivated." To William he spoke of "the indigestible Midi of Bourget and the Vicomte Melchior de Vogüé." The tense and gentlemanly fellow-guest observed all the amenities; his novel *Le Maître de la Mer* was found tucked away among a mass of French books in Lamb House years later, inscribed "À *mon eminent confrère*, Henry James, *en souvenir des bons jours passés près de lui au Plantier de Costebelle*."

IV

The week at Le Plantier passed quickly enough. "I treat the *Affaire*," Henry wrote to William, "as none of my business (as it isn't), but *its* power to make one homesick in France and the French air is not small. It is a country *en décadence*." There were sundry sociabilities, of which we have no record save that on one occasion Lady Randolph Churchill, who was editing an elaborate

hardbound journal called *The Anglo-Saxon Review*, paying a call
on the Bourgets, made James promise to do a story for her. Since
he was to be decently paid for it, James promised almost immediate
ate delivery and he was to spend a goodly part of his subsequent
visit to Venice, keeping his promise. We judge that there were
walks and talks at Le Plantier—wide-ranging talks about current
literature and the literary situation in France—for shortly afterwards
wards James was to write a brief and sketchy essay summing up
the French century. He called it "The Present Literary Situation
in France." Published in the *North American Review* six months
after his visit to the Bourgets, it contained James's one public
allusion to the Dreyfus case. In discussing Jules Lemaître as critic,
he expressed regret that when Lemaître finally had developed a
conviction it had turned out to be one of the "ugliest"—"his voice
was loud, throughout the 'Affair' in the anti-revisionist and anti-
Semitic interest." Bourget and Vogüé were mentioned only in
passing in the article, in which James did not conceal his feelings
that men of the second rank now held sway in the Republic. He
praised Bourget for having learned his trade in "the school of
reflection not hitherto supposed to be that of the novel." His
subject was always "an idea" and he was capable of regarding an
idea "as a positive source of excitement." But he also said of his
friend that the outer world to him was "a large glass case equipped
with wheels, stoves and other conveniences, in which he moves
over his field very much as a great American railway-director
moves over his favourite line in his 'luxuriously-appointed' private
car. For the consciousness inhabited by M. Bourget *is* luxuriously
appointed. I only regret that it is impossible we should here
accompany him on one or two of his journeys." As for the Vicomte,
comte, James quietly brushed him off with, "If I write the name of
M. de Vogüé, it is only that M. de Vogüé too is critically eminent,
and that I am obliged to pass him by. Consummately clever, yet
without having created a manner, he is, perhaps, as but one of a
number, the best instance of how the most characteristic French
aptitude may assert itself even in dull days." As usual James

confined himself to prose; he would doubtless have had other things to say had he touched poetry. His end-of-century view was more retrospective than contemporaneous. "The great historians are dead—the last of them went with Renan; the great critics are dead—the last of them went with Taine; the great dramatists are dead—the last of them went with Dumas; and, of the novelists of the striking group originally fathered by the Second Empire, Émile Zola is the only one still happily erect."

One episode from James's visit was to linger in Bourget's memory. It occurred on an evening when they sat by the fire and Bourget complained of the difficulty he had—and he spoke English fluently—in understanding certain verses of Kipling's. He mentioned in particular "McAndrew's Hymn." Henry James took the book from his hand. He moved over in front of the fire. The hymn contained indeed terminology that might have given an English reader pause—"thrust-block," "coupler flange," "crosshead jibs." According to Bourget, James spontaneously began to read the poem in idiomatic French: a feat of translation which the French writer admired and recounted years later to Mrs. Humphry Ward.

v

"I've been here a week and depart tomorrow or next day. It has been rather a tension," Henry wrote early in April from Le Plantier to his brother. A day or two later he journeyed to St. Raphael and by easy stages proceeded to Genoa. If Hyères had induced tension, he now felt relief, for he wrote a lively and affectionate letter to Minnie Bourget. "I am full," he told her, "of grateful memories and blessed pictures. The beauty and harmony and nobleness of your eternal medium—that nothing can injure, diminish or disturb—has added a great stretch to my experience." And he all but wrote a short story, in his "international" mode, as he described to Madame Bourget the curiosity of some British females at the *table d'hôte* at St. Raphael.

One of them, by the way, (who had the longest chin in Europe and bicycled over that afternoon from Costebelle!) has a villa near Le Plantier and succeeded in worrying out of me the shy confession of where—at Costebelle—I had been staying.

"And where did you come from?"

"Well—from Hyères."

"Ah, you've been at Hyères? What part of Hyères?"

"Well—properly, rather, the part near Costebelle."

"*Near* Costebelle—do you mean *at* Costebelle?"

"Well, yes—it *was*, I suppose at Costebelle."

"And at what hotel?"

"I was not at a hotel."

"Then where were you?"

"I was staying at a villa."

"Ah!—where was the villa?"

"Well—up rather high; out of the way, thank heaven!"

A silence.

"Not at La Luguette then?"

"No."

"And not Le Bocage either."

"No."

Another silence.

"But with some English friends at all events?"

"No."

"Then with some French."

"Well, yes—more or less French!"

"Ah, the Léotauds?"

"No."

"Oh, I see—higher up?"

"Yes—*much* higher up."

"Ah, the P. Bourgets?" (*breathlessly*)

"Well, yes, with M. and Mme. Bourget."

Sensation—quick conversation of lady with other lady on her right and prosternation of both so great that I was really left in peace (on that side) for the rest of the dinner. Your name is a talisman.

The clatter and chatter of Genoa came up into his hotel room as he wrote his letter to Minnie Bourget. He felt a great joy in the sunny warmth of the Italian air and the shuffle below of Italian feet. He was recovering again "the little old throbs and thrills" of his old Italian journeys.

THE BROODING TOURIST

HE HAD FALLEN IN LOVE WITH ITALY THIRTY YEARS BEFORE, NEVER again—as he put it—to fall out. In the eyes of his young manhood, Italy had been "a dishevelled nymph." Now, in his own middle age, the nymph seemed to have grown stout and orderly and become a votary of "progress." Later in Naples he would look with suspicion at big advertisements and "restorations" designed to please touring Americans and the perpetual horde of Germans from over the Alps. In Rome there were irrecoverable changes. He had known the last days of Papal Rome when Pio Nono was still carried through the streets and the Middle Ages and the Renaissance were piled high on antiquity. The *Risorgimento* had secularized the city and straightened out too many corners. His "little personal Florence" remained in spite of everything. He could still manage with it, but the "very modern Rome" could not come up to his old sensations and memories—the years of his horseback rides in the Campagna and his visits to the great palaces where expatriate Americans like William Wetmore Story, whose life he was now supposed to write, lived in high style and undemocratic grandeur. He had now known Italy during three decades. In spite of the pleasure of recovered sights and sounds (as in Venice, where the plash of the water, the dustless air, the sun on marble and stone delighted him), he felt a certain oppression. He was aware of "the tone of time," and he hated the desecrations and erasures. But there were new sensations and new pictures as well. He was not one to allow nostalgia to efface immediate reality. Still there was a change in his manner of looking. He had called himself of old "the sentimental traveller"; in England he had been "the observant stranger." Now in Italy he was "the brooding tourist."

I

He did not linger long in Genoa. A couple of days—visits to friends on the Ligurian coast—and he was off to Venice where he had promised to stay with the Daniel Curtises at the Palazzo Barbaro on the Grand Canal. He had spent painful weeks in the water-city in 1894 after Miss Woolson's death; but he confronted these memories and allowed older ones to reassert themselves. In a bravura passage in a travel sketch he wrote but did not immediately publish, he described the "dignity of arrival" by water at the Barbaro. With a touch of swagger, he adjured his readers, "Hold to it that to float and slacken and gently bump, to creep out of the low, dark *felze* and make the few guided movements and find the strong crooked and offered arm, and then, beneath lighted palace-windows, pass up the few damp steps on the precautionary carpet — hold to it that these things constitute a preparation of which the only defect is that it may sometimes perhaps really prepare too much. It's so stately that what can come after? —it's so good in itself that what, upstairs, as we comparative vulgarians say, can be better." Still the *piano nobile* of the Curtises had its grandeur; it was a high historic house, with "such a quantity of recorded past twinkling in the multitudinous candles that one grasped at the idea of something waning and displaced, and might even fondly and secretly nurse the conceit that what one was having was just the very last." There was no future for such manners and customs and the comprehensive urbanity of his host and hostess; but he would not bother with the future; it was better to stay with the picture into which Venice resolved itself. During this visit the Palazzo Barbaro placed itself more vividly than ever in James's imagination, superimposed itself on memories of earlier years. There is still a legend that he wrote *The Wings of the Dove* while he stayed there. He actually wrote this novel entirely in Lamb House, three years later; but he did work at the Barbaro on this occasion, instead of proceeding quickly to Rome, as he had planned. He lingered for almost a month in Venice, partly to fulfill his promise to Lady Randolph Churchill, and wrote for her *Anglo-Saxon Review* "The Great Condition," a variant on his earlier stories about women with a "past."

If he gave this task as his primary excuse for delay, there were other reasons as well. One was the presence of a charming older woman, a fellow-guest, Miss Jessie Allen. To read the opening pages of "The Beast in the Jungle" is to get a sense of the kind of Italianate comradeship that developed gradually between the two. Miss Allen was of a distinguished English family and knew the great noble houses of the Scottish border, there was a legend that she had been raised to be a lady-in-waiting at the court, but did not possess the requisite lineage. At any rate she was a grand lady, full of good talk and lively gossip; and a delightful companion in the alleyways and tiny curiosity shops of Venice. They wandered in the twists and turns of the passages, dipped into cool chapels when the heat became insufferable, evaded the parent-like vigilance of the Curtis servant Angelo, went for long gondola rides. Shortly atfer leaving Venice, James reported to Ariana Curtis that Miss Allen wrote thirty-page letters, "very agreeable ones, reflecting the life of unbridled luxury and perpetual country house." Also that "she is very faithful—and seems to lead a labyrinthine life." His own letters to her would be long and humorous and filled with verbal gallantries: more than two hundred survive. Miss Allen, in her house at 74 Eaton Terrace, for the next fifteen years would pour tea for Henry James whenever he was in London.

We gain a picture of his stay with the Curtises between the

lines of "Two Old Houses and Three Old Women," memories of Venetian glimpses and visits which he printed, ten years later, in *Italian Hours*. It is there that he described his arrival at the Barbaro, and an occasion when the Curtises were host to German royalty, to the Empress Frederick.

Such old, old women with such old, old jewels; such ugly, ugly ones with such handsome, becoming names; such battered, fatigued gentlemen with such inscrutable decorations; such an absence of youth, for the most part, in either sex—of the pink and white, the "bud" of new worlds; such a general personal air, in fine, of being the worse for a good deal of wear in various old ones.

It was a picture to see the little Empress in the *piano nobile*, a throwback to 1830. "You profit to the full at such times by all the old voices, echoes, images—by that element of the history of Venice which represents all Europe as having at one time and another revelled or rested, asked for pleasure or for patience there; which gives you the place supremely as the refuge of endless strange secrets, broken fortunes and wounded hearts."

He carried away another picture as well. There was a meeting with three Venetian sisters, the old women of the title of his article, and a touch of revived interest in George Sand and her Venetian adventures with Musset and Dr. Pagello: for the old ladies pointed to the house in which George Sand had lived after the first stage of her romance with Musset at the Danieli. Publication of a large biography of Sand in the ensuing months would enable James to write anew of this novelist who had charmed him in his youth even if this publication was "a tub of soiled linen which the muse of history, rolling her sleeves well up, has not even yet quite ceased energetically and publicly to wash." And then the three sisters—he did not name them—took James (and probably Miss Allen) to see their own house, the seat of an ancient Venetian family in decline. The visit prompted in James a peroration that was a recall of the old palazzo in the Rio Marin in which his own Juliana of "The Aspern Papers" had lived with her memories of lost moments. "The charming lonely girls, carrying so simply their great name and fallen fortunes, the despoiled *decaduta* house, the unfailing Italian grace, the space so out of scale with actual needs, the absence of books, the presence of ennui, the sense of the length of the hours and the shortness of everything else—all this was a matter not only for a second chapter and a third, but for a whole volume, a *dénoûment* and a sequel."

II

To visit Venice was to pay homage to his oldest friend in that city —to Mrs. Arthur Bronson. They had met long ago at sea when he crossed to embrace Europe permanently; she had played cards in the salon with Anthony Trollope; and in later years, in the Casa Alvisi, she had received Henry James and Robert Browning, and provided cigarettes and good talk and a splendid balcony on the Grand Canal directly opposite the weight and mass of the Salute. He had celebrated the Casa Alvisi in a notable essay on the Grand Canal in the early 1890's as "the very friendliest house in all the wide world, and it has, as it deserves to have, the most beautiful position. It is a real *porto di mare*, as the gondoliers say—a port within a port; it sees everything that comes and goes, and takes it all in with practised eyes." In the essay James also alluded to the fact that Mrs. Bronson had restored the near-by Madonnetta and lit the red spark of a lamp within the shrine of painted and gilded wood, for the worship of the *gondolieri*.

He found her now at La Mura, at Asolo, a sadly aged and limited figure—she who had once ruled over the Canal. It did not minister to James's sense of the past to arrive with the flabby and unhappy son of poets—"Pen" Browning; and in the little house, which he had always found uncomfortable, he got a painful picture of the waning of a life once filled with ease, power and relaxed and open-handed generosity. "That eternal glass cage," he was to write to Mrs. Curtis, "and that little swarm of beneficiaries." Mrs. Bronson had become "the strangest mixture of folly of purchase and of discomfort about necessaries." There wasn't an easy chair in La Mura for her to be ill in, or for him to sit comfortably in. They had an immense quantity of talk after the years of his absence. But Mrs. Bronson was helpless and demoralized, "a great deal of rheumatism, an enormous appetite, not a scrap of possible action," with two nurses, a flock of servants and queues of shopkeepers trying to sell her antiques. Asolo still had its old charm; the plain stretched away like a purple sea from lower cliffs of the hills and the white *campanili* of the villages. Here the fumbling red-velvet carriage of provincial and rural Italy had served Mrs. Bronson instead of her gondola; they had long before made trips to Bassano, to Treviso, to high-walled Castelfranco. Mrs. Bronson remained alert and fresh "for pleasant surprises and proved sincerities"; these no longer included excursions and explorations. She was "of this world that she so much loved," but she would not be for long. This was to be James's last vision of her. At her death he wrote one of his finest eulogies, that was also a eulogy of his own dead Venice, the Venice he would revive in a poignant novel already shaping itself in his thoughts.

III

He was overdue in Rome, where the Waldo Storys awaited him in the old many-roomed apartment of William Wetmore Story at the Barberini. But James had no desire to stay with them; he preferred to be near the Spanish Steps, and he put up at the Hôtel de l'Europe, where he had a sitting room that looked on the Piazzetta Mignanelli. To Bourget he wrote, "Rome is always Rome—at this moment generally empty and quiet but more and more 'modern' as I grow more and more antique." To Howard Sturgis he described it as "a warmish, quietish, emptyish, pleasantish (but not maddeningly so), altered and cockneyfied and scraped and all but annihilated Rome." There were however social traps on all sides. He halfheartedly examined the large Story archive—"this preposterous Story job": letters from the Brownings, his old friend Lowell, Charles Sumner, the accolades of the world bestowed upon this amateur sculptor who had left a great studio filled with strained awkward statues. It was clear to him that he could write Story's life with ease; but not perhaps with much pleasure. Three or four months would suffice. He would have to fill out the gaps with his own Roman memories. "There will be all the Rome I can put into so small a compass, and as little Story as I can keep out," he told Grace Norton. Story's "vast marble shop" he described as "a huge system and workshop of marmoreal Bedizenment of Billionaires."

For the rest, he paid calls as always and continued to tour—and to brood. He went to Castel Gandolfo to visit the Humphry Wards in their rented villa, where Mrs. Ward was strenuously composing an "Italian" novel, and promised to return for a stay; he took two English ladies, the literary Angelina Milman and a friend, to look at Hadrian's Villa and the Villa d'Este; and he called with pleasure and some regularity at the studio of John Elliott and his wife, the former Maud Howe whom he had known for many years, daughter of Julia Ward Howe. He liked Elliott's work and he liked their charming place near St. Peter's—a flowered terrace on the roof of the Palazzo Accoramboni. Elliott was working on the ceiling for the Boston Public Library; and with great ingenuity he had turned the vast apartment into a comfortable home; he cultivated roses on the terrace in a series of hanging gardens which bloomed throughout the year. James admired the view—they looked down into the square of St. Peter's and also on Castel Sant' Angelo and beyond to the Pincio and the Villa Borghese, the Campagna and the Alban and Sabine hills. Maud Elliott was a niece of Mrs. Luther Terry who still lived at the Odescalchi Palace where James had often visited in the 1870's; and he met again, after the long years, the indomitable Baroness Von Rabe, whom he had once found so formidable (when she was Annie Crawford) and who was now elderly and widowed. Maud

Elliott gave a dinner for her Aunt Annie on the terrace under the pergola and James was toasted in Orvieto and said with great solemnity—as a brooding tourist might—"this is the time when one lights the candle, goes through the house and takes stock." Such was, indeed, the nature of this—the all but last of his Italian journeys.

One day Maud Elliott told James of Julia Ward Howe's visit to Rome the previous winter when her beauty of old age—she was seventy-eight—had been remarked upon everywhere, so that she was referred to as a living Holbein, and all the artists had raved about her. Out of this grew one of James's charming late stories, "The Beldonald Holbein."

Maud Elliott reported on James's visit to her mother: "Did I write you how delightful Henry James's was? We saw him constantly while he was preparing the material for a life he is to write of Mr. Story. He is now old bacheloresque, but so dear, though a wee thought cranky."

On another day at the Elliotts' Henry James was introduced to a strapping American sculptor from Boston, of Norwegian birth. His name was Hendrik Andersen—it sounded very like the name James had given to the sculptor he had created long ago, Roderick Hudson. Andersen was of "magnificent stature," Henry later wrote. He was much taken by his ingenuity, his sincerity, his seriousness, and his handsome blond countenance. The sculptor responded to James's interest. He invited him to his studio in the Via Margutta. The place, the Roman art atmosphere, the young aspiring handsome American—it was as if James were back in the 1870's, in the days when he had frequented studios and smoked cigarettes with the American artists and talked art in this very street. James listened to Andersen and to his grand dreams. He wanted—like Roderick Hudson—to do large statues, big conceptions. The novelist took him to lunch. They talked until it was time to have dinner. They continued to talk. In the studio James took a fancy to a small terracotta bust Andersen had done of the young Conte Alberto Bevilacqua. The novelist praised it highly, and praised the sculptor's promise. But what he was praising was the charm of youth and what he was enjoying above all was a reliving of the past. He was for the moment young again. To encourage the sculptor, James took the unusual step of purchasing the bust of Conte Alberto. The price was $250, the sum he usually got for a short story. Andersen said he would pack it carefully and ship it to Lamb House. He promised too that he would come to England to visit James.

THREE VILLAS

MRS. HUMPHRY WARD IN A ROMAN VILLA, WRITING ONE OF HER novels—with an Italian background! The thought fascinated Henry James. He was due in Florence to talk to William Wetmore Story's daughter, the Countess Peruzzi, who had married a descendant of the Medici; but he could not resist the invitation from the "irrepressible" Mrs. Ward to return to the Villa Barberini. He had liked its high position at Castel Gandolfo, the great slope of the Campagna seaward, the ruins of one of Domitian's villas far below, the view of the Alban lake and Monte Cavo. At the end of May when he began to find the heat of Rome uncomfortable he arrived at the Barberini for a stay of a couple of nights. He remained a week. "This place is a wondrous ravishment," he wrote to Daniel Curtis. "The villa itself bleak and bare, but the circumstances, garden, views, walks, drives, ramifications of every kind, the fullest splendour of the picturesque. It rains and almost freezes (yesterday it quite hugely *hailed!*) but pedestrianism triumphs—and the blood of Dr. Arnold."

Mrs. Humphry Ward—Mary Augusta Arnold—was granddaughter of the great Arnold of Rugby and the niece of Matthew Arnold, whom James had long ago met in Story's apartment in the Barberini Palace. Now he was visiting the niece in the villa of the same noble house, where the bee emblem of the Barberini was much in evidence. It was a seventeenth-century villa, massive but carelessly built. "We perch over the blue Alban lake by one set of windows—vast campagna by other sets," James wrote. "Mrs. Ward reads and writes hard. We had Mrs. (Maud Howe) Elliott out here yesterday to lunch." Maud Elliott in her memoirs speaks of her indignation against "the swarm of less important authors, Mrs. Humphry Ward among them" who somehow managed "to steal Henry James's time." Mrs. Ward had been stealing Henry James's time for years—and with his help. Something about her— perhaps her Arnold blood, certainly her high seriousness, her tremendous moral tone, her appeal to James's artistic wisdom, found him always ready to be kind to her. He had criticized her first novel—it dealt with an actress—and told her how he would have written it; and from that time on he assiduously rewrote—in his letters—all her novels. She took his criticism in good spirit, she knew it was well-intentioned; she seemed however unaware of some of its ironies. "One fears a little sometimes," James had written her of *Robert Elsmere*, "that he [Elsmere] may suffer a sunstroke, damaging if not fatal, from the high oblique light of your admiration for him." Perhaps James experienced a little the same oblique light; certainly he was astonished when Mrs. Ward wrote many years later asking his permission to quote from his letters in a late preface to the novel. "She asks my leave," he told Grace Norton, "to print and publish two letters of gratulation that I appear to have written her on the issue of *Robert Elsmere* . . . after the manner of testimonials in the advertisement of a patent medicine." He gave rueful assent; but admitted to himself that there had to be a streak of opacity in the otherwise intelligent and erudite lady.

Mrs. Ward had had enormous success with *Robert Elsmere*, the kind of success James envied. But then Mrs. Ward's subject was Christianity, and her "dissent" had even caught the eye of Mr. Gladstone. She had called upon the clergy to occupy itself with good works as well as with sin. She had been shocked by orthodox sermons which suggested that her kind of earnest and dedicated inquiries into Christian history might be heretical. Mr. Gladstone reviewed her novel under the portentous title, "*Robert Elsmere* and the Battle of Belief." They had met, the Prime Minister and the formidable bluestocking, and Mr. Gladstone had suggested Mrs. Ward was being "visionary." Mrs. Ward replied courteously but firmly that for Mr. Gladstone "the great fact of the world and in the history of man is sin," while for her the great fact was "progress." She was, ever after, a best-selling lady. James had satirized her kind of literary aspirations in "The Next Time," in the person of Mrs. Highmore, the woman who wished she could have an artistic rather than popular success. He, on his side, would have liked to win her kind of readers, but he knew he could not write her kind of novel. And he knew he could never tell her how to write *his* kind. Yet patiently, consistently, he lectured her on the art of fiction—*his* art—in all the years of their friendship. "She is incorrigibly wise and good, and has a moral nature as Patti has a voice," James wrote to Edmund Gosse, "but somehow I don't, especially when talking art and letters, *communicate* with her worth a damn. All the same she's a dear."

Perhaps because she was a "dear," Henry James had composed a brief tribute to her during the 1890's at the request of the *English Illustrated Magazine*. In sending it to the editor he wrote, "Alas, alas, I have found her deadly difficult to do and cursed the rash hour I undertook her." And when a correspondent asked him why he had written the piece, he replied that it wasn't "written," it was simply a gesture, an act of loyalty to an old friend. The essay is brief and polite. It pays tribute to the ascendancy of women in the field of fiction. And it praises Mrs. Ward's intellect, her "fine, moral ripeness, a genial much-seeing wisdom." Of the art of fiction, which he usually invoked in discussing novelists, there is not a word.

I

Mrs. Ward went about her novel-writing with great thoroughness. When she decided to write a novel about Italy on the *Elsmere* formula—one in which she would show "progress" as prevailing over Papal inertia—she felt a need to live herself into an actual background. In March, while Henry James was making his slow journey along the Riviera and basking in the sun at Hyères, she had arrived at the Villa Barberini. There was snow on the Campagna and a wind was moaning in the Alban Hills. "Oh, how cold it was that first night!" Mrs. Ward remembered years later. The villa was rudely furnished and without heat; the kitchen was fifty-two steps below the dining room; the Neapolitan cook was formidable. Humphry Ward, who was an editorial writer and art critic for *The Times* of London, predicted his wife would end up in a heated hotel in Rome. Even he did not reckon with the blood of Dr. Arnold. Stoves were brought in and made to burn; books were unpacked; the meagre furnishings were pushed about into comfortable positions, and Mrs. Ward's two daughters and the staff of servants were mobilized against the elements. Presently the warm days of April took possession. Mrs. Ward had her fill of Italian antiquity, beauty, romance. Visitors came from Rome to do her homage. Her daughter Janet Trevelyan, who was to be her biographer, remembered that the walls of Domitian's villa at the bottom of the hill echoed animated talk of Pope and Kingdom, Church and State—Mrs. Ward's favorite subjects. In her days at Oxford, where she had known Jowett and Pattison and lived next door to Walter Pater, she had been an absorbed student of ecclesiastical history.

In her memoirs Mrs. Ward recalled that "our earliest guest" in the villa was Henry James; but when she wrote this she telescoped the weeks of her Italian summer. He was actually one of the last guests—he came at the end of her three-months' stay. However she saw more of him than she had ever seen at her country place at Stocks, in England, where he occasionally week-ended, or in her drawing room, in earlier years, in Russell Square.

Mrs. Ward looked at James during this memorable visit with new eyes. In England she had known the social James, with his interest in society on the one hand and in his art on the other. Now she discovered the Italianate James—with his long reach to the Italy of the *Risorgimento* and his thorough knowledge of antiquity and the artistic resources of the Roman countryside; and when, in London or at Stocks, had she heard him speak Italian? She watched him in fluent conversation with a brown-frocked barefoot monk, from the monastery of Palazzola, on the farther side of the Alban lake; and what fascinated her was that this super-subtle super-sensitive cosmopolite of the English social world was drawing out the peasant on this Italian hillside, questioning him, looking into his face with searching eyes, and "getting at something real and vital in the ruder simpler mind." Mrs. Ward unbent and laughed when Henry James paced the dining room with her younger daughter Dorothy, who had charge of the household, searching for some formula by which they could convey to the cook in the lower depths that lately he had not been up to scratch, that guests were coming, that something nice in the way of a sweet would be helpful. The cook had once been a bandit; and being Neapolitan he should have a love of sweets. Mrs. Ward watched James treat this problem as if it were a high literary matter; he paused, he paced, he struck his forehead, he settled for *un dolce come si deve*, which became proverbial in the Ward household for "the tiptop thing."

What struck Mrs. Ward—and she seemed surprised—was that James too could be erudite; this apparently had never occurred to her. She remarked that he wore his learning lightly, "like a flower"; and in saying this she was probably remembering the compliment he had paid her in his letter on *Robert Elsmere*, "What a lot you know . . . your head carries it like a garland of flowers." Mrs. Ward found that James conveyed his knowledge of things Roman and Italian by indirect hints, a grave way of being politely certain that his listeners themselves knew all that he knew; then he walked "round and round the subject, turning it inside out, playing with it, making mock of it, and catching it again with a sudden grip, or a momentary flash of eloquence." The impressions of a man of genius, Mrs. Ward observed, were many, the number of words few. James made the fullest use of the resources of speech. Spoken James was more effective than written James, she found—in talk his living personality, his fun, his irony, prevailed, over "this involution, this deliberation in attack, this slowness of approach toward a point which in the end was generally triumphantly rushed."

"I can see still Mr. James's figure strolling along the terrace which roofed the cryptoporticus of the Roman villa,—the short coat, the summer hat, the smooth-shaven finely cut face, now alive with talk and laughter, now shrewdly, one might say coldly, observant—the face of a satirist—but so human!—so alive to all that underworld of destiny through which move the weaknesses of men and women." The picture in Mrs. Ward's memoirs is vivid, intimate: but Mrs. Ward was extending her memories of the future into the past. At the time of his visit to the Villa Barberini James still wore the beard he had grown long ago, during the Civil War. It was now sharply trimmed and spadelike, but remained a striking part of his public "image." The smooth-shaven finely-cut face was yet to be revealed.

I I

One afternoon James, with his hostess and her daughters, went on an excursion to the blue lake of Nemi visible on their horizon.

They passed on their way over the great viaduct at Ariccia, where Diana had been barbarously worshipped, as readers of Mrs. Ward's *Eleanor* would learn. Diana's priest was always a runaway slave who obtained office by killing his predecessor. In the late soft hours of the afternoon the landscape was bathed in golden light. Everywhere there were ruins and fragments, ghosts of the past—as Mrs. Ward would put it, "engulfed and engarlanded by the active present." They crossed the Appian Way and the high ridge above the deep-sunk lake; the crossing is described in her novel. The excursionists perceived the niched wall and the platform of the temple; they speculated that the historic spring, Egeria's spring, must be in an embrasure in the high wall—Egeria who had instructed Numa Pompilius, the second king of Rome, in modes of worship, and who had honored him with her love. The spring had been a sacred fount—and James's next novel would bear this title. He would allude briefly to Egeria in one of its passages. Whether on this day the novel, already sketched in his notebooks, was taking form, we do not know. What we do know was that James was reading portions of the proof of Mrs. Ward's novel, *Eleanor*, fruit of this visit, while he was writing his: and the idea of an Egeria—a woman who gives of herself to the enhancement of a man, prevails in different ways in both novels.

During this excursion however James's attention wandered elsewhere than with Diana or Egeria. Both in *Eleanor* and the Ward memoirs there is allusion to a dark-eyed youth, encountered among the strawberry beds in the vicinity of the temple of Diana Nemorensis then being excavated. The boy knew his way about the place and was full of talk of fragments and artifacts lying in the furrows of the freshly ploughed field. James walked beside him, unable to take his eyes from his face. He asked him his name and listened, and repeated it, the noble Greek name of Aristodemo. "It was a wonderful evening," Mrs. Ward remembered, "with a golden sun on the lake, on the wide stretches where the temple stood, and the niched wall where Lord Savile dug for treasure and found it; on the great ship timbers also, beside the lake, wreckage from Caligula's galleys, which still lie buried in the deepest depth of the water; on the rock of Nemi, and the fortress-like Orsini villa; on the Alban Mount itself, where it cut the clear sky." Aristodemo led the way. He was "straight and lithe and handsome as a young Bacchus," said Mrs. Ward, who also called him "a young Hermes in the transfiguring light." Henry James paused, his eyes on the youth; he surveyed the sunset scene. He murmured the name: his voice, said Mrs. Ward, caressed it—Aristodemo—a kind of caress of the boy himself. And then she quotes him as exclaiming—in a manner almost banal—"What a name! What a place!" The youth, aware that he had the center of the stage, was voluble about the diggings and the artifacts. He described to James a marble head he had found—yes, he!—complete, even the nose preserved. The sun sank, the enchantment lingered. "For me," James wrote to his hostess later, "the Nemi lake, and the walk down and up (the latter perhaps most), and the strawberries and Aristodemo were the cream"—and he said, as for emphasis, "I am clear about that."

III

Mrs. Ward's excuse for sending James proof of *Eleanor* was that she had introduced an American girl into her story. The plot placed her Egeria, a charming sentient woman named Eleanor Burgoyne, in a villa like the Barberini, and in the countryside James had seen. Eleanor is helping a temperamental cousin, a man named Manisty, with a book in praise of old and reactionary Italy. To this villa comes the young American, Lucy Foster, a very churchy young puritan, stiff and awkward, badly dressed—*gauche* in every way. Eleanor is in love with her cousin; and she becomes Lucy's Egeria as well: she gets her to dress her hair, induces her to put on more stylish clothes, brings out her latent beauty, and Manisty in due course falls in love with her. Lucy and Manisty however are proponents of differing philosophies. Lucy is anti-

Catholic and all for Mrs. Ward's progress and a democratic Italy. Manisty defends the past, the Pope, the Jesuits. In the long meandering plot Lucy and Manisty come together; and Eleanor ultimately dies, having endowed others and deprived herself of her love. The novel was a successful serial in *Harper's* and in the United States at one time was selling 1,000 copies a day—more copies in one day than an entire edition of some of James's works. In fact Harper had confined the printing of *The Awkward Age*, recently published, to exactly 1,000 copies, so little faith did they have in their author, and in this novel.

James's letters to Mrs. Ward about *Eleanor*, whose impending success he could foresee, are solid little private essays on the art of the novel as he practiced it. He thought Lucy Foster not sufficiently American. Her religious stiffness seemed to him untypical. The American reader would say, "Why this isn't *us*—it's English 'dissent' "—"keep in mind how very different a thing *that* is (socially, aesthetically etc.) from the American free (and easy) multitudinous churches, that, practically in any community, are like so many (almost) clubs or Philharmonics or amateur theatrical companies." Nor did James think an obscure American girl would be shocked by Rome, the Pope, St. Peter's, kneeling, or anything of that sort. "She would probably be either a Unitarian or 'Orthodox,' (which is, I believe, 'Congregational,' though in New England always called 'Orthodox,') and in either case as Emersonized, Hawthornized, J. A. Symondsized, and as 'frantic' to *feel* the Papacy etc. as one could well represent her." And, he went on,

In that case I should say "The bad clothes etc. oh yes; as much as you like. The beauty etc. scarcely. The offishness to 'Rome,'—as a spectator etc.—almost not at all." . . . Had I looked over your shoulder I should have said: "*Specify*, localise, a little more—give her a *definite* Massachusetts, or Maine, or whatever, habitation— imagine a country-college-town—invent, if need be, a name, and stick to that."

He did not stop with this. He told Mrs. Ward he felt she was throwing her story too obviously at the reader; no suspense, no "crooked corridor," no attempt to keep him guessing for a while. Since Eleanor the Egeria was the focus, she should keep her at the "center," make her consciousness "full, rich, universally prehensile and *stick* to it—don't shift—and don't shift *arbitrarily*—how, otherwise, do you get your unity of subject or keep up your reader's sense of it?" He concluded his letter with: "Do let me have more of *Eleanor*—to rewrite!"

Mrs. Ward seems to have replied that the question of a "center of consciousness" represented an "old difference" between them. Moreover, she chided James for criticizing her novel before he had read it entire—she had sent him but the first instalments. This elicited from the novelist a 2,000-word answer. He apologized for anticipating what Mrs. Ward would write, and he did not think there was an "old difference" between them; to say so made it sound as if he had a fixed idea about how a novel should be written. There were five million "rules"—as many as there were subjects—and each rule arose from the artistic situation in each case. He admitted he was "a wretched person to *read* a novel—I begin so quickly and concomitantly, *for myself*, to write it rather —even before I know clearly what it's about." Nevertheless there were certain things he could say, and one was that the artist must know what he is doing and how he is doing it. The story must get its unity not from the personality of the author—as apparently Mrs. Ward had argued—but from the nature of the subject. He exonerated himself from prejudging what her novel would be like by adding that he did not have the feeling, from what Mrs. Ward had shown him, that she did know how she was "doing it." "The promiscuous shiftings of standpoint and centre of Tolstoy and Balzac for instance (which come, to my eye, from their being not so much big dramatists as big *painters*—as Loti is a painter), are the inevitable result of the *quantity of presenting* their genius launches them in. With the complexity they pile up they *can* get no clearness without trying again and again for new centres. And they don't *always* get it."

What James was defending so ardently was not only his kind of novel—which Mrs. Ward could never write—but the method of limited "point of view"; he anticipated the criticism that this might restrict the freedom of his story-telling. When *Eleanor* was published a year later he offered Mrs. Ward extravagant praise, calling it "a large and noble performance," although confessing that in reading the work he had "recomposed and reconstructed *Eleanor* from head to foot." After the *éloge*, he damned the book as having an essential weakness—Lucy wasn't a genuine antithesis to Eleanor, she had "no logical force"; moreover, "irony should at its hour have presided" in the novel. Mrs. Ward however saw only the praise in the letter and she printed it almost entire in her memoirs.

There was one page in *Eleanor* which James read with a certain humor and irony of his own. Mrs. Ward had included a brief scene, irrelevant to the story proper, in which she introduced a man of letters, a poet, who visits Eleanor's villa. He was named Mr. Bellasis, and he figures only as a "walk-on" character. She made him stuffy, arrogant, self-important. "So you have read my book?" is his first question and then he wants to know whether Eleanor has reread it. "My friends tell me in Rome that the book cannot really be appreciated except at a second or third reading." The physical Bellasis does not resemble James; but something in the way Mrs. Ward made him talk sounds familiar. Mr. Bellasis has no use for critics, and he talks of style: "Why the style is done with a magnifying glass!—There's not a phrase—not a word that I don't stand by," he says. When Mrs. Ward sent James her first instalment he answered: "I've read every word, and many two or three times, as Mr. Bellasis would say—and is Mr. Bellasis, by the way, naturally—as it were—H.J.???!!!"

We do not know whether Mrs. Ward answered his question.

\ I V

A few days after his visit to the Villa Barberini, Henry James was
standing on the deck of the little steamer that took pilgrims—and
brooding tourists—from Sorrento to Capri. Far aloft, on the great
rock, was pitched "the amazing creation of the friend" who was
offering him hospitality—the San Michele of Dr. Axel Munthe.
The puffing little boat had carried with it a flock of Germans and
Americans. Above and below, through the blue of air and sea,
there was a great confused shining of hot cliffs and crags and
buttresses. James sat on the deck and meditated on "the splendid
couchant outline." The deck was empty. The "happy brotherhood
of American and German tourists, including, of course, many
sisters," had scrambled down into little waiting rocking tubs, and
after a few strokes, popped systematically into the small orifice of
the famous Blue Grotto. There was a moment when they were lost
from view—the psychological moment during which an observer,
sitting on the peaceful deck, could "find himself aware of how
delightful it might be if none of them should come out again." As
the wave rose over the aperture there was a most encouraging
appearance that they perfectly might not reappear. "There it is.
There is no more of them," James mused. His imagination erased
them. "It is a case to which nature has, by the neatest stroke and
with the best taste in the world, just quietly attended."

His visit to Munthe was to be an affair of twenty-four hours, a
side-trip from another visit he was paying in Naples. He had met
the famous society doctor on the train to Rome, almost a month
before, and had received several pressing invitations to come to
him at Capri, to the villa reared by Munthe among blocks of
ancient marble on the site of the ancient villa of Tiberius. At the
same time no less pressing invitations had come to James from
Sorrento, from the popular Italianate-American novelist F. Marion
Crawford—son of the sculptor Thomas Crawford and nephew of
Julia Ward Howe—to visit his elaborate villa at Sant'Agnello di
Sorrento where relatives of the American Wards and Howes gath-

ered for familiar and happy festivities. James had scarcely known Marion Crawford when he used to visit Marion's mother and stepfather, the Luther Terrys, in the Palazzo Odescalchi in his Rome of the early 1870's. Now, in the fulness of time, the occupant of modest Lamb House was finding the later generation in villas that spoke of great affluence; in the case of F. Marion Crawford a best-selling prosperity not unlike Mrs. Humphry Ward's. To his intimates James wrote that Crawford was "a prodigy of talent—and of wealth! It is humiliating."

The Italianate Americans, in their cushioned ease, had always been devotees of amateur theatricals and musical evenings, and during James's stay at the Villa Crawford his host would invite to his great terrace after dinner the usual local quartet—violins, guitar, flute, the musical barber, the musical tailor, saddler, joiner —the humblest sons of the people and exponents of Neapolitan song. The novelist had planned a brief visit here. However Crawford announced a grand *festa* to celebrate his wife's birthday, and James promised to return after his side-trip to Munthe's.

The Munthe week-end proved a continuous *divertissement*. There was first the fantastic villa itself with its loggias and its statued pergolas hanging dizzily over splendid views. The white arcades and the cool chambers offered at every step some fragment of the past, a rounded porphyry pillar supporting a bust, a shaft of pale alabaster upholding a trellis, some mutilated marble image, some bronze that had roughly resisted the ages. "Our host," James was to write, "had the secret; but he could only express it in grand practical ways." Still, it was a place "out of which the long summer squeezes every secret and shadow."

James however as always also had a feeling of discomfort; the villa of black Tiberius had overhung the immensity of Capri and this evoked "the cruel, the fatal historic sense . . . to make so much distinction, how much history had been needed!" The air still throbbed for James "and ached with it, as with an accumulation of ghosts to whom the very climate was pitiless, condemning them to blanch for ever in the general glare and grandeur." Munthe in his memoirs attributed to James the statement that San Michele was "the most beautiful place in the world." But the private record, a letter to Venetian friends, gives us James's direct impression—"a creation of the most fantastic beauty, poetry, and inutility that I have ever seen clustered together." Munthe also had, James remarked, an "unnatural simplicity." The novelist seems to have enjoyed however the local feast day of St. Anthony. He visited the crowded chapel and square, finding the "robust odour" of the peasantry "thick and resisting," but delighting in the color, the ribbons, the draperies, the general impression of the festival as "holy and merry and noisy as possible."

Munthe held open house that afternoon. Huge straw-bellied flasks of purple wine were tilted for all the thirsty—and the general thirst was great. Three hundred flocked through the long, pillared portico "where everything was white and light save the blue of the great bay as it played up from far below or as you took it in, between shining columns, with your elbows on the parapet." Sorrento and Vesuvius were close to James; Naples furthest off melted into the middle of the picture—into shimmering vagueness, and the long arm of Posilippo.

When the wine-drinkers were gone the musicians came, as at the Villa Crawford, and the dancers of the tarantella. "It was all purple wine, all art and song, and nobody a grain the worse. It was fireworks and conversation—the former, in the piazzetta, were to come later; it was civilisation and amenity. I took in the greater picture, but I lost nothing else; and I talked with the contadini about antique sculpture. No, nobody was a grain the worse; and I had plenty to think of. . . . It was antiquity in solution, with every brown mild figure, every note of the old speech, every tilt of the great flask, every shadow cast by every classic fragment."

After Munthe and Capri, the novelist had a few more days with the Crawfords, days of a continually festive kind. "It was a treat to have Mr. James in the house," one of Crawford's sisters remembered. "His keen interest in everything, his utter absence of 'side,' the exquisite urbanity which tempered every expression of his unerring judgment of men and women; above all, his amazing humility about his own achievement, made up a most endearing personality. We all felt quite poorly the day Henry James left the Villa."

The summer heat was over the land. James did not linger. He paid his visit to the Countess Peruzzi in the mountain coolness of Vallombrosa, where he also saw much of her brother, Julian Story, the sculptor's son. While in Florence, James's hotel room was rattled and shaken early one morning by an earth shock. "Praise be to earthquakes of small calibre," he remarked; a little more would not have been at all amusing. Early in June he was in Paris; crossing the Channel July 7, he went straight to Folkestone and to Rye. He had been away nearly four months. Lamb House, with its refurbished fireplaces and reduced fire hazards, seemed to him a haven of coolness and greenness. "Oh, it is a joy to be once more in this refreshed and renovated refuge!" he wrote to Edward Warren. He had indeed had enough of travel, he who had been so ardent a traveller of old. He had had enough of villas built or rented with the proceeds of best-selling novels. Almost a decade would elapse before he would go again to the Continent.

A YOUNG SCULPTOR

I

A FORTNIGHT AFTER HENRY JAMES'S RETURN FROM ITALY THERE arrived at Lamb House, carefully packed, the bust of the Young Conte Alberto Bevilacqua which James had purchased from Hendrik Andersen in the Via Margutta. The novelist set it in the niche of the newly remodelled chimneypiece in his dining room where it would face him during lonely repasts. It would stand there for years—the neat amateurish head and shoulders of boyish adolescence, somehow weighted and lifeless, for Andersen did not care for such small and trivial things as busts: his touch was heavy. His dream was of great equestrian statues gleaming in the sun; he wanted to work in the soaring and the colossal; his vision was of huge American cities displaying form-filled fountains—sculpted by Hendrik Christian Andersen. But he was young and obscure, and it was a new experience for him to receive a letter from a famous novelist in far-off Rye, in England, which told him, "I've struck up a tremendous intimacy with dear little Conte Alberto, and we literally can't live without each other." Henry James added: "He is the first object my eyes greet in the morning and the last at night." Equally exciting for Andersen was the famous writer's saying that Bevilacqua was "so living, so human, so sympathetic and sociable and curious." It would be a life attachment, he said—"Brave little Bevilacqua, and braver still big Maestro Andersen."

The bravos rang loudly in the ears of the hopeful artist. He had been working in comparative obscurity, making such friends as he could among Roman-Americans and dreaming his dreams, as James's Roderick Hudson had done a quarter of a century before. To have James tell him that his little Bevilacqua would be a "life attachment" seemed an augury of friendship, intimacy, patronage.

And when James wrote that the bust would "make many friends here," Andersen immediately assumed this to mean James had written an article about him and his work. The novelist was quick to correct this impression. "I'm afraid I said something (accidentally) that misguided you to suppose I have written in a journal . . . I haven't." He had simply meant that the bust would be visible in its niche to his many friends who came to Lamb House.

Andersen had planned to leave for New York that summer. In the light of James's praise, and his invitation, it seemed to him a good idea to go to America by way of Rye. James was delighted. He had hardly expected so prompt a response. It came when he was downcast and weary. His trip to Italy had made him feel old; and in Rye he felt lonely. To have a splendid eager youth come rushing to his side at this moment of the midsummer made James feel that someone still cared and that he was not cut off from the world. Andersen was hardly the "nervous nineteenth-century Apollo" the novelist had made of Roderick Hudson; he was strong and handsome, and full of energy. To be sure, he talked a little like Roderick—he wanted to do statues of Love, Equality, Peace, great abstractions, as Roderick had proclaimed his plans for Adams and Cains and Beauty, Wisdom, Power, Genius. Sensing that Andersen had dreams of grandeur, James warned him that Lamb House was hardly a *palazzo* or even a villa. "I feel you to be formidable, fresh from your St. Peterses, Vaticans and Trattorie Fiorentine—formidable to my small red British cottage and small plain British *cuisine*—but you will be very welcome."

I

The relationship between the two had its complexities from the first. James looked at Andersen with an inward vision of his own youth, his distant Roman days. On his side, Andersen saw a kind, indeed a benignant, fatherly figure, who might aid him in the hard climb to fame and fortune. He made himself agreeable, with a show of modesty on the one hand and of ambition on the other. It is doubtful whether James saw, at the beginning of their friendship, much beyond the chiselled countenance, the flaxen hair, the big frame, the vitality of the young sculptor. That Andersen lacked the intellectual and moral force—or the will to discipline—James demanded of himself in art was hardly perceptible at first, and it is doubtful whether James cared. Nor was Andersen's grandiosity—which James sensed—likely to have troubled him. Youth was entitled to its dreams; the grander the better, so long as they were anchored in realities, as his own had been. James's feeling of tenderness and affection for Hendrik Andersen, and the appeal of the young man's physical qualities, sufficed. Andersen, on his side, knew he was admired, and responded warmly; but it is doubtful whether he had the depth to discern just how profoundly he touched James, and how much the aging novelist felt attached to him from the first. Andersen seems to have thought mainly of how "useful" James could be to him.

Coincidence indeed added a few charming touches. Henry and Hendrik—they bore the same name. The Hendrik evoked in James also the old name of that river which had nourished his young senses between Albany and New York; he had bestowed the name of Hudson on his first hero. And then his birthday and the sculptor's fell in the same month. They were second sons. They had talented brothers. Hendrik's elder brother, Andreas, was a skilful painter. From the first, James treated Andersen as if he were his *alter ego*. He tended to endow him with his own feelings about art—which may explain his later chagrin at discovering that Hendrik had no such feelings. Hendrik in the presence of the novelist possessed a longer past than he knew. The old Henry and the young—it was as if James had been re-fashioned out of his old memories and his old passions. A warm nostalgia filled their hours together during the sculptor's first visit to Lamb House. James seemed unaware of his own illusions. And it is doubtful whether he fully realized at first that the youth's presence had filled him with that precious essence that men have called from time imme-

morial—love. He bestowed on Andersen his own taste, his own
high standards, his own feeling for beauty. He looked into the
mirror and saw smiling and healthy youth instead of his obese and
aging self. The image charmed—one might say it enchanted.

11

We have no record of their talk, but it is possible to imagine its
course in the light of the epistolary record and James's retrospective allusions. It was casual, easy, spontaneous. James was always
to be happiest when his objects of affection were not too intellectual, not burdened with literary trappings. That was why he felt
comfortable with the sailors and the lifeguards. Andersen met this
qualification splendidly; he was singularly unlettered (James
would later chide him for his spelling), and singularly self-cen-
tered. They talked of art, work, career, success, how to confront
and woo the world; they discussed the old subjects of James's
professional life, they spoke of intimate things, family, friends,
affections. So Roderick and Rowland had talked long ago. The
novelist could offer the wisdom of his decades and Hendrik
listened with tender deference. They cycled to Winchelsea and
back. They sat under the big mulberry tree in the Lamb House
garden at the summer's richest hour. The splendid bignonia threw
its red flowers up and down the south wall; the big purple clematis
flushed as if in competition and envy. Andersen was all sincerity
and respect—and Henry James was full of warm feelings. He was
unexpectedly happy. One judges that Andersen's deference contained no awe; he was not one to be shy. Forgotten for the moment by Henry was pride of reputation, envy of the best-sellers,
the weight of the world. He lived for a small, a cherished idyll,
of happy summer moments. And with his curiosity and questioning, he learned more intimately the simple facts of his new-found
friend's life. Hendrik Christian Andersen was a remote relative
of the teller of fairy tales—"little Hans," James would call him,
as if to give him the stamp of literature, but adding promptly

that the "little" was uttered "without prejudice to your magnifi
cent stature." The sculptor had been born in Bergen, Norway, and
brought to America as a child by his immigrant parents. The
family had lived at Newport in genteel poverty, where however
the Howes and La Farges, and other old families, had taken an
interest in the talented Andersen children. There were three sons,
all artistic. Besides the painter there was the youngest brother, a
musician; and there was a young sister. The father was an alco-
holic; ultimately he would be shipped back to Norway to drink
away the years. The mother was long-suffering and devoted. The
boys had little schooling; they had to go to work early. With some
help from well-wishers, Hendrik had gone to art school in Boston;
then he had lived in the Latin Quarter in Paris and attended the
École des Beaux Arts. He showed much skill in drawing, and a
painting of his concierge's daughter attracted attention; he tended
to stylize his subjects in imitation of the sixteenth-century Clouet,
court painter to François I. His emphasis was on clarity and
draughtsmanship. After a while, he decided that he did not want
to follow in the footsteps of his brother, the painter. He took up
sculpture and went to the Holy City where the secrets of Michelangelo were still remembered, and where he presently joined the
art-life in and around the Piazza del Popolo. At the end of the
nineteenth century all was still hope and hard work—a familiar
story of zeal, dedication and the dream of Arcadia. A great tenderness seems to have been evoked in Henry James as he listened. He
had liked Hendrik from the first; and when the three-day visit was
over he became aware, in a strangely troubled way, that he had
deeper feelings for him than he had ever had perhaps for anyone
outside his own family. To the Elliotts in Rome, in whose apartment he had met Andersen, he wrote, "That most loveable youth,
as he strikes me, Hans [sic] Christian Andersen, turned up in due
course nearly a fortnight ago—came down, that is, spent two
days and was as nice as could be; then whirled himself off into
space after making me grow quite fond enough of him to miss

him. I think he really liked his little visit, and was cooled and comforted, perhaps even a little braced."

We cannot doubt this—nor that Henry himself had been much comforted and braced. "I would with joy have put him up for ever so much longer," the novelist added, but Andersen had gone on to New York to try his fortune there. James told the Elliotts he had "distinct confidence" in his future. It took courage, said Henry, to be a sculptor. Andersen "doesn't, somehow, make one positively alarmed for him. But I shall watch over him there—as I hope to hear from him—with a great deal of anxiety, all the same, as well as sympathy."

In the letters he began to write now to the young sculptor he hovered a great deal over him; he had advice and encouragement for his protégé and an abundance of love. The letters show also an ache of absence unusual for James. "I was absurdly sorry to lose you when, that afternoon of last month, we walked sadly to the innocent and kindly little station together and our common fate growled out of the harsh false note of whirling you untimely away. Since then I have *missed* you out of all proportion to the three meagre little days (for it seems strange they were only *that*) that we had together. I have never (and I've done it three or four times) passed the little corner where we came up Udimore hill (from Winchelsea), in the eventide on our bicycles, without thinking ever so tenderly of our charming spin homeward in the twilight and feeling again the strange perversity it made of that sort of thing being so soon *over*. Never mind—we *shall* have more, lots more, of that sort of thing!" He hoped he could put him into his Watchbell Lane studio, "and we shall be good for each other; and the studio good for both of us." And James added, "I feel in you a *confidence*, dear Boy—which to show is a joy to me."

A few weeks later: "It *was*, last August—our meeting—all too brief, too fleeting and too sad. You merely brushed me with your elbow and turned me your back. I walked up from the station, that soft summer morning of your departure, much more lonely than I should have thought three days of companionship could, in their extinction, have made me."

James felt "confidence" in Andersen, but he was to discover, as the months passed, that the "loveable youth" would have to be loved at a distance. They were to have in all only half a dozen meetings and at long-spaced intervals. Andersen was too busy with his career, his ambitions, his excess of confidence. He came again to Lamb House two years later, after abandoning New York, and only after much pleading on James's part; and once more some months afterwards. They met in America in 1905; they met in Rome in 1907. Each meeting brought a renewal of affection, renewed and often intense outpourings from James, who wrote to Andersen with a freedom not to be found in any of his other letters. The greater part of this attachment seems to have been expressed in words, in an ache of loneliness, in touches of jealousy, in a kind of brooding hurt that the young maestro was not properly pursuing his genius under the old Master's direction. In his old age, James would pour out ironies and protests at Andersen, as he denounced his pretensions and his larger-than-life statues. The ironies however would be lost on the rigid and unimaginative Andersen.

I I I

Two significant elements set apart James's letters to Hendrik Andersen—the saddest and strangest perhaps in his entire *epistolarium*—from all of his correspondence up to this time. The first is the quantity of physical, tactile language: James repeatedly offers his *abbraccio*—puts out his arms to embrace the younger man, pats him tenderly on the back—in words. While these speak for a certain physical intimacy in their meetings, they can be seen also as forms of endearment in one who was overtly affectionate in public. There is abundant testimony that James in his late years embraced friends at his club or at a railroad station in the Latin fashion, with much patting on the back. Bernard Shaw has told how during a visit to Lamb House, James crossed the length of garden to kiss him on both cheeks, in the French style, as if he were bestowing the Legion of Honor. Shaw told this story with a vivid sense of amazement and amusement (for his own affections were always deeply interred in his wit). All this embracing and laying on of hands and tender benedictions in James's letters to Andersen may signify nothing more than a well-known demonstrative Jamesian hug. Nevertheless there is a quality of passion and possession in the reiterated "I hold you close," "I feel, my dear boy, my arms around you," or "I meanwhile pat you affectionately on the back, across the Alps and Apennines, I draw you close, I hold you long." James is at his most mothering—but also most intense—in letters written to Andersen in 1902 on the death of the sculptor's elder brother, when he enjoins him, as from Olympus, to "lean on me as on a brother and a lover."

The sense that I can't *help* you, see you, talk to you, touch you, hold you close and long, or do anything to make you rest on me, and feel my participation—this torments me, dearest boy, makes me ache for you, and for myself; makes me gnash my teeth and groan at the bitterness of things. . . . I wish I could go to Rome and put my hands on you (oh, how lovingly I should lay them!) but that, alas, is odiously impossible. . . . I am in town for a few weeks but I return to Rye April 1st, and sooner or later to *have* you there and do for you, to put my arms round you and *make* you lean on me as on a brother and a lover, and keep you on and on, slowly comforted or at least relieved of the first bitterness of pain —this I try to imagine as thinkable, attainable, not wholly out of the question. There I am, at any rate, and there is my house and my garden and my table and my studio—such as it is—and your room, and your welcome, and your place everywhere—and I press them upon you, oh so earnestly, dearest boy, if isolation and grief and the worries you are overdone with become intolerable to you. . . . I will *nurse* you through your dark passage. . . . I embrace you with almost a passion of pity.

The pity endured, but it would turn to mockery and irony: for the dead brother's widow, the former Olivia Cushing, subsidized Hendrik Andersen, and the giant men and women began to emerge in his studio. Huge fountains, a "world city," were sketched—with no visible signs of public interest, although a few exalted patrons gave their names to the latter project. James's letters, brilliant statements on the discipline and scale of art, belong however to a later time.

The second element in the correspondence is James's unusual and reiterated cry for the absent one. The pain of separation is strong. Two years after the first visit James is writing, "I miss you —keep on doing so—out of all proportion to the too few hours you were here—and even go so far as to ask myself whether visits so damnably short haven't more in them to groan, than to thank, for." In 1903: "Don't 'chuck' me this year, dearest boy, if you can possibly help it." In 1904 he signs himself "your poor helpless far-off but all devoted H.J. who seems condemned almost and never to be near you, yet who, if he were, would lay upon you a pair of hands soothing, sustaining, positively *healing*, in the quality of their pressure." In 1905: "We must hold on in one way or another till we meet. It is miserable how little, as the months and years go on, we *do*." In 1906: "The months are added to the months and we only don't meet." In 1911, when James is sixty-eight and Hendrik is thirty-nine, there is a final clinging to a hopeless wish, the tired words of an old man: "It's a sad business, this passage of all the months and years without our meeting again save in this poor way [that is by correspondence]. I wish to heaven we could relieve it a little by finding ourselves again fondly face to face. I want to see you—and I so hold out my arms to you. Somehow it may still come—but it seems far off. Well, may life still be workable for you, with the mighty aid of art. *Ci vuol anchea* little intimate affection too, *pure* (as they say) *che diavolo!* Therefore let us manage it somehow." And in 1913, when James is seventy, he still speaks with a kind of faint and forlorn hope that perhaps they "will meet (and still embracingly) over the abyss of our difference in years and conditions."

The embraces were postponed; the abyss remained; it had been temporarily bridged at the first, and James's search—*che diavolo* —for affection, *pure*, as he had said, had long been turned elsewhere. But there lingered this particular love, which flickered up whenever he heard from Andersen, even when it was smothered by the sculptor's failures in perception, his indifferences, or his insensitive belief that he could induce James to be among the sponsors of his plan to build a city *de chic*. The question that may be asked is whether the use of the term "lover" and the verbal passion of the letters was "acted out." The question, if relevant, cannot be answered. We simply do not know. Most Victorians kept the doors of their bedrooms shut: certainly Henry James did. Some might judge the question irrelevant in the life of a writer who had defended himself for so many years against sex, and had exalted the intellectual and emotional rather than the physical in human relations. It is perhaps too easy to assume in our time that the "physical" would have to be a consequence of so much epistolary passion. It well might be: but it would be presuming too much to insist on its inevitability, particularly in the absence of Andersen's letters to James. We must remind ourselves also, in weighing this delicate and ambiguous evidence, that James had hitherto tended to look at the world as through plate-glass. Andersen seems to have helped James emerge from behind that protective wall. If we let our fancy run, we might think of him as opening James up to sensory feeling to a greater degree than had been the case earlier; perhaps the touch of those strong fingers of the sculptor's hand may have given James a sense of physical closeness and warmth which he had never allowed himself to feel in earlier years; and it is this which we perhaps read in his letters. Certainly a great fund of affection was there, and it was openly expressed. Allowance must be made for James's long puritan years, the confirmed habits of denial, the bachelor existence, in which erotic feeling had been channelled into hours of strenuous work and the wooing of *mon bon*, the available and compliant muse of the writing table. One also must remember that James had a fear of loss of masculinity.

His highest praise of a writer—as with Turgenev—had been to stress the "masculine" in his work. He had rigorously, in the inhibited Victorian fashion, transferred the seat of affection to his intellect; he had argued in his discussion of Maupassant that it was not the physical side of man, but his reflective side, that is most characteristic. James was constitutionally incapable of belonging to the underworld of sex into which Oscar Wilde had drifted. These elements must be weighed in any consideration of James's intimate life. Somerset Maugham used to enjoy telling his friends of an alleged attempt by Hugh Walpole to violate the Master, and of James's passionate recoil—"I can't, I can't!" Since Maugham's feud with Walpole was notorious, we must regard the anecdote with suspicion; yet it may testify to an understandable reticence and even fear and anxiety in James. We may speculate endlessly on this theme, without discovering the answers. One thing is clear. The "heavy" Andersen, whose brightness would fade so quickly, inspired feelings in Henry James akin to love—to a love such as Fenimore had had for him long before she ended her life in Venice. She had written of her loneliness and complained of the years that passed between their meetings as James now wrote to Andersen. She had known what it was to have the object of her love fail her, fail to recognize the depth of her feeling. This James would in due course learn from Hendrik.

For the rest, it is perhaps useful to invoke the inspired comment of Geoffrey Scott, in his *Portrait of Zélide*. Discussing the passion that developed between Madame de Charrière and Benjamin Constant, Scott observes that psychologically "the character of their relation was abundantly clear;—technically the inquiry would be inconclusive."

THE THIRD PERSON

HENRY JAMES HAD RETURNED FROM ITALY VAGUELY DEPRESSED. HE had fed much more on "established memories" than on new impressions. There had been too many changes; there were too many intruding ghosts. "All was charming, but all was haunted," he wrote to Francis Boott. He set aside for the moment the proposed biography of Story; almost four years would elapse before he wrote it. Perhaps it also had in it too great an assemblage of ghosts. And if he had found the life of his fellow-writers in their fine villas—Bourget, Mrs. Ward, Crawford—amusing, it nevertheless made him aware of the difference between their "success"— and his. Then, just before leaving Rome, he received word that his brother William was coming abroad for his health. This was another—a very loud—clock-stroke of the years. William had seemed to Henry the embodiment of restless energy, a mind and body constantly questioning and active: now he was on his way to take the cure at Bad Nauheim, like so many elderly invalids. Seven years had passed since the brothers' last meeting.

Thinking that William and his wife Alice would go first to England, Henry offered them his London flat, at the moment tenantless. But the two sailed directly for Germany. Henry soon learned the essential facts. Dr. Baldwin of Florence happened to be at Nauheim, also taking a cure. He examined William and reported to the novelist that his brother had developed a serious heart condition—a valvular lesion. Baldwin did not minimize its seriousness, but he was full of hope. Henry wrote to the doctor that what he had learned made him "rather sick and sore and sad; so narrow a squeak does he seem to have had." Physiological details always terrified him and he would try to believe, he said, "in the reality of the rescue." To William he wrote that he was deeply moved by Baldwin's "inscrutable physiological definiteness"; and he added, "oh, how I want you convalescent and domesticated here!" Henry too began to worry about his heart. "I am coddling my organ at such a rate that I no longer bicycle up anything less level than a billiard table," he wrote to Dr. Baldwin. Fortunately he had a billiard table of some twenty miles in the area of Rye.

I

A few days after his return from Italy, Henry learned that his landlord had died and that Lamb House was for sale. The price was £2,000 or about $10,000. This was substantial for the time, yet reasonable given the excellent condition of the house and the increasing value of Rye real estate. Henry had no difficulty in making up his mind. He had lived himself sufficiently into the house to know that he wanted it. However, he had very little ready money, and not much practical knowledge about financing such a purchase. He wrote promptly to Germany to his brother, who had for a long time handled his finances in America, to summarize the arguments for and against his making what would be the largest expenditure of his lifetime. He began in so portentous a tone that he had a second thought, and reassured William with a "don't be alarmed" and "I don't mean that I've received a proposal of marriage." He seemed once again to be the younger brother asking for guidance—even while announcing he had made up his mind. He was certain he could obtain a loan from his banker. Rye was becoming increasingly popular; the new golf course was attracting visitors, and so on. His letter ran to many pages. He told William he had wept "tears of joy at the thought of acquiring this blessed little house so promptly and so cheaply." William, in the midst of debilitating baths and general fatigue, took Henry at his word. He had not yet seen the house; but Dr. Baldwin had, and William asked him whether he considered it worth $10,000. Baldwin was physician to royalty. His conception of houses was on a palatial scale, and he had spent only one night in Lamb House. It had struck him as a kind of rural *pied-à-terre* for the London-identified novelist. He therefore judged $10,000 to be "a very extravagant price." William passed the word along to Henry.

The effect of this on Henry was registered in a lengthy letter of anger and frustration. William had sent "a colder blast than I could apprehend." Forgetting that he had asked for his brother's opinion, Henry exclaimed, "I do, strange as it may appear to you, in this matter, know more or less what I'm about . . . I am not yet wholly senile." Brushing aside the question of cost, he told William his fondness for Lamb House was reason enough for acquiring it. As for Baldwin's opinion, the doctor had "scarcely appeared to me to appreciate the place at all." He wasn't qualified to judge. "PLEASE, drop the subject altogether—with Baldwin. I *hate* its being talked of with anyone but Alice." Henry said he had taken counsel every step of the way with Edward Warren. The architect considered the house not only worth the price, but also an excellent investment. Moreover, Henry had learned that he needed only $4,000—£800—since the rest represented a mortgage he could take over at 4 per cent. He wouldn't have to borrow any money.

The obsessed pleading of the reply and the self-justification revealed anew how vulnerable Henry was to anything William might say. A word of disapproval and the novelist was taken back to the days when William repulsed him at their play. "*You*, after all, have bought and built etc.," Henry wrote, "and I have never wanted faith! I *may*, of course, have made a mistake—anyone, everyone, always may." But he added that he would have been utterly depressed and shown no faith in himself "or any courage for *any* act" if he had not taken advantage of this opportunity. His sense of inferiority and his anger were also transferred to more recent history; and there was a note of pathos as he wrote:

My whole being cries out aloud for something that I can call my own—and when I look round me at the splendour of so many of the "literary" fry, my confrères (M. Crawford's, P. Bourget's, Humphry Ward's, Hodgson Burnett's, W. D. Howellses etc.) and

I feel that I may strike the world as still, at fifty-six, with my long labour and my genius, reckless, presumptuous and unwarranted in curling up (for more assured peaceful production) in a poor little $10,000 shelter—once for all and for all time—*then* I do feel the bitterness of humiliation, the iron enters into my soul, and (I blush to confess it), I *weep!* But enough, enough, enough!

II

Enough, enough, enough! His sense of outrage abated. William's Alice offered a loan from her personal funds. Henry gracefully declined; he no longer needed it. He apologized to William. He had felt, he said, "the impulse to *fraternize*—put it that way—with you, over the pleasure of my purchase, and to see you glow with pride in *my* pride of possession." This was the heart of the matter. For Henry, in spite of his childhood sense of rivalry with his elder brother, had always wanted his approval. The episode resembled very much the days of their boyhood—Henry could not play with William and the older boys; Henry could not own a house; Henry wasn't qualified—for anything! Some such ancient jumble of emotion out of the faraway world of the "mere junior" had been reawakened. The boy Henry would have done anything for a loving glance from William, a pat on the back. Now he shifted his old sense of second-class status to his relationship with his affluent *confrères. They* had elaborate villas. He was entitled at least to a small hermitage. William had once again—this time in the most innocent way imaginable—hit one of the novelist's exposed nerves.

Just how exposed this nerve was we know when we remind ourselves that not quite five years had elapsed since *Guy Domville*. The rejected author, the scorned brother, were one; and the power of this old hurt had been amply illsutrated in the fate of little Miles, and the other little boys, and in his retreat to the "safety" of the feminine world—as in some of Henry's old fantasies, and as in the bad novel (*Confidence*) he had written when William had

married Alice, in which he had used his familiar nickname of
"Angel" for a fictional "Angela." Transformed into Angela, he
could be jealous, kittenish, devious, spiteful and offer himself the
armor and consolations of his assumed sex. Whenever William
was close at hand, Henry resorted to these feminine defenses. And
then, too, the central symbol of this feminine world—the symbol
of the House—was involved. Poynton, Bounds, Eastmead, Bly,
Covering End, Paramore where young Owen Wingrave had died:
the houses of his tales had suddenly become the reality of Lamb
House.

III

William James, his wife and young daughter Peggy arrived at
Lamb House early in October of 1899. The brothers had last met
during William's sabbatical year in 1892. In the intervening years
the two had passed into late middle age. Henry had had his crisis;
William's fame as philosopher had continued to grow. A snapshot
of the brothers taken a few months after this time clearly shows their
established relationship—William stands upright, his arm around
Henry's shoulders; at the same time he pulls himself a little away
from him. Henry's head is sharply and stiffly inclined toward him,
as if he wished to lay his head on his shoulder. The picture has an
intimacy as of a couple posing for a camera, with Henry held
firmly but at arm's length in William's arm.

William felt tolerably well after his Nauheim cure. He responded with his old painter's sense to the greenish-yellow autumn
light in which Rye was bathed. He found the town, with its
miniature brick walls, houses, nooks, coves and gardens alternately
suggestive of English, Dutch and Japanese effects. Lamb House
itself seemed to him like a toy compared with his own large New
England house in Cambridge; he wondered "how *families* ever
could have been reared in most of the houses," they were so small.
He characterized his brother's house as "a most exquisite collection of quaint little stage properties," and his brother as still

interested above all "in the operations of his fancy." He found
Henry's face calm, his spirit "equable." In general he had his old
view of his younger brother—that he was a "powerless-feeling" but
an agreeable if slightly temperamental fellow. He did however
perceive that his life in this out-of-the-way town must be lonely,
yet he said the novelist was in equilibrium with his loneliness. This
was William's fixed picture of Henry: and every time he saw him
abroad, after an interval, some such vision of him was recorded.
"Harry is a queer boy," he had written to his wife some years
before, "so good and yet so limited, as if he had taken an oath not
to let himself out to more than half his humanhood in order to
keep the other half from suffering, and had capped it with a
determination not to give anyone else credit for the half he
resolved not to use himself. Really it is not an oath or a resolve,
but helplessness." As usual, Henry was "helpless" only in William's presence. As usual, he was reticent, closed-in, on his guard,
full of awe and respect, making no allowance for his own reputation and achievement. They related to one another intellectually
as adults. Emotionally they were still back in Fourteenth Street, in
the 1850's.

In these circumstances it can be understood how much anxiety
Henry, through the admiring eyes and affections of long ago, felt
over William's illness. At first William took everything in his old
stride, save that he tired easily after his walks. He sat in the
garden, he read, he worked at the Gifford lectures he hoped to give
at Edinburgh on the varieties of religious experience. But within a
fortnight he began to complain of being unwell again, and quite
suddenly one day he had a return of the terrible chest pains he had
experienced in America. Alarmed, Henry and Alice took him at
once to London and installed him in De Vere Gardens, with its
spacious rooms and big sky windows. They called in the eminent
heart specialist Bezly Thorne, a younger Harley Street man well
versed in the latest theories concerning heart ailments. He ordered
the unwilling William to bed, put him on a strict no-starch diet.

This time the philosopher obeyed. As Henry put it, he at last "consented to be really ill." And watching him, the novelist became aware that William was "a graver and more precarious case than I had dreamed of."

After three weeks of this regimen the patient improved. Thorne then dispatched him—it was December by now—to Malvern for hydropathic treatment. Here the bitter cold of the season and the rigors of the baths quickly made William ill again, and after about ten days he rushed back with Alice to London. Henry however in the interval had let his flat for the coming year. He met the two on their arrival from Malvern, put them in a hotel, and then, next day, brought them back to Rye.

In the waning days of December, in sad and wintry Rye, where the storms raged and the wind roared, the brothers and the sister-in-law awaited the coming of the last year of the old century. Its advent had been announced that autumn by the guns in South Africa—the trumpets, as they would prove, of the new era. The brothers had been together as young men in the other war, the War between the States, which Henry invariably recalled—and he wrote early in the new year of remembering "the general sense, the suspense and anxiety, stricken bereavement, woe and uncertainty of that—and more still of the special sense of young men, sons and brothers, of one's friends, many magnificent, *égorgés* in their flower. Such grey battalions of ghosts!"

Once again William showed improvement. Henry built great fires in his reconditioned fireplaces; and writing to Rosina Emmet he could report just before Christmas that "the quiet, the private conditions, the sunny outlook (for we *have* sun), the garden, the birds, the rest, the comfort, the sense of protection from *me!*"— the novelist caught his slip, and corrected it without erasing it—"by which I mean *by* me; all these things make so much for his gradual improvement." He later spoke of how he had been "worried, depressed, tormented in a high degree." "My spirits were in my boots about him and my time all went in trying to create for him here an atmosphere of optimism and an illusion of ease." To Miss Reubell he wrote: "I have always regarded him as the pillar of my family life, and to see him down while I am up bewilders and disorientates me." In these moments William's wife Alice became for Henry a counterpart of his own mother. He was seeing her for the first time at close quarters; they had hardly known each other in earlier years, and he grew greatly attached to her—"I bless the high heaven hourly for her." He spoke of the renewed sight she gave him "of what a woman can do for a man. Her devotion, her courage, her cheer, her ability and indefatigability, her ingenuity and resource in his service, are pure magnificence. She is *always* in the breach."

Peggy spent Christmas at Lamb House with her parents and uncle. As William grew stronger it was settled that he would go to the Riviera, to escape the hardest part of the English winter. A wealthy French *savant*, admirer of the philosopher, had made available to him his fine little château at Costebelle, not far from the Bourgets. In mid-January Henry escorted his brother and sister-in-law to Dover and saw them aboard the Channel steamer. To William's oldest son, who two years before had visited him, he reported that the philosopher was "distinctly on the mend and has extreme vitality (in spite of everything), but is handicapped by his excessive nervous delicacy and agitability, so that he doesn't get the good, much of the time, as it were, of the *facts*. He reads, talks, moves about, eats, sleeps, comports himself generally in a very different manner from a month ago. He *looks* far better."

I V

In Henry James's early stories, at the time of the Civil War, it is fairly easy to see the presiding emotions. In the tales which now tumbled from his desk one finds a complex network of old themes, reawakened by the anger he felt at William's seeming hostility to his acquisition of a home—anger which he could not discharge more directly, since his brother was seriously ill. The new stories contain a fund of the feline, and strange notes of cruelty. They are brilliant and decidedly unpleasant, and the old theme of revenge is stated in new and shrill terms. In James's earlier writings, revenge was often renounced—a guilty backing away from the violence it required. The narrator still shrinks from such passions, but this only dramatizes Mrs. Grantham's ferocity in "The Two Faces." She is a woman scorned. Insult moreover is added to the injury when Lord Gwyther, after jilting her, turns round and asks her to help introduce his inexperienced child bride into society. Mrs. Grantham complies—the bride is "overloaded like a monkey in a show." She herself provides the proper contrast by attiring herself with *éclat*. We are left with the narrator's horrified vision of two faces: May Grantham's, savagely triumphant, and the "feverish frightened" countenance of her young victim. In "The Beldonald Holbein," the tale derived from Julia Ward Howe's triumph of elderly beauty in Rome, we also look at two faces: that of the beautiful and proud Lady Beldonald, who uses her plain companion to enhance her own beauty; and the companion, whose plain face triumphs. She is seen as a perfect Holbein. In "The Special Type" there is a sacrificial lady who helps the male egotist marry the woman he wants, but takes her own quiet revenge. The theme will be used in "The Tone of Time," in which a woman painter is asked by a lady to supply her with the "portrait" of an imaginary husband. Instead of imagining a face, the lady painter puts on canvas the countenance of the man who long ago jilted her, only to discover that this man figured in the life of the very woman for whom she is painting the "portrait." A terrible jealousy seizes her; she will not surrender the picture at any price; hating the man, she loves him enough to want to keep his remembered likeness for herself; and she is jealous enough to refuse his image to the other woman. If we realize that in these stories Henry is casting himself as the jealous woman, we recover elements of the little ballets of his old novel *Confidence*. These had incorporated his jealousy of his sister-in-law. They are like a series of *pas-de-trois*, in which the

sex of the dancers is really irrelevant: what matters are the emotions they incarnate—old love, old jealousy, old anger—of the
little Henry who yearned with all the intensity of his being for
acceptance by his brother. In a more benign and pathetic mood,
the legend of childhood took still another form that autumn in a
tale Henry wrote just before William's arrival from Germany—before he began to feel the old envy again. He named it "Broken
Wings." In it a writer-lady and a painter-man avoid one another at
a country house. They had been in love years before; yet each
believed the other to be too successful for them to have a life
together. Then they both discover they have had their fame
without the financial reward that goes with it. Life together is now
possible; their wings "broken," they can face the future and recognize their old love. It is a wishful parable in which Henry equates
his own recent failures with William's broken health. He seems to
be saying in the story that perhaps now, at long last, he and
William, their wings broken, are on the same footing—in the
same boat.

.These three-cornered ballets and tugs-of-war in the inner life of
the novelist represent in essence the feelings of a brother scorned
who equates himself with scorned women. Nothing had changed
in James's inner world; what had changed was his adult power of
fantasy. His tales are richer and more jewel-encrusted; but they
show him still trying to resolve old problems, even as in the
themes of murdered little boys and surviving little girls. There
could be also morbid variants, such as "Maud-Evelyn," in which
the stiff young man gives up the living woman he is courting to
love a young woman whom he has never known—and who is dead.
It is a tale of a kind of *folie à trois*, in which the girl's parents
pretend their daughter lives. The young man falls in with their
pretense; he even pretends that he marries her. He goes further
still—pretends that she has died as his wife. He moves in fantasy
from courtship of a ghost to becoming a ghostly widower.

This venture into morbidity—to a feeling of the deadness of his
past—had its counterpart, however, in a different kind of tale: a

good-humored story to which James gave the significant title of "The Third Person." One of his slightest ghost stories, it is eloquently biographical. It was written while William and Alice were with him that cold December of 1899. Its principal characters are two elderly ladies who live in the ancient town of Marr, "a little old huddled, red-roofed, historic south-coast town," high and dry on its hilltop from which the sea has long since receded. The cousins have inherited a fine old brick house in which two hundred years of the "little melancholy, middling, disinherited" town have "squared themselves in the brown, panelled parlour, creaked patiently on the wide staircase and bloomed herbaceously in the red-walled garden." We are in Rye, we are in Lamb House. Presently the two spinsters became aware of the presence of a man, who carries his head always distinctly to one side. He appears and vanishes—he haunts one and then the other. With the aid of the local clergyman, who knows the history of the place, the third person is established as an ancestor who had lived in the old house and who had been hanged for smuggling—that is why his head is so mournfully tilted. For a while the cousins enjoy having a man about the house—even if he is a ghost. But they have also tense little jealous moments. In the end they decide the troubled spirit must be returned to its rest. Each has her own theory, and the tale peters out in a joke—a smuggled paperback, a Tauchnitz Continental edition banned from England to protect copyrights, effectively allows the ghost's brooding spirit to depart.

This was perhaps the most direct statement of the themes recurring in Henry James's creative consciousness that winter. William, laid low by his heart attack, was as shorn of his power as the hanged smuggler; the two women competing for him might be Henry and Alice; or they belonged to the perpetual triangles of the Jamesian childhood and youth, with either himself or William cast as "third person"—depending on the situation. It had been an eternal ballet, a shuffling of the same figures into familiar combinations involving not only the parents but that other third person in the family, the devoted Aunt Kate. Ghosts might be laid in tales: but they had a way of returning in life. They still could be aroused at a given signal, by anything that might touch an ancient hurt.

THE VISITABLE PAST

ONE DAY THAT AUTUMN HENRY JAMES HAD TAKEN THE BRIGHTON train from London and gone to Rottingdean to have lunch with the Kiplings. They were back from America, and "the great little Rudyard," inspired by the Boer War, had been spouting patriotic verses and publishing them in the press. On the day of James's visit, he had written a new poem. He seemed to thrive on violence and declamation and measureless chauvinism. James couldn't swallow these "loud brazen patriotic" mouthings. It was like exploiting the name of one's mother or one's wife. Two or three times a century—perhaps. But every month!

He took the return train in the thickening dusk. F. N. Doubleday, Kipling's American publisher and friend, had talked to James about his doing another volume of ghost stories like "The Turn of the Screw." Thinking of this, he seemed to see, as the train sped him back to London, "the picture of three or four 'scared' and slightly modern American figures," against European backgrounds, rushing from place to place to escape their haunted state—only to find each place just as haunted as the last. His travellers were "hurried by their fate—from one of these places to the other, in search of, in flight from, something or other." It would be, he noted, a "quasi-grotesque Europeo-American situation."

In search of, in flight from, something or other. He did not apply this to himself when he recorded it some months later in his notebooks; yet the statement contained James's essential life experience in eerie form. He had been the archetypal American in flight from home; he had gone in search of "something or other" in the great House of Europe, with its centuries of bloodshed and bric-à-brac. And now his brother William had reminded him again—had brought into his immediate experience the things from which he had taken early flight: the life of Cambridge, Boston, New York, the glaring daylight of a world that confined him to old taboos and prohibitions, the invisible barriers of his childhood and youth.

The uncanny moment passed. The train sped him into the city. And James did not then write the story: all he could do was record the emotion and the terror. Instead, he set down a scenario for a tale of a young American who walks into a house he has just inherited in London—to find himself in the past. Part of his Brighton-to-London fantasy was incorporated into this scenario. which conveyed an idea of something inescapable: of the past carrying with it its future; of the future going back to its past. Some such brooding nightmare sense of time and history, involving Europe and America, was woven into his plan—perhaps the thought of his own old and recent travels, when in Venice, Rome, Naples he had found the present invaded at every turn by his personal past. He had a title for his story almost from the first. He would call it *The Sense of the Past.*

I

James wrote the opening chapters of his story in the early days of 1900, a time when men are inclined to be unusually conscious of the clock and the calendar. The idea, fascinating in its possibilities, proved extremely difficult to develop. He could get his young man back into the old house and back into the past of 1820: that was easy enough. But how arrange for his escape to the twentieth century? The choice of 1820 was carefully made. James did not

want to venture into a century he did not know. It would have
meant "research," and the kind of factitious "historical" background he disliked. The year 1820 was his "visitable past." It was
the period of his father's boyhood, the remembered family background. The visitor from the New World, trapped in an old house,
in the Old World, the man from the present moving from city to
city in a haunted past, enjoying the past—yet fearing it—this had
been a part of his experience, and it was a part of his theme.
Wonderful as James's evocation and sense of old things were, he
had always been able to enjoy the past from the perspective of a
delightful, a comfortable present. The past had the charm of
remembered lamplight and candlelight, in the new era of electric
light. There was much of the past in his memories of his grandmother in Albany, in her old-time clothes, reading books with the
candle set between her eyes and the printed page. This was
distinctly a "visitable" past, the kind to which Fanny Kemble used
to transport him during long winter evenings by her fireside; or
some of the crusty ancients who like her could go back to the
eighteenth century, within the panelled walls of old London clubs
and drawing rooms, which also had belonged to other centuries.

In invoking a "visitable past," James in reality suggested his
ambivalence toward old things, toward Europe itself. His horseback rides long ago in the Campagna had given him an uncanny
—and uncomfortable—feeling of ancient empires: of the insolence of power, the primordial cruelty and brutality of man. He
liked the sense of the backward centuries, but he shuddered at
their violence. The unreachable centuries partook of nightmare:
they held within them man's accumulated evil, the terror of the
ages. His early stories had fabled this—the tale of the Emperor's
topaz that still carried within it all its old evil; it had had to be
recommitted to the past—thrown into the Tiber. Or his tale of the
Valerii, the excavated Juno which threatens the Italianate-American marriage and must be re-interred if the present is to be
preserved. The distant past could choke the present. The visitable

past was easier to accept: it was palpable, reachable, and it ministered to a faint antiquarian interest. Out of such ambivalent
feelings, James wrote his fragment of *The Sense of the Past*,
seeking to recapture a "Turn of the Screw" horror in it by having
his twentieth-century man blunder cheerfully into history—and
into the terrible discovery that he is its prisoner. Trapped in the
past! To be unable to escape into kindly, sheltering, secure and
easy immediacy—that could be the ultimate nightmare!

And yet in the opening pages of this story there is one of James's
delicate passages in celebration of the past—the one washed of its
centuries of misery, its dirt, its bad smells—the "clean" past of the
historian:

He wanted the hour of the day at which this and that had
happened, and the temperature and the weather and the sound,
and yet more the stillness, from the street, and the exact look-out,
with the corresponding look-in, through the window and the slant
on the walls of the light of afternoons that had been. He wanted
the unimaginable accidents, the little notes of truth for which the
common lens of history, however the scowling muse might bury
her nose, was not sufficiently fine. He wanted evidence of a sort for
which there had never been documents enough, or for which
documents mainly, however multiplied, would never *be* enough.
That was indeed in any case the artist's method to try for an ell in
order to get an inch.

It was of course the artist's method, and more particularly the
novelist's. The young historian in *The Sense of the Past*, pausing
in the doorway of the house that will admit him to the world of
1820, has the thought that "it was for the old ghosts to take him
for one of themselves." This was interesting as a thought—but
also frightening. It may account for Henry James's failure to
finish this book.

I I

The story James planned was composed essentially of his personal myth. His young historian, Ralph Pendrel, is an American who has never been abroad; but he possesses a sense both of art and of history. He wants to marry a young New York matron with the picturesque name of Aurora Coyne, a name which expresses both the Homeric rosy-fingered morning of America and its monetary materialism. She will have Pendrel if he will promise to keep his national virginity—stay away from Europe. Going to Europe has become commonplace, an adventure of the mob. Pendrel's uniqueness is that he has always been a part of the new America, and Aurora feels that he must shape his future within the land of the future: build it out of American materials without the adulteration of Europe, the past of other lands. Pendrel's dilemma, in the artificial comedy of the opening chapter, is that he not only wants to go to Europe, but that there is a particular incentive for him to do so. Like his author, he has just acquired—indeed in his case inherited—an old house, the house of the English Pendrels, located in Mansfield Square in London. The last of the English line had read Ralph Pendrel's brilliant *Essay in Aid of the Reading of History* and had rewarded his kinsman for his piety toward the past. In bestowing the house he has, so to speak, made Pendrel custodian of the family past. Far from being an American claimant, like James's early hero in "A Passionate Pilgrim," Pendrel may make his pilgrimage with the feeling of full possession. At the end of the first part of the novel, written in January 1900, Aurora and Ralph reach a vague accord. She knows she cannot persuade him to stay in the United States. But she may agree to marry him if, after his adventure, he returns to America—and then promises to remain.

The ensuing two or three chapters, all James wrote at the time, take Pendrel to London. His visit to the house in Mansfield Square reminds us of James's own close stock-taking in Lamb House; and in his nightly wanderings he studies an old family portrait of a young man painted in unusual pose. His back is turned, looking, one gathers, into the past rather than the future. In these pages we feel James's masterly touch in the ghostly genre:

the sense of the eerie grows for Pendrel, he expects to encounter some sign, some portent, some apparition. Lighting his candle late one night he does—it is the finest and spookiest moment of this section—and perceives himself in one of the mirrors holding his candle aloft to light his way. But he now has his shock: it is not a reflection in a mirror. It is himself, descended from the picture, his *alter ego* out of the past, who wants to visit the present as he wants to visit the past. It is Pendrel who must now turn his back, take up the pose in the picture: and the man in the picture will replace him.

Leaving the house, Pendrel has the certitude that on his return he will change places with his ghostly double, his dead ancestor. Before embarking on this adventure, before his possible disappearance into history, he has a long talk with the American Ambassador whom James set down in the image of the most significant of the American envoys he had known at the Court of St. James's— James Russell Lowell. Pendrel on the eve of the twentieth century tries to explain to the Ambassador that he is about to go back to the nineteenth—to 1820. The Ambassador listens, comments, and understandably thinks him harmlessly mad. "I *am* the Future. The Future, that is, for *him*; which means the Present, don't you see—?" Henry James's *Time Machine* story (he had recently read Wells's book) or his fantasy of the Connecticut Yankee in the Court of King Arthur (or indeed of Dorian Grey) did not get far beyond this point. The Ambassador takes Pendrel to the entrance of the house in Mansfield Square: from the pavement he watches the young man take hold of the knocker, hears the rat-tat-tat, and sees his supreme pause before he enters and "before the closing of the door again placed him on the right side and the whole world as he had known it on the wrong."

In January 1900 James abandoned his story at this exciting moment. Later that year, in the summer, he picked it up again, but could not go on with it. He was much too interested in another novel, dealing with other "ambassadors." He would not turn to this manuscript again until 1914 made him want to escape from a terrible present into a remote past. At that point several further chapters were written, and part of a scenario, which suggests how difficult James found his theme. He was not comfortable with his handling of an imprisoning past: the history of the Pendrels, which in the later chapters becomes an almost commonplace tale of the kind James had written during the Civil War. One catches a glimpse of the Civil War young men James had created—even Pendrel seems to be one of them; and of his long dead cousin Minny Temple; and the formidable and fearful James family mother, and a sister, whose unpleasant brother is still another incarnation of the William of long ago. The atmosphere of James's early tales, the vivid past of the novelist rather than of the remoter 1820, is to be felt in these late pages. That James should come to this at the outbreak of a new war suggests indeed that in this respect also we are dealing with a reliving of crucial moments at the time of the story's genesis: the Boer War, William's presence, the purchase of an historic house—the uneasy feeling that in acquiring the house he was re-enacting the adventure of this long-ago "passionate pilgrim"—and above all his malaise at the thought that he might be trapped in the past, *his* past. These were the thickly overlaid memories and emotions which prompted this novel. It was a story too large for him to write, a plot that would remain unresolved in his own experience. By 1914 it would be too late. *The Sense of the Past* remains a fragment of what might have been a very great ghost-novel, James's ultimate discovery—had that been possible—of how to complete his journey into himself.*

III

There was still another meeting of recent and old experience in *The Sense of the Past*. In Ralph Pendrel, contemplating himself

. . . .
* In another form the fragment caught the public imagination, twelve years after James's death, when it was dramatized as the play *Berkeley Square*.

as a figure seemingly reflected in a mirror, but in reality confronting an *alter ego*, a "double" out of history, we may see the visage of the three-day visitor of the past summer, Hendrik Andersen. The ghostly fantasy gives us a glimpse into the power of the imagination to reweave and combine old and new in the symbolic language of the mind. The vision of Ralph in Mansfield Square was the vision Henry James had had of his younger self during the fleeting hours spent with the young sculptor. He had felt his own past stirring in this youthful presence: he had *seen* his *alter ego*, had been involved in a double play of identity: the man out of the picture, standing facing him in the old room, holding his candle aloft, "the young man brown-haired, pale, erect, with the high-collared dark blue coat, the young man revealed, responsible, conscious, quite shining out of the darkness." He had wanted to see his face in the portrait, but it had been looking the other way. Then he saw it: "the face—miracle of miracles, yes—confounded him as his own."

To return to the past was to meet oneself. The present Henry James, writing these pages as the century ended, heavy with middle age, was living in the future of the young Henry James who had written about a young sculptor in Rome or, as he puts it to the re-invoked Lowell, on behalf of his character: "I *am* the Future, the Future, that is, for *him*." This was hardly a myth of Narcissus. It was the attempt of an aging man to accept the hard fact of his aging, and to tell himself that he could be both old and young at the same time. He could possess his past; he need not be swallowed up by it. *The Sense of the Past* was Henry James's way of bringing together all the fancies that his charged imagination had been dredging up, inventing, modifying, in the attempt to recover the integrity of his self—that identity diminished in boyhood by the dramas of rivalry and made sovereign by escape into Europe: an historical past, in which Henry James had always intensely lived the life of the present. Small wonder that he would use the phrase "the visitable past," in talking of his tale of Venice,

"The Aspern Papers"; and Venice itself had been, in his imaginative life, the symbol of a dead past and a living present, both death-in-life and life-in-death, as he had shown in his story of the haunted Juliana and the publishing scoundrel, a dozen years before.

Encased in the pages of James's unfinished novel, we find the essential elements of what he himself would call "the Americano-European legend"—*his* legend, and the legend of the· world he had peopled. For him there had been the great drama—the voyage out of the men of England to the New World. In the fullness of time there had come the voyage back. His father had made it long ago when he revisited County Cavan in Ireland with his man, black Billy Taylor; he himself had made it in the memorable voyage of 1869, which he had retold in "A Passionate Pilgrim." And then there had been the great—the single great—adventure of his life: his embrace of Europe—of a past that had set him free. It set him free, but not without exacting its touch of nightmare, the nightmare of doubt that things might have been otherwise, had he stayed at home, or the feeling at moments that he might be immersed, shut in, lost, damned, beyond all rescue in the maelstrom of history. He would borrow from *The Sense of the Past* seven years later, for his tale of "The Jolly Corner," to try to see himself in the American past *as he might have been* had he stayed at home. For the moment the vision of Hendrik "shining out of the darkness" remained with him—Hendrik who now had taken a studio in New York and was attempting to make his way in America, the land of the future, while James watched from the land of the past.

A RAGE OF WONDERMENT

THE REMARKABLE THING ABOUT HENRY JAMES'S LIFE DURING THE crowded autumn of 1899 and well into the new year was that he worked—in spite of distractions, anxieties, interruptions—as if constantly pursued by the furies. If ever there was an "economic motif" in his writing, it existed during these weeks. He wanted to pay for Lamb House and he turned out tale after tale, a series of articles, and the scenarios for two novels which his agent circulated among the publishers. He had acquired an agent after much hesitation. Howells had urged this step on him long before. A brief period with the old firm of A. P. Watt did not prove fruitful; and James recognized that his wares required special handling. Once he left London, his need for help became acute. To this end he enrolled himself in the literary "stable" of James B. Pinker, a man who in a very short time made himself indispensable to James, as he did to all his authors. He was an experienced former magazine editor, unobtrusive, thoughtful, respected in the literary world. His clients would be the most distinguished in the annals of literary salesmanship: James, Conrad, Wells, Kipling, Bennett and others, a veritable roll-call of late Victorians and Edwardians. Wise, shrewd, tactful, friendly, he reviewed James's confused copyrights, a heavy accumulation of literary properties representing thirty-five years of continuous toil; he found new publishers; he reopened old relations. James spoke of "the germs of a new career" as Pinker began to place his work.

From this time on James's correspondence with his agent offers us a clear picture of his work and his earnings. The record of the winter of 1899–1900 is striking. For a while James produces a story a week—and most are sold at Pinker's standard price of £50 per story, that is about $250, a large sum for the time. "Paste" is sent by James late in the summer of 1899: two articles follow and are sold at $375 each. The records show the following: September 8,

"The Beldonald Holbein"; September 17, "Broken Wings"; September 24, "The Special Type"; October 3, "another short tale," not named; October 11, "The Faces" (later called "The Two Faces"); in December, "Miss Gunton of Poughkeepsie" and "The Third Person." James writes an article on "The Future of the Novel" for a many-volumed "universal anthology," a travel piece, "The Saint's Afternoon," recalling his wine-bibbing day at Munthe's. The scenario for *The Sense of the Past* is dispatched and an early scenario for *The Ambassadors* which will be rewritten late in 1900 into the long "preliminary statement" which has survived. In the thick of winter, three more tales are produced, "The Tone of Time," "Flickerbridge" and "The Story in It." William Heinemann, who considered himself a friend of James's and had published all his work from *The Spoils of Poynton* to *The Awkward Age*, balked at dealing with an agent. Pinker promptly established new relations for the novelist with Methuen and with Constable. The tales of that autumn and winter were rapidly assembled into the volume, *The Soft Side*, for which Pinker obtained a $500 advance.

In the spring James began another short story, planned at 8,000 to 10,000 words. This one however ran away from him. By June it had become a short novel, *The Sacred Fount*, which Pinker sold to Methuen in England and to Scribner, a publisher who had long wanted to have James, in America. Thus began for the novelist a relationship in New York which would endure beyond his lifetime. The money for the initial payment on Lamb House had been speedily earned. Self-confidence was restored; and James had margin in his bank. The furious pace of production moreover would not stop. Three large novels lay ahead, as well as several major essays, the promised biography of Story and a series of other projects. They would account for the rest of the novelist's life.

I

The novel which had begun as an anecdote and jumped from 10,000 words to 70,000 was dispatched to Pinker at the beginning of the summer of 1900. "A fine flight into the high fantastic," James called it, describing it to Howells; and to Pinker he wrote, "It is fanciful, fantastic—but very close and sustained, and calculated to minister to curiosity." The novel has ministered to curiosity ever since. When it came out, Henry Adams told Mrs. Cameron that "Harry James has upset me" and that John Hay had found the novel "close on extravagance." Adams went on to say, "I recognized at once that Harry and I had the same disease, the obsession of the *idée fixe*. Harry illustrates it by the trivial figure of an English country-house party, which could only drive one mad by boring into it, but if he had chosen another background, his treatment of it would have been wonderfully keen. All the same it is insanity, and I think Harry must soon take a vacation, with most of the rest of us, in a cheery asylum." In a later generation, Edmund Wilson would strike a similar note, finding the book "mystifying, even maddening." Perhaps Adams discovered in *The Sacred Fount* echoes of Surrenden Dering, for the Newmarch of the novel is that kind of lavish establishment; and in the novel James continued to show an antipathy toward the English country-house and large week-end parties that contrasted with the relish he had taken in them fifteen or twenty years before. He had expressed this sharply in the tale "Broken Wings," in which his artists speak of the quantity of imagination they must furnish the rich—as the latter "have none themselves."

The Sacred Fount is of a piece with the work of this period—it is the last of the experimental series which extends from *The Spoils of Poynton* through the tales of the little girls and the record of their "range of wonderment." James's later preface uses the word "range", although one wonders whether he might not have written the word "rage." These novels as we saw were studies in the "phantasmagoric," in the ways in which the mind and the emotions, coping with realities, tend to invest them with beauty, terror and mystery. (*The Sacred Fount* is the only novel James wrote in which he used a first-person narrator like that of his tale of the governess in "The Turn of the Screw." James did not believe in the use of this device in long stories, where he felt it tended to make for a "fluidity of self-revelation"; but in this novel the mystified "I" is essential to his scheme.)

The unnamed narrator is turned loose among the week-enders at Newmarch. We are confined to his observations and theories. These are sufficiently fantastic to have created almost as much bewilderment among readers and critics as James's celebrated ghostly tale. We accompany the "I" as he goes to Newmarch on the train; and here, meeting some of the other guests, he is struck by the fact that Mrs. Brissenden, who has married a man much younger than herself, has grown remarkably young. Later he will see that her husband, "poor Briss," has grown appreciably older. Out of this he evolves his generalization: people are capable, vampire-like, of draining one another: Mrs. Briss is acquiring her youth at the expense of her husband. Then he discovers another guest, Gilbert Long, "a fine piece of human furniture," a man hitherto possessed of a banal mind, who he now discerns has become alert, intelligent and witty. The logical narrator decides that someone is being drained by Long of wit and intelligence. The narrator's week-end quest is to discover this particular "sacred fount," the one that has ministered to Long. His candor and his inquisitiveness are resisted by his companions; we are never sure whether they treat his inductions with genuine interest or are merely humoring him as an incorrigible bore. He is far from boring as a narrator. He may be vain, self-preoccupied, obsessed, but he also has the artist's touch, the wider imagination—and he imagines a great deal. He judges those around him as if they were objects in an inquiry. For one of the week-end guests he does have, however, a marked sympathy. She is his "suspect"; once beautiful and intelligent, she now seems drained of life. Her name is May Server. The narrator sees her fluttering restlessly and unhappily "like a bird with a broken wing."

In a word, *The Sacred Fount* is a kind of adult *What Maisie Knew*, and the narrator who wants to know everything discovers invariably that inquiry, especially into the lives of humans, has well-defined limits. He assures himself that he is not using the methods of "the detective and the keyhole." The ugly thought crosses his mind that he is perhaps "nosing about for a relation that a lady has her reasons for keeping secret," but he is reassured by the perceptive artist, Ford Obert, R.A., one of his fellow-guests. An inquiry, Obert explains, is honorable so long as the investigator sticks to "psychologic evidence." He observes that "resting on psychologic signs alone, it's a high application of the intelligence." James, in this way, justifies what had always been his greatest art—that of seeing *into* human behavior. Of all writers, he was the novelist perhaps most in tune with what people really said behind the masks they put on. The aggressive emotion that masquerades as a cutting witticism; the euphoria that disguises depression; the endearment that compensates for animus; the pleasant remark that is accompanied by a hostile gesture; the sudden slip of the tongue that reveals the opposite of what is intended—James had learned long ago to read the truths of such data.

But within *The Sacred Fount* there seems to be an uneasy questioning: "Have I been right? How can I be sure?" A little voice whispers that omniscient novelists can be wrong as well as right. "People have such a notion of what you embroider on things," Mrs. Briss tells the narrator. Her assaults on his self-confidence are particularly violent: "You see too much. . . . You talk too much. . . . You're abused by a fine fancy. . . . You build up houses of cards. . . . You over-estimate the penetration of others." These are some of the charges she brings during her long final talk late at night with the speculating mental detective. Her parting shot is, "I think you're crazy." Mrs. Briss, to be sure, may be trying to cover up an involvement of her own; for the reader often suspects she is having an affair with Long, the "heavy" who is believed by the narrator to have drained Mrs. Server's wit. Certainly her remaining with the narrator into late evening, and her intense need to set him right, suggest that in spite of her coolness she is in some way disturbed by his "investigations." The effect of the final dialogue is to echo how reality can come barging in and destroy the fine fruits of theory. "You're costing me a perfect palace of thought," the narrator pathetically accuses Mrs. Briss. He feels indeed that his palace has become a house of cards. He fights for "my frail, but, as I maintain, quite sublime structure." But he is left shattered on the battlefield. "I *should* certainly never again, on the spot, quite hang together, even though it wasn't really that I hadn't three times her method. What I too fatally lacked was her tone." With these words the novel ends.

I I

In *The Sacred Fount,* James wrote the last of his series of tales of curiosity and wonder, his inquiry into the extent to which man lives not by bare realities but by the embroidery of these realities within his mind. There had been Maisie's little world, "phantasmagoric" with "strange shadows dancing on a sheet," and the world of the governess, frightened by her own thoughts. The world of the imagination, James seems to tell us, arrives at its own truths, and its own beauties; but it can hold within it the terror of the unreal, the delicate uneasy balance between thought and fact, man's eternal struggle between what is and what might be. "Light or darkness," says the narrator in *The Sacred Fount,* "my imagination rides me." In this novel the question of "reality" is resolved into a little scene in front of a glass-covered pastel of a young man without eyebrows, like a circus clown, and a pale and livid face. He holds an object, some work of art, that appears on closer examination to be "the representation of a human face, modelled and coloured, in wax, in enamelled metal, in some semblance not human. The object thus appears a complete mask, such as might have been fantastically fitted and worn." The narrator remarks that this is the picture "of all pictures, that most needs an interpreter."

The interpretation is not offered: or rather, James leaves us with two interpretations which cancel each other out, thus inviting the reader to put his own imagination to work. One of the spectators calls the picture "the mask of death." The narrator however argues that the face in the pastel is more dead than the mask. He would call it "the mask of life." Thus, what is seen as life by one is seen as death by the other: and May Server adds a further touch—perhaps out of her own depleted life—by discerning a grimace on the mask. The mask of life, if it is that, has indeed had a grimace for Mrs. Server: and in the cliché of opera, the clown's mask of laughter always conceals a breaking heart. But the mask is art—the face is life. And the art which is a grimace and a mask can express —in James's view—more life than life itself. We are reminded in this little "set" scene of James's tale of "The Real Thing" and the hidden meaning of "The Figure in the Carpet"—the "real thing" was simply itself, photographic. Art transfigured reality.

The symbolic scene contains within it the essence of *The Sacred Fount*. The older woman has assumed the mask of youth, while her husband has taken on the mask of age. But the symbol-pastel suggests something else as well. It reminds us that the obsessed narrator is trying, in his compulsive way, to arrive at the meaning and unity of his abundant impressions. If the same picture can yield opposite meanings, how real—or how phantasmagoric?—are his own "discoveries"? How much does he really see?—how much does he read into what he thinks he has seen? The narrator wonders whether he is indulging too freely in this "idle habit of reading into mere human things an interest so much deeper than mere human things were in general prepared to supply?" He enunciates in effect the law of the artist—the burden of the charged and creative imagination, which (James implies) continues to function in the creative being as regularly as "the organ of life," the beating of the human heart.

The pastel scene in the gallery of Newmarch may perhaps hold within it also a personal memory of James's—a remembrance of the afternoon he had spent long ago, in the time of his first fame, with Flaubert, listening to the French novelist read Théophile Gautier aloud. Flaubert had been supreme among his peers in translating the ugliness of existence into the beauty of words; and he had bellowed the sonnet at James—about pastels of beauties, lying in antique shops or among the stalls on the quays, with specks of mud on the glass, the melancholy beauty spots of time on the faded and the dead:

> Le vent d'hiver, en vous touchant la joue,
> A fait mourir vos œillets et vos lis. . . .

The poet had described the sad smile on the pastel faces at the memory of vanished gallantries, vanished lovers, vanished life. It is significant that in the Newmarch scene it is the fading beauty, May Server, who sees the grimace on the mask. And she is described as having a grimace on her own countenance as well.

III

The themes of this perhaps undervalued novel begin to disengage themselves: the aging process, the invulnerability of art, indeed the "madness of art," which insists on seeing more than the immediate "real," and the vulnerability of love. In trying to decipher the "story" of *The Sacred Fount*—the equations of who is "draining" whom—critics have failed to see that the most touching and most beautiful theme within this novel resides in the person of the unhappy May Server. Her children have died; love has died; she flits pathetically from man to man, "the absolute wreck of her storm," yet remains a person to whom "the pale ghost of a special sensibility still clung, waving from the mast, with a bravery that went to the heart, the last tatter of its flag." One almost seems to recognize her as the parable-figure for the other side of her creator, not the intellectual-imaginative side, but the James whose children—his fiction, his tales, his plays—seemed to die when launched in the world and who still tried to face society as the "personality" he had been. May Server's broken wing is the broken wing of the writer in his recent pathetic tale about himself and his brother. More important, she becomes the haunting figure of James's awareness of his loneliness, the passing of youth, the passing of success. He had had his good years; he had had his fame—and now it all seemed like a house of cards. And he was vulnerable—as vulnerable as the lovely fragile May Server, who needs love, who craves affection, and seeks someone, as she flits in her loneliness like a ghost about the grounds at Newmarch —strange, beautiful, alienated from the impersonal and the gross, the social falsity, the lies and conventions of "society." Love depletes, James seems to say—not simple physical love, which offers momentary solace to the senses, but the love that is "the great relation": the states of feeling and being which humans engender in one another. The passages devoted to May Server in *The Sacred Fount* are suffused with poetry and pathos, and lead us to the narrator's—to James's—vision of the ravage of love: "I saw as I had never seen before what consuming passion can make of the marked mortal on whom, with fixed beak and claws, it has settled as on a prey. She reminded me of a sponge wrung dry and with fine pores agape. Voided and scraped of everything, her shell was merely crushable."

At last James, the egotist and "man of the world," a great intellectual and artistic phenomenon, was allowing himself to feel not only the beauty of art, into which ugly life constantly intruded, but was recognizing that his exquisite "palace of thought" was not enough. One had not "lived" if one had not loved; one had to know the ache of love, the pain of absence, the need for communion with the beloved; one had to *feel* love, not as he had felt it in all the novels he had written—novels about egotists seeking power, seeking the world, seeking the high places of art and life, as Roderick, Isabel, Newman had sought them; or the helpless, crushed by the absence of power and recognition, like young Hyacinth.

Henry James's work had never dealt with love, save as a force destructive of—or in competition with—power and aesthetic beauty. Now, at the very last of the century, when in his loneliness in Lamb House he reached out to his younger friends, and mourned the absence of the bright young sculptor, and saw in the mirror the gray streaks in his once glossy brown-black beard, he knew the deepest ache, felt it with all the strength of his genuis. This was the new awareness, the new insight. He was vulnerable: he too could love. Yet he still had the armor of his egotism. For the narrator of *The Sacred Fount*, who so busily tries to ferret out the secrets of his various couples, is still more interested in himself and his great strength of mind, his problem-solving power, than in the persons who furnish him with his facts. Only May Server touches him, with the poetry of her loss and her struggle to survive:

She went through the form of expression, but what told me everything was the way the form of expression broke down. Her lovely grimace, the light of the previous hours, was as blurred as a bit of brushwork in water-colour spoiled by the upsetting of the artist's glass. She fixed me with it as she had fixed during the day forty persons, but it fluttered like a bird with a broken wing. She looked about and above, down each of our dusky avenues and up at our gilded tree-tops and our painted sky, where, at the moment, the passage of a flight of rooks made a clamour. She appeared to wish to produce some explanation of her solitude, but I was quickly enough sure that she would never find a presentable one.

It is at this moment that the narrator sees how "crushable" May Server is; what survived out of the wrack and ruin of her storm was her still striving consciousness—"with a force that made it struggle and dissemble. This consciousness was all her secret."

In this trivial, artificial yet often beautiful tale, Henry James embodied the last stage of his "self-therapy," his long struggle to bring into balance his world of art with the human values of the world, the beauty of his vision with the tawdriness and ugliness of reality. He could now write his last books. The way was clear. He could stop looking at the past, and its entrapments; he could ask himself what uses the past may have for the present. The question that formed itself on his lips now, that brought with it perhaps the deepest ache, that he whispered to himself—or wrote into his notebook—was "too late." Was it "too late? too late? too late?" out of this old remark of Howells to Sturges would grow—in the cleared vision of his sensibility, in his renewed power as artist—the history of the middle-aged American returning to Paris, starting over again the same voyage Henry James had made a quarter of a century before. He had settled then in the French capital, and written a novel about an American in Paris—a romantic tale of an American's quest for the refinement and beauty and nobility of the Old World. Christopher Newman was about to become Lambert Strether.

THE GREAT RELATION

TOO LATE? TOO LATE? TURNING THE PAGES OF ONE OF TURGENEV'S novels at this time, in the English translation—he had read it long before in French—James drew a pencil line beside the words, "Youth, youth, little dost thou care for anything!" The title of the novel was *First Love*. He was discovering the insolence of youth; he knew himself young in thought and even in strength, and yet it was an anguish to contemplate the ravage of time. "I like growing old: 56!" he had written to Henrietta Reubell, "—but I don't like growing *older*. I quite love my present age and the compensations, simplifications, freedom, independences, memories, advantages of it. But I don't keep it long enough—it passes too quickly." He asserted his power every day as he dictated to MacAlpine (who remained his part-time typist), and expressed his irritation as the elements turned the roads to mud, immobilized his bicycle and made walking difficult. Rye seemed at such times like a prison; its winter months were long, its tempests noisy.

Shortly after Hendrik's visit, Henry James had begun to reach out to younger friends to mitigate his solitude. He now felt a new and strong affection for them. To Morton Fullerton in Paris, to Howard Sturgis (not to be confused with Jonathan Sturges), to A. C. Benson—indeed to any charming and civilized young man who came to him with introductions from friends, young men like the studious and amiable Gaillard Lapsley, sent by Mrs. Gardner from America—James offered the hospitality of his home, the rural distractions of Rye, an anxious avuncular affection.

James had known Morton Fullerton for a decade. They had spent many pleasant hours together in Paris, whenever James was there: Fullerton worked for *The Times* of London and was accused by his editors of writing news dispatches in long Jamesian sentences. In the novelist's letters he had been "my dear Fullerton" from the beginning. Now he is addressed as "dearest boy," and the letters are warm—and importunate. Had Fullerton been working too hard? He surely needed a rest, what with the Dreyfus case and the vagaries of French politics—of course at Lamb House! "You shall be surrounded here with every circumstance of tranquillity and comfort, of rest and consecration. You talk of the *real thing*. But that is the real thing. *I* am the real thing." Fullerton was ready to concede this: but he was embedded in Paris; he rarely crossed the Channel. Elegant in his morning coats and striped trousers, looking more like a diplomat from the Quai d'Orsay than a journalist, with his fine big mustaches and melancholy eye, he was *un homme de cœur*, a genial poetry-quoting sentimentalist from New England—every inch the gentleman journalist. He had lived himself into a Gallic way of life. He would become so French in the end that he would shift from *The Times* to *Le Figaro*, and write articles in French on American politics and American life. He sent James the latest books. He responded to his affectionate letters. But he seldom left Paris. A few years later, Edith Wharton would be charmed by him, and for a time they would be intimate friends, perhaps even—gossips said—lovers. On the shelves at Lamb House there remained a seventeenth-century volume Fullerton had found on the quays—he was a versatile bibliophile—and inscribed elegantly in French to James. It was a book of dialogues between two French *élégants*, Aristide and Eugène, who discourse on life, on nobility, on art, on emblems. We may see the gift as emblem of the civilized communion between novelist and journalist. Fullerton's inscription told how busy he was in Paris, how much he longed for "a quarter of an hour" to call his own. Such were the delicacies of this friendship.

To Fullerton, late in 1900, James wrote one of his grandiose letters, a confessional document couched in the majesty of the late style. James was reading proof of *The Sacred Fount* at the time; and Fullerton once again had told him that he was prevented from visiting Lamb House. He also asked James one of his thoughtful questions—what had been the "port" from which the novelist believed he had taken sail; what had been, as the French might put it, the *point de départ* of his life? James rose to the question with all the organ tones of his prose. First there was regret that Fullerton could not visit him and he put this in a sweep of Olympian resignation:

I *am* face to face with it, as one is face to face, at my age, with every successive lost opportunity (wait till you've reached it!) and with the steady swift movement of the ebb of the great tide—the great tide of which one will never see the turn. The grey years gather; the arid spaces lengthen, damn them!—or at any rate don't shorten; what doesn't come doesn't, and what does does.

So Lambert Strether would soon meditate aloud to Little Bilham, in Gloriani's garden, in *The Ambassadors*. In his letter, James told Fullerton he discerned some "obscurity of trouble" in his tone and he wondered whether he mightn't be of help. "Hold me then *you* with any squeeze; grip me with any grip; press me with any pressure; trust me with any trust." As for the question about his "port of departure," this might require "a large synthesis." Yet James felt he could "in a manner answer"—

The port from which I set out was, I think, that of *the essential loneliness of my life*—and it seems to be the port also, in sooth, to which my course again finally directs itself! This loneliness (since I mention it!)—what is it still but the deepest thing about one? Deeper, about *me*, at any rate, than anything else; deeper than my "genius," deeper than my "discipline," deeper than my pride, deeper, above all, than the deep counterminings of art.

I

Within this awareness of "the essential loneliness of my life," the loneliness of being which was both his art and his alienation as artist, James now moved toward a greater and deeper understanding of the essences of human experience: that life was to be viewed not as some puzzle, as the narrator of *The Sacred Fount* viewed it, but as a question of human relations. He spoke of "the great relation" between man and woman, "the constant world renewal," as he elegantly phrased the physical and moral relation —in a word, love, in its deepest meaning which he had not yet probed in his novels even after all these years. In such fantasies as *The Sacred Fount* we see James still in bewilderment before the exigencies, depredations and vulnerabilities of love; but in his essays of this time there is a clairvoyance and vision new in his writings. His mind could grasp what his feelings were still probing. It is strange, perhaps, that at this moment James should have written two essays on Italian writers. He had never written on Italians; he would never do so again. He seized upon them we may imagine because they offered him the special critical "case" and the opportunity to express what lay closest to his thought. This was that life was not a matter of who slept with whom, or of tearing a passion to tatters, but of understanding and feeling—as he put it in his essay on Matilde Serao, the Neapolitan novelist. One could not get to know people simply by their "convulsions and spasms." It was not "the passion of hero and heroine that gives, that can ever give, the heroine and the hero interest, but it is they themselves, with the ground they stand on and the objects enclosing them, who give interest to their passion."

Love, at Naples and in Rome, as Madame Serao exhibits it, is simply unaccompanied with any interplay of our usual conditions —with affection, with duration, with circumstances or consequence, with friends, enemies, husbands, wives, children, parents, interests, occupations, the manifestation of tastes. Who are these people, we presently ask ourselves, who love indeed with fury— though for the most part with astonishing brevity—but who are so without any suggested situation in life that they can only strike us as loving for nothing and in the void, to no gain of experience and no effect of a felt medium or a breathed air?

If the novelist begins to treat physical sex in a close and intimate way, James argued, a strange thing occurs. On the eve of the sexually liberated century he set down these prophetic words:

The very first reflection suggested by Serao's novels of "passion" is that they perfectly meet our speculation as to what might with a little time become of our own fiction were our particular conventions suspended. We see so what, on its actual lines, does, what *has* become of it, and are so sated with the vision. . . . The effect then, we discover, of the undertaking to give *passione* its whole place is that by the operation of a singular law no place speedily appears to be left for anything else; and the effect of that in turn is greatly to modify, first, the truth of things, and second, with small delay, what may be left them of their beauty.

In an essay on D'Annunzio, written in the autumn of 1903, this question was pursued to its ultimate end; for in that essay, based on James's close readings of a series of D'Annunzio's novels in the original (they remained in his library, heavily marked), he analyzes the dangers of an art which blows aesthetic gold dust over life's uglinesses, and masks with serious beauty the empty passions of persons possessed of nothing but their senses. Love in D'Annunzio is fragmented; it has no relation to human values. It is a simple physical act; the total beauty of his novels "somehow extraordinarily fails to march with their beauty of parts." In this James was giving new meaning to old ideas expressed in his essay "The Art of Fiction," that a novel could not be better than the quality of the novelist's mind. Faced with the erotic, and choosing two Italian novelists of the time who offered him illustration not available among English writers, James now speaks of the totality of love that will find expression ultimately in his symbolism of *The Golden Bowl*. He does not espouse the aesthetic view, which would seek beauty in order to look away from ugliness. His requirement is for both ugliness and beauty, the lies and deceptions as well as the truths of life; for only by knowing the lies is it possible to know the truth. "The vulgarity into which he [D'Annunzio] so incongruously drops," James wrote, "is, I will not say the space he allots to love-affairs, but the weakness of his sense of 'values' in depicting them."

At the end of the essay he uses a striking image to characterize the emptiness of novels that isolate the physical from the act of living:

Shut out from the rest of life, shut out from all fruition and assimilation, it has no more dignity than—to use a homely image —the boots and shoes that we see, in the corridors of promiscuous hotels, standing, often in double pairs, at the doors of rooms. Detached and unassociated these clusters of objects present, however obtruded, no importance. What the participants do with their agitation, in short, or even what it does with them, *that* is the stuff of poetry, and it is never really interesting save when something finely contributive in themselves makes it so.

This passage would lead Max Beerbohm to draw one of his celebrated cartoons of Henry James. He would portray the bewildered novelist, heavy-jowled, kneeling in a hotel corridor, before two pairs of shoes, a man's and a woman's, placed beside the shut door. The witty cartoon was of course a joke; but for the wider public it too literally portrayed a state of bewilderment that did not in reality exist. It belonged to the mental detective of *The Sacred Fount*, not to the Henry James facing into the new century. In this simplification of wit Beerbohm expressed the opposite of what James was now saying. The mature statement resides in the plea that the novel use the fullness of life, and attempt new divinations and discoveries. D'Annunzio illustrated for James how much a novelist could overlook: he had seen "neither duration, nor propagation, nor common kindness, nor common consistency, with other relations, common congruity with the rest of life." Great territories were open to the "future of the novel"—certainly to the novel in the English-speaking world. The English novel had done very well, wrote James, in dealing with the pirate and the pistol, the police, the wild and tame beast—but it had not yet studied "whole categories of manners, whole corpuscular classes and provinces, museums of character and condition." Instead it had taken for granted that "safety lies in all the loose and thin material that keeps reappearing in forms at once ready-made and sadly the worse for wear." With these views James expressed his faith in the beauty and elasticity of the fictional form. For novels fulfilled one of man's deepest needs. "Till the world is an unpeopled void," he said, taking Stendhal's image, "there will be an image in the mirror." Everything would depend on the novelist's art. "So long as there is a subject to be treated, so long will it depend wholly on treatment to rekindle the fire."

Recording these views in his essays, James gave intellectual utterance to feelings adumbrated in his stories—and in this meeting of sentience and idea, his intellectual power and his new openness to feeling, he showed his readiness for a *vita nuova*. The masterpieces he would write were already sketched in his notebooks.

II

In his "deep well of unconscious cerebration," Henry James had moved slowly from sickness to health. He had taken backward steps into the black abyss in order to discover his power of self-recreation, and now he had emerged again a whole man in spite of assaults and misfortunes. Step by step, James's imagination had found, had wrought, the healing substance of his art—the strange, bewildering and ambiguous novels in which somehow he had recovered his identity so that he might be again a strong and functioning artist. In this process he had opened himself up—life aiding—to feeling and to love. He had taught himself to accept middle age, and to face great loneliness, and had turned again and again for solace to the discipline and difficulty of his craft. His self-discoveries had not healed every hurt; certain nerves would remain exposed and vulnerable. There would be moments again and again when the depths of his sadness, his inner mourning, and his deepest anger, would blacken the light of day. Nevertheless he could weather storms within himself as never before. In this indirect soothing of his soul, the frigid wall of his egotism had been breached to an enlarged vision of the world, and a feeling at last of the world's human warmth.

During the last summer of the century, at the urging of Howells, James picked up again *The Sense of the Past*, but a short struggle with it showed him clearly that this was not what he wanted to write. He wanted to write the story, long buried in his notebook, about the middle-aged American who arrives in Paris wondering whether he is rediscovering human experience and life's values "too late." With his message of "live all you can"—his *cri de cœur* that was now Henry James's as well—he was a protagonist who could express James's new will to life and being, the belief in himself and his old power as artist. "We open the door to the Devil himself," he wrote to one literary lady, describing the act of art and of life he daily performed, "the Devil himself—who is nothing but the sense of beauty, of mystery, of relations, of appearances, of abysses, of the whole—and of *expression!*"

Beauty, mystery, relations, appearances, abysses! These words seemed to contain all the stages through which James had passed in his six-year purgatorial journey. To Howells he wrote, as he set aside *The Sense of the Past*, "preoccupied with half a dozen things of the altogether human order now fermenting in my brain I don't care for 'terror' (terror, that is, without 'pity') so much as I otherwise might." He was no longer willing to write his ghost story; he no longer felt trapped by his past. And one day that spring, confronting himself again in the mirror, he had had a sudden impulse—he would shave off his beard. It had hidden his face since the days of the Civil War. He was prepared now to shed an old identity, to divorce himself from his youth, his past, to be a new man—in the new century. On May 12, 1900, he wrote to his brother William that he had been unable to bear any longer his increased hoariness, "it had suddenly begun these three months since, to come out quite white and made me *feel*, as well as look, so old."

Now he felt "*forty* and clean and light." He had made his face correspond to a kind of physical youth he could feel again. A new face for the new century! "I am told," he wrote to Grace Norton, "this shaven me is wholly another person from the old, of all the years." Now, the massive forehead, the great dome, the smooth cheeks, the strong line of the nose, the full sensuous lips, and the deep blue penetrating eyes showed to the world another, a strong visage. The benignity of an archbishop, the aspect of an elder statesman, formidable in utterance and style—the Henry James whom the younger men now coming up around him would address as *cher maître, maestro*—master. And daily now, in the brightening summer that heralded the twentieth century, *The Ambassadors* took its shape in the garden room of Lamb House.

HENDRIK C. ANDERSEN
From the portrait by Andreas Andersen

HENRY JAMES IN ROME
From a photograph by Count Giuseppe Primoli, 1899

HENRY AND WILLIAM JAMES AT RYE
From a snapshot, 1900

A RAGE OF WONDERMENT
From the caricature by Max Beerbohm

NOTES AND ACKNOWLEDGMENTS

I WISH TO EXPRESS MY THANKS TO THE PRESIDENT AND FELLOWS OF Harvard College for continued access to the James papers; to Mr. John James, grandson of William James, for the invaluable help he has given me; to Dr. William H. Bond, librarian of the Houghton Library for generosities shown me prior to and since his assumption of the librarianship and to Miss Carolyn E. Jakeman of his staff for her help over many years.

I am no less indebted to C. Waller Barrett and the Barrett Library of the University of Virginia; the director of libraries at New York University, Dr. Charles F. Gosnell and the university librarian John E. Frost; the Henry W. and Albert A. Berg Collection of the New York Public Library, Astor, Lenox and Tilden Foundation and its curator, the late Dr. John D. Gordan; the Beinecke Library at Yale and its librarian, Dr. Herman W. Liebert, the curator of the American Collection, Mr. Donald Gallup, and Miss Marjorie G. Wynne, research librarian; the Morgan Library and its director, Mr. Frederick B. Adams, Jr. I have worked also at the Princeton Library, and the New York Historical and Massachusetts Historical Societies, and have received material from the Library of Congress and the Bancroft Library, University of California (Berkeley).

I wish to express particular thanks to the Miriam Lutcher Stark Library of the University of Texas for generous help in making available to me certain of their James letters, notably those to Miss Robins, Lady Bell and the Waldo Storys.

In England, Sir Rupert Hart-Davis, Mr. Simon Nowell-Smith, Mr. Alan Bell of the National Library of Scotland, Dr. A. N. L. Munby, librarian of King's College, and Mr. C. R. Dodwell, the librarian of Trinity, at Cambridge, have been of great assistance. I wish to thank also the Borough of Hove, Libraries and Museum Department and the borough librarian Mr. Jack Dove; also the County Archivist, Cheshire Record Office.

The late Mr. Alvin Langdon Coburn allowed me to use for purposes of illustration certain of his unpublished photographs of Lamb House.

Mrs. Stanley Hawks generously made available to me the papers of her father, the late Dr. W. W. Baldwin of Florence and Rome. Particular mention should be made of Mr. Roger Senhouse, my host at Rye, where I re-explored the neighborhood and visited Point Hill, Playden. Burgess Noakes, whom I saw on this occasion, and with whom I had long talks, gave me many insights into the life at Lamb House early in the century. Leonard Woolf and Mrs. Ian Parsons continued my access to the Elizabeth Robins material after the death of Miss Robins's executor, the late Dr. Octavia Wilberforce. A considerable part of this archive is now at New York University. Lady Hart-Davis, before her untimely death, had rendered me many valuable services, particularly in copying certain documents in England indispensable to my work. I also wish to thank Mr. Donald Brien; my wife, Dr. Roberta R. Edel; Mr.

George Stevens and the following, who in one way or another have rendered assistance:

Professor Joseph M. Backus; Mrs. George Bambridge; Mrs. Theodocia Bird; Mr. Jean Bruneau; Prof. Irving U. Buchen; Mr. Herbert Cahoon; Mr. C. E. Carrington; Gen. Daille; Mr. J. T. Frederick; Prof. Max H. Fisch; Mr. Charles E. Feinberg; Mr. Richard Garnett; Prof. Robert L. Gale; Mr. Alan Gauld; Mrs. Sheila S. Grant; Mrs. Deenagh Goold-Adams; Lady Halsey; Mr. R. W. Ketton-Kremer; Mr. Lachland Phil Kelley; Prof. Philip Kolb; Prof. Dan H. Laurence; Mr. R. McAllister Lloyd; Lady Meyrick; Rev. K. S. P. MacDowall; Mr. George Painter; Sir George Pollock, Bart.; Miss Sybille Pantazzi; Mr. Howard C. Rice, Jr.; Lady Rosebery; Mr. Morton Rosse; Mr. Halsey Thomas; Mrs. Renée Tickell; Countess de Sartiges and Mrs. John Hall Wheelock.

In 1963 a grant-in-aid from the American Council of Learned Societies enabled me to explore certain archives in London and Paris and to revisit Rye. I had originally visited Lamb House during the tenancy of the late E. F. Benson, when the furniture and library were still in place and prior to the destruction (during the Second World War) of the garden room. In 1965 I wrote certain of these chapters while Resident Fellow at the Center for Advanced Studies at Wesleyan University and I wish to express my appreciation to Mr. Paul Horgan, then director of the Center, for many kindnesses shown me. The John Simon Guggenheim Memorial Foundation renewed my fellowship and provided me with the leisure for the writing of the most difficult portions of this work and parts of the final volume. I wish to thank Dr. Gordon N. Ray, president of the Foundation, for his kind assistance on various occasions in connection with this work.

My specific indebtedness to certain institutions and individuals are recorded in the notes which follow. In view of the elaborate details contained in my annotation of the earlier volumes, I have made these notes as brief as possible. I have used initials for the principal members of the James family. Other abbreviations in the notes are N = *The Notebooks of Henry James* (1947); GN = Grace Norton; RLS = Robert Louis Stevenson; NY Ed = New York Edition of the Novels and Tales of Henry James.

BOOK ONE: *An Excess of Simplicity*

The Scenic Idea: Sir Compton Mackenzie kindly allowed me to see HJ's letters to the Comptons, subsequently published by him in *My Life and Times*, Octave Two (1963); Lady Alexander made available the unpublished letters to Sir George Alexander. A. E. W. Mason, *Sir George Alexander and the St. James's Theatre* (1935). Gosse 17 Nov. 91; 20 Apr. 93; WJ 21 Mar. 93. N 133-34. Edel, *Complete Plays of HJ* (1949).

The Northern Henry: Gosse 29 Jan. 89; 17 Oct. 90; 27 Apr., 13 May 91. William Archer, 3 July, 5 July 91; the unpublished letters to Archer were made available by Lt.-Col. C. Archer. James's papers on Ibsen were reprinted in *Essays in London* (1893) and *Notes on Novelists* (1914). Mrs. (later Lady) Bell 7 Oct., 10 Oct., 16 Nov. 92; Robins 25 Nov. 94.

Saint Elizabeth: Dan H. Laurence, *Bernard Shaw: Collected Letters 1874-97* (1965). Elizabeth Robins, *Ibsen and the Actress* (1928); *Theatre and Friendship* (1932); *Both Sides of the Curtain* (1940); *Raymond and I* (1956). Lady Bell, *Letters of Gertrude Bell* (1927), *Landmarks* (1929). Allen Dent, *Mrs. Patrick Campbell* (1961). Bell 4 Mar. 93, 26 May 1912. In 1937 I had two meetings with Miss Robins, and subsequently corresponded with her about HJ.

Oscar: Sir Rupert Hart-Davis, *Letters of Oscar Wilde* (1962). Bell 23 Feb. 92, 27 Apr. 93; Reubell 25 Feb. 92; Robins 7 Apr., 5 June 93. In his preface to *Tenants*, HJ says the play was inspired by a tale by Henri Rivière published "some five-and-twenty-years ago, if not more, in a single number of La Revue des Deux Mondes." This was "Flavien," *Revue* 1 Nov. 74. Reubell 23 June 93.

The Young Bard: Broughton 5 Dec. 90; Gosse 10 Dec., 6 Aug. 91, 17 Mar. 92, 25 June 94; RLS 13 Jan., 30 Oct. 91; Curtis 14 July 93; WJ 10 Aug. 94; GN 25 Dec. 97; Robins 11 Dec. 91; Howells 12 Dec. 91; Bourget 12 Dec. 91; Mrs. Sands 12 Dec. 91; Sir John Clark 13 Dec. 91; Reubell 13 Dec. 91; Fullerton 18 Jan. 92; Kipling 30 Oct. 1901, from Harvard typescript: the original has never turned up. Wolcott Balestier, *The Average Woman* (1892). Anna Balestier 30 Jan. 1900; 1 Jan. 1910.

A Romantic Fable: RLS 12 Jan., 18 Feb., 30 Oct. 91; 19 Mar. 92. Janet Adam Smith, *Henry James and Robert Louis Stevenson* (1948). George Monteiro, *Henry James and John Hay* (1965). Adams to Mrs. Cameron 11 Jan. 92. W. C. Ford, *Letters of Henry Adams* (1938). Clark 8 Jan., 23 Jan.

82, 10 July 83, 13 Dec. 91; Gosse 17 Dec. 94; Mrs. Sitwell 20 Dec. 94; Mrs. RLS 26 Dec. 94.

Preparations: For the documentation of this chapter see Edel, *Complete Plays* (1949); Lady Lewis Dec. 94.

The Three Critics: Shaw, *Collected Letters* (1965); St. John Ervine, *Bernard Shaw* (1956); Arnold Bennett, *Journals* (3 vols. 1932); Reginald Pound, *Arnold Bennett* (1952); Leonard Woolf, *Beginning Again* (1963); Leon Edel and Gordon N. Ray, *Henry James and H. G. Wells* (1958); H. G. Wells, *Experiment in Autobiography* (1934); *Complete Plays* (1949). Minnie Bourget 5 Jan. 95; WJ 5 Jan. 95.

The Last Domville: Sources for this chapter are given in *Complete Plays* (1949). *Guy Domville*, included in that volume, was reprinted separately in 1960 together with my reconstruction of the events of the first night, and the reviews by Shaw, Bennett and Wells. Bernard Shaw long ago described the *Guy Domville* evening to me, remembering in particular details of the clumsy drinking scene. I also had the personal recollections of two members of the cast, Dame Irene Vanbrugh and Franklyn Dyall; and, among those in the audience, of W. Graham Robertson and Elizabeth Robins. Arnold Bennett wrote to me that he did not think the hostile gallery was "anti-American." I also discussed HJ and the theatre with Sir Johnston Forbes-Robertson and his wife, Gertrude Elliott; and with W. Morton Fullerton, H. M. Walbrook, Edith Wharton, Gertrude Kingston, H. Granville-Barker and Allan Wade.

BOOK TWO: *The Black Abyss*

Postscripts: Documentation of this chapter is also to be found in the *Complete Plays*. New material used includes letter to Mrs. Compton 15 Mar. 95; W. E. Norris 10 Jan. 95. Gosse, *Aspects and Impressions* (1922).

Embarrassments: The visit to the Archbishop of Canterbury is recorded in N 178; preface to NY Ed, XII; A. C. Benson 11 Mar. 98; and in Benson's *Memories and Friends* (1924). For details of the *vastation* see Edel, *Henry James: The Untried Years* (1953). WJ 2 Feb. 95. "London Letter" in *Harper's Weekly*, 5 June 1897. N 143, 183. Mrs. Wister 10 Nov. 95; Benson 5 Aug. 95; Baldwin 16 Nov., 25 Nov. 95; Howells 22 Jan. 95.

The Young Heroes: Axel Munthe, *The Story of San Michele* (1929). Preface to NY Ed, XI. Scudder 5, 27 Oct., 10 Nov. 90. Preface to NY Ed, XVII. N 118, 184. I am indebted to Mrs. Stanley Hawks, daughter of Dr. Baldwin for many details about her father's life.

Discoveries: N 187-189; 208; 269; 317; 333; 346; 347-48. See also preface to *Complete Plays*.

In Ireland: HJ, *Notes of a Son and Brother*, Chap. 8. Frances R. Morse 22 Mar. 95; Mrs. Gardner 23 Mar. 95; WJ 28 Mar. 95; Theodora Sedgwick 30 Mar. 95. Sir F. Maurice and Sir George Arthur, *The Life of Lord Wolseley* (1924). HJ unpublished letters to Lady Wolseley.

A *Squalid Tragedy:* Hart-Davis, *Letters of Oscar Wilde* (1962). WJ 23 Apr., 28 Apr. 95; F. Boott 28 Apr. 95; Baldwin 2 June 95. Phyllis Grosskurth, *John Addington Symonds* (1964); I wish to thank Mrs. Grosskurth for allowing me to see some of her notes for this work, in particular a fuller text of Gosse's letter to Symonds of 24 Feb. 90. N 57. Symonds, 22 Feb. 84; Gosse 7 Jan., 21 Apr. 93, 8 Apr., 25 Apr. 95; Bourget 5 June 95; Curtis 4 May 93, 1 Mar. 95. Hart-Davis in *Letters of Wilde* suggests that the Member of Parliament was Richard Burdon Haldane, who in his *Autobiography* (1929) described a visit to Wilde in Wandsworth Gaol. Haldane was a member of the Home Office committee investigating prisons. According to Hart-Davis, Haldane urged Wilde to "use his prison experiences as a subject for literature." He also persuaded the Home Secretary to transfer Wilde to Reading and obtained books for him. Oscar Cargill, *Novels of HJ* (1961), attributes to me a statement that James sent gifts to Wilde "in Dartmoor prison." I have no knowledge of this and doubt whether HJ did (nor was Wilde ever in Dartmoor prison).

The Two Romancers: RLS 8 June 93; AJ 31 Dec. 78; Theodore Child 10 Oct. 83. Information supplied by the late Lucien Daudet, who made available to me HJ's and Meredith's letters to his father. GN 4 Jan. 88, 4 May 92. N 151, 155, 269. Gosse 22 Aug., 8 Sept. 94; 28 Apr. 95; Wolseley 30 May 95; WJ 1 June 95; Edith Bronson (Contessa Rucellai) 2 June 95; Baldwin 2 June 95; Daudet 22 Apr., 2 June 95; Reubell 20 June 95; R. U. Johnson 24 June 95. G. V. Dobie, *Alphonse Daudet* (1949); Léon Daudet, *L'Entre Deux Guerres* (1932), *Quand Vivait Mon Père* (1940), *Memoirs* (translated by A. K. Griggs, 1926); Lucien Daudet, *Vie d'Alphonse Daudet* (1941). James's contract with Harper for translation of the Daudet *Port Tarascon* is in the Morgan Library. Edmund Gosse, essay on Daudet in *French Profiles* (1905). Siegfried Sassoon, *Meredith* (1948). Lionel Stevenson, *The Ordeal of George Meredith* (1953). James's tribute to Daudet, *Literature* 25 Dec. 97.

The Figure in the Carpet: Baldwin 2 June 95. N 207. Reubell 21 July, 10 Nov. 95; Gosse 9 Aug. 95; Mrs. White 29 Aug. 93; Ellen Terry 24 Aug., 31 Aug. 95. Clare Benedict, *The Benedicts Abroad* (privately printed). Boott 11 Oct. 95; WJ 20 Aug. 95. N 211-12. Scudder 12 May, 8 June, 3 Sept., 4 Oct., 10 Oct., 6 Nov., 9 Nov., 18 Dec. 95. N 224-25.

BOOK THREE: *The Turn of the Screw*

A *Quiet Hermitage:* Reubell 10 Nov., 19 Dec. 95; Gosse 7 Nov., 19 Dec. 95; Mrs. Wister 12 Nov. 95; Daudet 10 Nov. 95; WJ 18 Dec. 95; Bourget 19 Dec. 95; Curtis 19 Dec. 95; Millais 25 Dec. 95; Howells 30 Mar. 96. N 245-46. Shorter 24 Feb., 26 Feb., 6 May 96; see Clement Shorter, *Letters to an Editor* (privately printed). Norris 4 Feb. 96; Preface to NY Ed, X. Warren 22 May 96; WJ 29 May, 24 July 96; Lady Lewis 26 June 96; Reubell 6 July 96; GN 12 Sept. 96; Boott 3 Sept. 96. In 1963 I was able to visit Point Hill, Playden and inspect the house and the terrace. The view remains very much as HJ described it. Point Hill was rented from the architect, Sir Reginald Blomfield; see *Memoirs of an Architect* (1932).

Houses and Old Things: I have here adapted portions of my preface to *The Spoils of Poynton* written for The Bodley Head Henry James (1967). I am indebted to Mr. J. F. B. Watson for showing me the "old things" in the Wallace Collection which HJ had photographed as frontispiece. Preface to NY Ed, X. See also my preface to *The Other House* (1948) and to the play in *Complete Plays* (1949).

Paradox of Success: Ethel Sands 6 Aug. 96; E. L. Godkin 31 Aug. 96. James's tribute to du Maurier appeared in *Harper's Monthly Magazine*, Sept. 1897. N 97. Bourget 16 Oct. 96; GN 16 Oct. 96.

A Fierce Legibility: Fullerton 25 Feb., 1 Mar. 97; Curtis 20 Apr., 24 Aug. 97; Mrs. Wister 6 June 97; Frances Morse 7 June 97; Bourget 8 Feb. 98; Mrs. Gardner 3 Apr. 98. *Harper's Weekly*, 26 June 97, reprinted in *Notes on Novelists* (1914). Reubell 2 July 97; WJ 7 Aug. 97.

A Faint Convergence: *Harper's Weekly*, 21 Aug. 97, reprinted in *Notes on Novelists* (1914). See also J. S. G. Simmons, "Turgenev and Oxford," *Oxoniensis*, XXXI, 146-151 (1966).

A Question of Speech: Mrs. George Hunter (Ellen Emmet) 23 July, 27 July 97; Rosina Emmet 2 Feb. 97; WJ 1 Sept. 97; Gosse 11 Aug. 97; Curtis 24 Aug. 97; Warren 27 Aug. 98. The late Miss Leslie Emmet gave me her recollections of Dunwich and her visits to Lamb House. I am indebted to Mr. Michael O'Shaughnessy, who knew Rosina Emmet in later years, for the anecdote about her vowels. "The Question of Our Speech" (1905); "The Speech of American Women," *Harper's Bazaar* (Nov.-Dec. 1906, Jan.-Feb. 1907); "Old Suffolk" in *Harper's Weekly*, 25 Sept. 1897, reprinted in *English Hours* (1905).

Lamb House: Lamb House is now the property of the National Trust. Edward Warren 15 Sept., 16 Sept. 97; Mrs. Waldo Story 30 June 97; Benson 1 Oct. 97; William Blackwood 15 Oct., 28 Oct. 97; Howells 16 Oct., 27 Nov. 97; Mrs. WJ 1 Dec. 97. The invaluable letters to Edward P. Warren were kindly placed at my disposal by his son Mr. Peter Warren before he presented them to the National Trust for Lamb House.

The Little Boys: Preface to NY Ed, XII; HJ, *A Small Boy and Others* (1913), Chap. XIX; T. S. Perry's recollection in Percy Lubbock, *Letters of HJ* (1920), I, 6-9; Steele MacKaye, *Epoch* (1927), I, 70. Preface to NY Ed, XVII. Correspondence relating to "The Turn of the Screw" is published in Lubbock *Letters* I: Dr. Waldstein 21 Oct. 98; H. G. Wells 9 Dec. 98; F. W. H. Myers 19 Dec. 98; A. C. Benson 11 Mar. 98; Howells 16 Mar. 98. See also Sir James Mackenzie, *Angina Pectoris* (1923) 209-10: "Case 97. Male. Aged 66. Examined 25 Feb. 1909." Also R. MacNair Wilson, *The Beloved Physician: Sir James Mackenzie* (1926). A posthumous paper on Mackenzie and James by Dr. Harold Rypins, entitled "Henry James in Harley

Street," appeared in *American Literature*, XXIV, No. 4 (Jan. 1953), 481-92.

The literature on "The Turn of the Screw" is vast, but most of it is conjectural. As early as 1916 readers began to question the sanity of the governess. Miss Edna Kenton in "Henry James to the Ruminant Reader," *The Arts*, VI (Nov. 1924), drew attention to the fact that the governess alone sees the ghosts. Edmund Wilson's well-known essay reprinted in *The Triple Thinkers* (1948) offered the hypothesis of the governess as a neurotic; earlier Prof. Harold C. Goddard had suggested in a paper, posthumously published (*Nineteenth Century Fiction*, XII, No. 1 June 1957), that the governess was mentally unbalanced. He also discussed the effect such a person might have on children. In *The Psychological Novel* (1955) I drew attention to the devices used by James in telling the story, and questioned the credibility of the governess. Fantasy interpretations have included an hypothesis that little Miles survived and was in reality Douglas; that James knew one of Freud's case histories (there is no evidence that James ever heard of Freud); that the housekeeper, Mrs. Grose, was actively hostile to the governess; and that the governess is in reality performing psychotherapy on little Miles. Perhaps James's most important statement about the governess is to be found in his preface to NY Ed, XII, when he speaks of her keeping "crystalline her record of so many intense anomalies and obscurities" and adds "by which I don't of course mean her explanation of them, a different matter."

BOOK FOUR: *The Great Good Place*

Two Diaries: The diary of WJ's oldest son, Henry, was made available to me by his widow, the late Dorothea James. The excerpts from Mrs. Field's diary were printed by M. A. De Wolfe Howe in *Memories of a Hostess* (1922). This diary is in the possession of the Massachusetts Historical Society.

A Russet Arcadia. WJ 20, 22 Apr., 1 June, 11 Oct. 98; Mrs. WJ 19 Dec. 98; Margaret Warren 6 Mar., 2 May 98; Ellen Hunter 5 May 98; GN 25 Dec. 98; Reubell 19 Oct. 98; HJ Jr. (nephew) 11 Sept., 23 Sept. 98; Mrs. Fields 20 Aug., 5 Sept. 98; Boott 27 Dec. 98; Edward Warren 21 Jan., 22 Jan., 25 June, 5 Oct. 98; Mrs. Curtis 1 Aug. 98. HJ's article "Winchelsea, Rye, and 'Denis Duval' " was included in *English Hours* (1905).

A Summer Embassy: WJ 15 June 97; 20 Apr. 98; Howells to HJ 17 Apr. 98; HJ to Howells 27 Nov. 82, 4 May 98; Curtis 11 May 98; HJ Jr. (nephew) 24 Feb. 99. N 269. Frances Morse 23 Apr. 98; Reubell 27 Feb. 1901. Abigail Adams Homans, *Education by Uncles* (1966); W. C. Ford, *Letters of Henry Adams* 1892-1918 (1938); Ernest Samuels, *Henry Adams* (3 vols.) (1948-1965); George Monteiro, *James and Hay* (1965); Thurman Wilkins, *Clarence King* (1958). GN 2 Aug. 82; Clark 13 Nov. 82, 10 July 83; HJ to Hay 5 Dec. 82; Hay to HJ 9 Dec. 82, 14 Feb. 94, 3 Apr. 1900; AJ 3 May 84. Prof. Edward Chalfont kindly made available to me King's comments on HJ.

Brother Jonathan: Boott 27 Dec. 98; Reubell 15 Dec. 1901. The Sturges

fragment is dated 23 Nov. 98. Benson, *The Diary of Arthur C. Benson* (n.d.)
46-48. Benson 16 Jan. 1900. See also Leon Edel, "Jonathan Sturges," *Princeton
Univ. Library Chronicle,* XV, No. 1 (Autumn 1953).

The Awkward Age: NY Ed, IX; Edmund Wilson, *The Triple Thinkers*
(1948). N 192-4. Bourget 23 Dec. 98. Preface to NY Ed, XI. I have used
certain portions of my preface to The Bodley Head *The Awkward Age* (1967)
in this chapter.

The Little Girls: Preface to NY Ed, XI. James, *A Small Boy and Others*
Chap. XXII. N 268-9. A. F. de Navarro 27 Feb. 99; Warren 27 Feb. 99.
N 155, 232, 348.

BOOK FIVE: *The Sacred Fount*

L'Affaire: Mrs. Gardner 6 Mar. 99; Warren 25 Feb. 98, 6-7 Mar., 13 Mar.
99; Bourget 26 Sept. 98; Brewster 11 Feb. 98. In his letter to Edward Warren
25 Feb. 98 HJ says, "I worked off a part of my feeling yesterday by writing
to Zola." A search among Zola's papers at the Bibliothèque Nationale has not
turned up this letter. Mrs. Ward 22 Sept. 98; WJ 2 Apr. 11 May 99; Urbain
Mengin 11 June 1900. *North American Review,* Oct. 1899, 488-500; Bourget,
Outre-Mer (1895). Minnie Bourget 8 Apr. 99.

The Brooding Tourist: Italian Hours (1909), "Two Old Houses and Three
Old Women," "The Grand Canal," "Casa Alvisi." Mrs. Curtis 10 May,
31 May, 15 June 99; Bourget 15 May 99; Sturgis 19 May 99; GN 7 Sept. 99;
WJ 3 June 99; Maud Howe Elliott 21 May, 26 May, 4 June 99; Curtis 31
May 99. Maud H. Elliott, *Three Generations* (1923); *John Elliott* (1930).

Three Villas: Curtis 31 May 99; Mrs. Ward 9 Dec. 84; June 88; 18 Oct. 93,
24 May 98, Gosse 22 Aug. 95; GN 12 Mar. 90, 10 Aug. 1909; RLS 19 Mar.
92. The essay on Mrs. Ward was reprinted by James in *Essays in London*
(1893). Mrs. H. Ward, *A Writer's Recollections* (2 vols., 1918). James,
Italian Hours (1909), "The Saint's Afternoon and Others." Maud H. Elliott,
My Cousin F. Marion Crawford (1934); Axel Munthe, *Story of San Michele*
(1929); Mrs. Hugh Fraser, *Reminiscences of a Diplomat's Wife* (1912);
Warren 9 July 99.

A Young Sculptor: Andersen 19 July, 21 July, 27 July, 9 Aug., 7 Sept., 23
Oct., 22 Dec. 99; 30 Nov. 1900; 5 Oct. 1901; 9 Feb., 15 Nov. 1902; 30 Apr.,
23 Aug., 22 Sept., 1903; 10 Aug. 1904; 28 Dec. 1905; 31 May 1906; 16 Aug.
1911. Maud H. Elliott 20 July, 16 Aug., 27 Aug. 99. Shaw himself told me
of James's affectionate embrace.

The Third Person: WJ 31 July, 4 Aug., 9 Aug. 99; Boott 5 Feb. 1900;
Warren 1 Aug., 14 Aug. 99; Rosina Emmet 20 Dec. 99; Reubell 25 Oct. 99;
HJ Jr. (nephew) 11 Jan. 1900.

The Visitable Past: Preface to NY Ed, XII, p. x; N 299-300. C. E. Norton
24 Nov. 99; Pinker 2 Jan., 17 Jan. 1900; Howells 29 June 1900.

A Rage of Wonderment: Pinker 19 June, 25 July 1900; Sturges 10 July

1900; Howells 9 Aug. 1900. I have used a portion of my preface to *The Sacred Fount* (London: Hart-Davis, 1959) in this chapter.

The Great Relation: Reubell 12 Nov. 99; Fullerton 16 Sept., 2 Oct., 1900. HJ "The Future of the Novel," in the *Universal Anthology* (1899); the essays on Matilde Serao and D'Annunzio were reprinted by HJ in *Notes on Novelists* (1914). The first appeared in the *North American Review*, Mar. 1901, the second in the *Quarterly Review*, Apr. 1904. Mrs. Cotes 26 Jan. 1900; Howells 9 Aug. 1900.

Index